WHY I AM NOT AN ARMINIAN

ROBERT A. PETERSON AND

MICHAEL D. WILLIAMS

InterVarsity Pre~

Downers Grove, Illinois

InterVarsity Press
P.O. Box 1400, Downers Grove, IL 60515-1426
World Wide Web: www.ivpress.com
E-mail: mail@ivpress.com

InterVarsity Press® is the book-publishing division of InterVarsity Christian Fellowship/USA®, a student movement active on campus at hundreds of universities, colleges and schools of nursing in the United States of America, and a member movement of the International Fellowship of Evangelical Students. For information about local and regional activities, write Public Relations Dept., InterVarsity Christian Fellowship/USA, 6400 Schroeder Rd., P.O. Box 7895, Madison, WI 53707-7895, or visit the IVCF website at <www.intervarsity.org>.

Design: Cindy Kiple

Image: Courtesy of Northwest Nazarene University

ISBN 0-8308-3248-3

Printed in the United States of America ∞

Library of Congress Cataloging-in-Publication Data

Peterson, Robert A., 1948-
Why I am not an Arminian/Robert A. Peterson and Michael Williams
   p. cm.
Includes bibliographical reference and index.
ISBN 0-8308-3248-3 (pbk.: alk. paper)
1. Arminianism. I. Williams, Michael, 1952 May 25- II. Title.
BX6195.P48 2004
230'.49—dc22

                                   2003027948

| P | 19 | 18 | 17 | 16 | 15 | 14 | 13 | . 12 | 11 | 10 | 9 | 8 | 7 | 6 | 5 | 4 | 3 | 2 | 1 |
| Y | 19 | 18 | 17 | 16 | 15 | 14 | 13 | 12 | 11 | 10 | 09 | 08 | 07 | 06 | 05 | 04 | | | |

Peterson and Williams do not fall prey to a rant against Arminianism. Their work displays an irenicism and charity that serves as a model for other authors. Even Calvinists may disagree with some of their arguments, but at the end of the day Peterson and Williams demonstrate that Calvinism is biblically grounded and Arminianism is not. This book is ideal for those who wonder what the debate between Calvinists and Arminians is all about.

THOMAS R. SCHREINER, *Professor of New Testament,*
The Southern Baptist Theological Seminary

Those who have been unclear about the issues separating Calvinists and Arminians will find here a carefully reasoned, understandable exposition of Calvinist theology. The authors treat their dialogue partners fairly, even compassionately, asking hard questions while avoiding triumphalism or caricature. *Why I Am Not an Arminian* will be a genuine help to anyone wanting to better understand the nature and application of salvation in Christ.

ROBERT A. PYNE, *Professor of Systematic Theology,*
Dallas Theological Seminary

A quick glance at this volume's title might give someone the impression that the book is a harsh, polemical attack on Arminianism. Nothing could be further from the truth. Though clearly written from a Reformed evangelical perspective, *Why I Am Not an Arminian* is an even-handed and careful critique of the Arminian approach to sin and salvation. To their credit, Robert Peterson and Mike Williams refuse to stack the theological deck in their favor by fairly evaluating only first-rate cases for Arminianism. After thoroughly addressing the historical context, theological concerns and biblical issues in a readable manner, Peterson and Williams show that even the best Arminian positions come up short. *Why I Am Not an Arminian* is a solid, valuable and biblically centered contribution to this never-ending discussion.

CHRIS MORGAN, *Associate Professor of Theology,*
California Baptist University

Peterson and Williams have addressed the historic debate between Calvinism and Arminianism with an irenic spirit and a zeal for truth. This is Christian scholarship at its best, characterized by biblical rigor, philosophical acumen, charitable expression and a willingness to engage opponents only after giving them a fair hearing in their own words. Not only are opponents treated fairly, so are the Scriptures. Peterson and Williams refuse to push the Bible into a box of easy answers and formula defenses. There are aspects of God' s sovereignty that will remain mystery until we are face to face with him. Peterson and Williams do not shy from the mystery but embrace it as an expression of the greatness of the God who makes us his own.

BRYAN CHAPELL, *President and Professor of Practical Theology, Covenant Theological Seminary*

Drs. Peterson and Williams write with a grace that goes far deeper than their commendable style. The authors' Arminian conversants are fairly represented from their best literature and answered with impeccable arguments that are scripturally compelling, philosophically and historically exacting, and gracefully irenic. *Why I Am Not an Arminian* is a book that you can get your head and your heart around—and be graced!

R. KENT HUGHES, *Pastor, College Church in Wheaton, Wheaton, Illinois*

I can hardly say enough in praise of this book. It is not flashy, but it is attractive. It models both clarity and charity. It does not fixate on pet Bible verses but covers seminal discussions in church history. At the same time it is Bible-centered in its presentation; it does not simply rehearse partisan opinions. In a new millennium, the church is looking for new direction. I believe Peterson and Williams offer it with this corrective but positive exposition of the faith. They promote church unity, aid clear thinking, and set forth divine teaching in constructive dialogue with human preference. Arminians, Calvinists and everyone in between are in the authors' debt.

ROBERT YARBROUGH,
Associate Professor of New Testament and New Testament Department Chair, Trinity Evangelical Divinity School

With fond memories we dedicate this book
to the Covenant Theological Seminary students
who took our elective course, "Calvinism and Arminianism,"
in the fall of 2001, and helped us wrestle with key issues:
Tim Bell, Brent Bergman, Mike Couvion, Keith Darrell,
Rob Fossett, Kim Goff, Donna Reinhard, Kyle Livingston,
Nancy Peterson, Phil Poe and Andrew Stewart.

CONTENTS

Acknowledgments 8

1 INTRODUCTION 9

2 AUGUSTINE AND PELAGIUS 20

3 PREDESTINATION: *Conditional or Unconditional?* 42

4 PERSEVERANCE: *Uncertain or Certain?* 67

5 ARMINIUS AND THE SYNOD OF DORT 92

6 FREEDOM: *Incompatibilist or Compatibilist?* 136

7 INABILITY: *Hypothetical or Actual?* 162

8 GRACE: *Resistible or Irresistible?* 173

9 ATONEMENT: *Governmental or Substitutionary?* 192

Names Index 217

Subject Index 219

Scripture Index 221

ACKNOWLEDGMENTS

We want to thank many friends for helping us in various ways in the writing of this book.

Those who took time to read our manuscript and offer suggestions: David Calhoun, Bryan Chapell, Jack Collins, Mike Honeycutt, David Jones, Chris Morgan, Bob Pyne, Mark Ryan, Ken Shomo and Dan Zink.

Ken Shomo, our teaching assistant, for painstakingly locating references and proofreading the manuscript.

Jim Pakala, Per Almquist and the rest of Covenant Theological Seminary's library staff, for cheerful and prompt assistance in finding resources and checking details.

Rick Matt, on the editorial staff of *Presbyerian,* for proofreading the manuscript and preparing drafts of the indexes.

Drew Blankman, our IVP editor, for patiently, kindly and competently guiding our book to completion.

1

INTRODUCTION

❧

J. I. Packer once observed that the very terms *Calvinism* and *Arminianism* represent an opposition: "The words are defined in terms of the antithesis, and the point is pressed that no Christian can avoid being on one side or the other."[1] This suggests that the two ideologies—whatever each might stand for in its own right—are to be considered mutually exclusive positions. An Arminian is by definition not a Calvinist, and a Calvinist could not also be an Arminian. Whatever one stands for, the other represents its opposing perspective and thus its denial. Unfortunately, as is so often the case, an inability to affirm the other easily becomes hostility toward the other. This is especially so with ideologies or doctrinal commitments that are openly contrary. That which we cannot affirm—for it represents the denial of our commitments—must be openly and vocally opposed.

Hence, we should not be surprised that the history of the debate between Calvinism and Arminianism has been one of intense and often mean-spirited confrontation. And it has been so from the very beginning, when the Dutch theologian Jacob Arminius (1560-1609) rejected some of the basic assumptions of the Calvinist soteriology that was being taught at the Geneva Academy under Theodore Beza. Those who agreed with Arminius's criticisms of Calvinism were called Remonstrants ("ones who

---

[1]J. I. Packer, "Arminianisms," in *Through Christ's Word: A Festschrift for P. E. Hughes,* ed. W. Robert Godfrey and Jesse L. Boyd III (Phillipsburg, N.J.: P & R, 1985), p. 121.

complained against" the Calvinist orthodoxy of their day). The bitter controversy that erupted in the Dutch church between the Remonstrants and the Contra-Remonstrants (as the Calvinists were called) would assume national importance in the second decade of the seventeenth century, and would eventually lead to the calling of the Synod of Dort in 1618. The synod condemned the views of the Remonstrants as heretical and removed Remonstrant pastors from their posts.

Since Arminianism began as a reaction to Calvinism, it might be expected that any defense of Arminianism would be obligated to enumerate the errors of Calvinism. Yet the polemical relationship is not one-sided. By and large, Calvinists feel duty bound to attack Arminianism at every possible opportunity. And far too often the debate between Calvinists and Arminians has failed to glorify God, promote understanding or honor one another as fellow members of the body of Christ. It is our aim, however, to treat our Arminian brothers and sisters in Christ as we would want to be treated.

People often assume that theological reflection is inherently polemical, that its job is to kick out the blocks from underneath the beliefs of others, that theology is properly done when one is being belligerent and adversarial. It is certainly true that polemics—showing why a particular belief is wrong—is part of the traditional kit of the theologian. The discipline of theology may even be depicted as having arisen for the purpose of polemical engagement with false understandings of the gospel and the Savior. The early church period (from the end of the New Testament era to the time of Nicaea [A.D. 325]) was typified by a wide range of belief concerning the nature of the Gospel and understandings of Jesus as the Savior and his relationship to God. Men like Irenaeus and Tertullian engaged in theological reflection in order to rid the church of heresy. Yet both men understood that polemics is no replacement for constructive theology and, indeed, that polemic is itself ultimately grounded in advocacy. Early Christian theologians opposed certain understandings of the gospel and the Savior because they were committed to the truthfulness of other positions, and those commitments informed and undergirded their arguments against false understandings. The work of the polemicist is never neutral or fully objective. Nor is it an end in itself. Polemic must serve advocacy. Polemic is subordinate to and serves theological construction.

Falsehood and truth bear an ironic relationship to one another. When one argues for a position as true, the argument includes an implicit denial of all counter claims. An argument in favor of supernaturalism implicitly denies naturalism. Arguing against a position or belief, however, does not automatically commend or advocate a counter belief. The false-choice fallacy, which suggests that if a claim is false, its counter claim is true, is false because a counter claim, even a claim that is designed to be the polar opposite of a known falsehood, may be just as false as the other option.

Positively stated, the false-choice fallacy suggests that constructive argument is stronger than the polemical. Even the argument that has a polemical intention is best couched as an affirmation. We say this for two reasons. First, the strictly polemical, an argument that is simply negative, commends no belief. Such arguments are valid only as warnings against that which is evil or dangerous (e.g., arsenic is not a suitable coffee additive; racism is evil). In theological discourse, however, polemic alone merely removes options without giving its hearer guidance into what should be believed. If a broadside against a particular view of the millennium gives people no guidance about how they ought to believe concerning a biblical vision of the future, it may only sour its hearers against all biblical eschatology.

The second reason polemic is best pursued through affirmative construction is simply that the best argument against false doctrine is the proclamation of truth. It was the faithfulness of early Christian apologists to the biblical depiction of Jesus as God incarnate who came to save sinners that put to flight the false understandings of Christ held by such heretical groups as the Ebionites and the Marcionites. The best defense is a good offense. And the best theological offense is fidelity to the Word of God.

11

Students often come to seminary with the idea that theology is fundamentally a polemical enterprise, that the truest mark of orthodoxy is that one shares nothing in common with that which is false. The student has been taught that a particular belief is false, even dangerous to the faith. It then becomes a matter of religious necessity to put as much theological distance as possible between oneself and the falsehood. And one does this by rejecting every point of the false doctrine. Indeed, orthodoxy is found in the rejection. The thought seems to be that if one rejects what is false, he will find truth. But truth is not merely the denial of falsehood. Truth must be sought, and sought for its own sake.

It might be argued that the most hotly contested debate within the churches of the Reformation has been the Calvinist-Arminian controversy. It is certainly the most long-lived. The debate has produced so much literature over four centuries that it is difficult to get a handle on. Further, the debate has been so dominated by caricature, epithet, shibboleth and anathema that clarity on the issues has suffered. Declaring the other side heretical has often been more important than finding the biblical truth. The Arminian believes that he is capable of making significant contribution to his own salvation, and this destroys the gospel. He is a heretic. The Calvinist believes that God has foreordained the salvation of some while damning all others, and thus destroys the gospel call to believe. He is a heretic. Of course, in our condemnation of all who demur from our own doctrinal insights—and we are always orthodox, of course—we are simply carrying forth a time-honored Christian approach toward those with whom we disagree over doctrine. Sadly, the perception has been created that all doctrinal commitment serves as an agenda of hatred, bigotry, divisiveness and intolerance.

Well, if polemic is so dangerous, why on earth would anyone write a book entitled *Why I Am Not an Arminian?* Doesn't that title demand a polemical presentation? And given the nature of this particular debate, doesn't a book like this promise to be just one more broadside against the heretical side? Well, yes, it does demand polemics, but we hope that we will not present the usual caricatures, name calling and easy dismissals. If we had our druthers, we would have preferred to write a biblical presentation of Calvinism, a *Why I Am a Calvinist* book. But InterVarsity Press prevailed upon us to write under this title so that the book would complement another title: *Why I Am Not a Calvinist*. Thus we accept the polemical nature of the project. And as Calvinists we will put forth our argument against Arminianism. But to be honest, our true goal is to commend and defend Calvinism. We believe that we are obligated to say this because the answer to the question "Why am I not an Arminian?" is that we are Calvinists. We believe that Calvinism is true to the intent and content of Scripture. Because of our commitment concerning the character of the biblical faith, we are not predisposed to be anti-Arminian but rather predisposed to affirm the fundamental tenets of Calvinism.

Calvinism and Arminianism do disagree regarding significant issues having to do with salvation, issues that we believe Calvinism rightly addresses and Arminianism does not. We believe that at certain points Arminianism presents a skewed picture of the gospel. The Synod of Dort was right to condemn the Arminian misrepresentation of the saving ways of God. Yet we do not think of Arminianism as a heresy or Arminian Christians as unregenerate. You see, calling someone a heretic is serious business. Heresy is not merely doctrinal error; it is damnable error. The heretic so mangles the gospel of Jesus Christ that it no longer communicates the grace of God in Jesus Christ. Heresy is such a corruption of the grace of God in Christ that it invalidates either Jesus as the Savior or grace as the way of salvation. The Arminian tradition does neither. The Arminian Christian believes that Jesus Christ is God come in the flesh to save sinners and that the saving work of Christ comes to the sinner by way of the grace of God received through faith. Whatever issues relevant to salvation we disagree upon, let us agree on this: the Calvinist and the Arminian are brothers in Christ. Both belong to the household of faith. The issue of debate is not between belief and unbelief but rather which of two Christian perspectives better represents the biblical portrayal of the divine-human relationship in salvation and the contributions of both God and man in human history.

Christians may disagree with each other, and disagree profoundly over issues close to the center of the faith, yet affirm one another as fellow believers. For some on both sides, we are sure that this might seem to subtract from the seriousness of the divide between Calvinism and Arminianism. We do not seek to devalue the issues of contention. They are real and important. The character of the elective love of God, the nature of human response to divine grace, and the relationship between God's sovereignty and human freedom are all issues of real disagreement between Calvinists and Arminians. But neither do we want to overestimate the debate. In the division between Christianity and Islam, the Arminian is our brother. In the contention between the gospel and the cults (e.g., Mormonism, Jehovah's Witnesses), the Calvinist and the Arminian stand together.

. With all of the foregoing in mind, we will seek to write under a number of self-imposed strictures that we hope will help us in addressing the issues of the contention without adding to the strife of the debate. Far too often, polemical works are not actually targeted at the other side of the debate. That is to say, they are not aimed at engaging the other side in discussion, or at seeking to persuade the other of the plausibility or truth of the author's own position. Many of the discussions we have read—from both sides of the debate—seem to be written to those who already agree with the author. The point often seems to be one of arming one's own troops, giving them ammunition for future firefights. We will not follow this strategy. We write as Calvinists to Arminians, as persons who hold the Word of God precious and worthy of our most careful reflection to other believers who share that same commitment of the heart.

In order to be heard by the other side, one must describe the commitments and doctrinal positions of the other party in such a way that the other person will recognize the description as a fair representation of what he or she actually believes. We have read descriptions of Calvinists that we suspect might fit someone but certainly do not do justice to our beliefs or those of most other Calvinists. Such writing aids neither party. It will not persuade the opposing side; nor will it inform and prepare one's own.

Therefore, to adequately describe the Arminian tradition, we will have to be careful with our sources. Both sides of this debate have advocates who do not represent the best of their own tradition, what we might call the majority report. We will seek to engage primary contributors representative of the Arminian tradition. The marginal, the eclectic and the extremist never represent the best of a tradition. Engaging such people allows the polemicist to set up straw men, i.e., people and ideas that are easy to discredit. We will seek to play the best team, representatives whom most Arminians themselves would want playing for them. By consulting some of our Arminian friends and paying attention to authors whom Arminian thinkers cite as precedent for their own arguments, we have selected a historical sample of Arminian thinkers and documents for examination. Jacob Arminius's "Declaration of Sentiments" and the "Remonstrant Articles" are crucial early sources for the Arminian reaction to Calvinism. The thought of John Wesley is the most significant of the eighteenth century. H. Orton Wiley's *Christian Theology* (1940-1943) became the modern standard, and Ray Dunning and Ken Grider have built upon Wiley's foundation.[2]

Genuine engagement demands that we will not employ guilt-by-association arguments. Even though a platypus has a bill that is ducklike in shape, it is not a duck. Only animals that waddle, quack and have duck parents are ducks. We Calvinists have been particularly guilty of the "if it quacks like a duck" smear. We have accused Arminianism of being Pelagian, Socinian, Erasmian, rationalist and liberal. And of course, since each of those ideologies is unorthodox, by association Arminianism too must be unorthodox. But merely saying the same thing on some particular point that a liberal theologian has said does not make one a liberal. Similarity is not sameness. And similarity does not necessarily indicate influence. Doctrinal similarity may be merely the result of different people

---

[2]H. Orton Wiley, *Christian Theology*, 3 vols. (Kansas City, Mo.: Beacon Hill, 1940-1943); H. Ray Dunning, *Grace, Faith and Holiness: A Wesleyan Systematic Theology* (Kansas City, Mo.: Beacon Hill, 1988); J. Kenneth Grider, *A Wesleyan-Holiness Theology* (Kansas City, Mo.: Beacon Hill, 1994).

coming to similar conclusions about some issue. The latter might even be totally unaware of the thought of the earlier thinker.

Polemics often degenerate into name calling. The principle we will use here is that we will not assign names or use descriptors in association with Arminians that Arminian theologians do not themselves employ. Rather than resort to name calling, we will seek to let people name themselves. Such a goal also demands that we refrain from making charges without clear evidence or from ascribing to Arminian theologians conclusions that they themselves refuse to draw. We should not push an adversary's position to what seems to us to be a natural consequence of the position. At best, such consequences might be a danger or tendency of a belief if overly emphasized. People usually live in the middle of their commitments rather than at their logical periphery. This is so because it is usually the case that one theological commitment within a tradition is moderated by other commitments. To no small degree, the very heart of the Calvinist-Arminian debate is about the nature of the relationship between divine action in salvation and history, on the one hand, and human responsibility in salvation and history, on the other. Both traditions seek to relate the human to the divine. Thus what is said about human agency in history will necessarily moderate statements about God's historical relationships. It would be easy to take the Calvinist commitment to the sovereignty of God in all things, push it to some "logical conclusion" through inference, and conclude that human beings have no proper role or agency in history, that they are but puppets trapped within an utterly amoral and deterministic stage play. Yet the characterization would not be one that many Calvinists would want to claim as their own. Indeed, the vast majority of us would strenuously object that we have been misrepresented.

As noted earlier, we write quite self-consciously from within the Calvinist tradition. Our ultimate goal is to commend a Calvinist understanding of the ways of God in salvation and history as being more biblical than the Arminian interpretation. But we also know just how daunting a challenge this is in contemporary culture. Judging by the way

Calvinism is so easily dismissed or denigrated in contemporary literature, we must face the reality that Calvinism is no longer considered a
viable theological tradition by many believers within modern Western
culture. In the popular mind, Calvinism belongs to the past. It is the
theological equivalent of belief in a flat earth or in bloodletting.

Why is Calvinism so unacceptable in modern society? Calvinism
stands for the doctrine that all of humankind is sinful, creatures turned
in upon themselves at the deepest core of their being such that they will
not—and cannot—make their way to God, retrieve their own lives or
earn their salvation. If humankind is to be saved, God must act. God
must be gracious. Human beings are utterly dependent upon the saving
grace of God. And apparently, God has not acted on behalf of all. He has
not chosen to be gracious to all human beings. Sovereign in his grace,
God reserves the right to shower his redemptive love upon a Jacob but
not an Esau, upon Israel but not Egypt, upon Peter but not Judas.

Because Calvinism holds that God is sovereign in his grace—that no
human being may presume upon grace or assume it as a given or avail-
able by right—we begin to see why Calvinism is so out of step with contemporary culture. Modern democratic society is committed to an egalitarian notion of equal opportunity for all. Any discrimination, any
favoring of one over another, violates our sense of fairness. If God is
good and worthy of our belief, he must be fair, giving each person the
same opportunity for redemption. Since Calvinism is predicated upon a
divine discrimination regarding the recipients of saving grace, it must be
rejected as contrary to all our enlightened and just conceptions of the
saving ways of God.

Along with this commitment to egalitarianism, modern culture has
also roundly rejected the traditional doctrine of original sin, the idea that
we are tainted by sin from the very beginning of our lives and unable to
commend ourselves to God for salvation. A recent poll of seminary students in the United States showed that the vast majority of them believe
in the essential goodness of human beings and our ability to contribute to
our salvation. But the Calvinist shows that he is a disbeliever in modernity

in that he accepts the ancient Augustinian doctrine of original sin (man is tainted from birth) and pervasive depravity (he cannot help himself).

And how do we play our part in our own salvation? A common belief in meritorious works is the third plank of contemporary Christian culture. Ben Franklin spoke for the American doctrine of merit in his *Poor Richard's Almanac* when he wrote that "God helps those who help themselves." The idea of advancement by personal merit is as American as our belief in our ability to achieve and our commitment to equal opportunity.

Calvinism does not fit the American ideal. We might even say that Calvinism is decidedly un-American in its fundamental commitments. Instead of standing for egalitarianism, it stands for discrimination, and a divine discrimination at that. Instead of recognizing human ability, the Calvinist contends that human beings are helpless. Rather than affirm a boot-strap doctrine of merit, the Calvinist insists upon the effectiveness of divine grace.

Why would anyone be a Calvinist then? The reason is quite simple. The gospel of Jesus Christ is countercultural. Arminians can claim that their position conforms to the sensibilities of modern democratic culture and that those of the Calvinist do not. They are right. The Arminian tradition may have more in common with prevailing cultural assumptions than the Calvinist tradition does. Yet we dare not impose our political ideals upon the King of kings. While democratic ideals seem to work well in the political arena, at least better than any of the known alternatives, those ideals are not transferable to every area of human endeavor, and where they have been artificially imposed on cultures (as was the case in Japan after the Second World War), they do not appear to conform to our natural experience of the world. Genetics is not egalitarian. The animal world is not democratic. Our argument here is not against democracy. We are both quite happy that we live within a democratic society. Rather, we intend to point out that the Reformation principle of *sola scriptura* stands for the notion that Scripture, and Scripture alone, is the final test of all doctrinal dispute and theological construction. The debate between Calvinism and Arminianism must be decided by Scripture.

For that reason, this book will focus on the theological exposition of Scripture. We do not naively claim, however, that we can do exposition in a vacuum, as if the terms *Calvinist* and *Arminian* were coined yesterday, for example. Rather, we will pursue our theological exposition in the context of two key events—the debate between Augustine and Pelagius in the early church and the controversy preceding the Synod of Dort in the early seventeenth century. Studying Augustine and Pelagius will help us locate Calvinism and Arminianism on the theological map. From that starting point we will examine the Scriptures concerning two topics debated in Augustine's time and still debated today: predestination and perseverance.

We will then investigate the original Arminian-Calvinist controversy that led to the Synod of Dort in 1618-1619. A discussion of incompatibilism and compatibilism immediately follows. Three more chapters on biblical themes ensue, treating inability, grace and the atonement.

2

AUGUSTINE
AND PELAGIUS

Ⰲ

The doctrines of sin and grace stand at the very heart of the Christian faith. And they stand together. Indeed, how a person understands sin (what is wrong with us) will all but dictate his understanding of grace (God's redemptive work in Christ to save us from sin). Conversely, what a person says about grace will implicitly communicate his understanding of sin as well. As solutions must fit the problems they address, and a physician prescribes a remedy that is appropriate to the ailment, so too sin and grace complement one another within the biblical drama of redemption and Christian theological reflection.

In the history of Christian thought, the clearest example of opposing views on the complementary nature of sin and grace is found in the Augustinian-Pelagian controversy of the early fifth century. Both principals of the controversy, Augustine, the bishop of Hippo, and the British monk Pelagius, consistently developed doctrines of the graciousness of God that were carefully tailored to their respective understandings of the nature of sin and its effects upon human beings. So stark is the difference between the theological visions of the two men, however, that Augustine and Pelagius have come to define the poles of debate concerning sin and grace. The whole Western theological reflection on sin and grace has oscillated between, on the one hand, Augustine's understanding of the crushing effects of original sin and the consequent emphasis upon salvation through grace alone and, on the other hand, Pelagius's teaching of sin as individual acts of free will and of grace as persuasive example of right action.

Yet, as we will see, the two poles, an emphasis upon divine grace and an emphasis upon human ability, have not had equal drawing power for the Christian tradition. To most thoughtful Christians, Pelagianism has represented a dangerous devaluation of the nature of divine grace and an overly optimistic portrait of inherent human ability. Thus the Augustinian pole has always enjoyed a greater attraction than the Pelagian. But Augustine's doctrine of the supremacy and all-sufficiency of grace in the salvation of sinners presents a vision that seemed for some to be too unrelenting in its affirmation that God's gracious action alone is operative in salvation. Human freedom seems to be bypassed, or even denied. While in succeeding centuries some theologians would affirm the Augustinian vision of the helplessness of the sinner, the sinner's absolute dependence upon the grace of God and the determinative role of divine predestination in salvation, many more would seek to qualify Augustine, or reject aspects of his doctrine. Whether it would be affirmation, qualification or denial, the Western theological tradition would work from the Augustinian pole rather than the Pelagian. Up until the Enlightenment revival of Pelagianism and the rise of theological liberalism, the story of the Western church's reflection upon sin and salvation would be written as "a series of footnotes to Augustine."[1]

AUGUSTINE

The basic contours of Augustine's understanding of sin and grace had been developed long before the beginning of the Pelagian controversy.[2] Already in his *Confessions,* which was written some years before Pelagius arrived in Rome and first came into contact with Augustine's teachings, we see a number of themes that will characterize his later anti-Pelagian

---

[1]Jaroslav Pelikan, *The Christian Tradition: A History of the Development of Doctrine* (Chicago: University of Chicago, 1971), 1:330.
[2]J. N. D. Kelly, *Early Christian Doctrines* (New York: Harper & Row, 1958), p. 330.

writings. Augustine recounts his early life as one of bondage to sin, a life "stuffed with iniquity." Reflecting upon what we might call a mere youthful indiscretion, the theft of some pears from a neighbor's orchard when he was a boy, Augustine would later write:

> The fruit was not particularly attractive either in color or taste [yet we] . . . stole all the fruit that we could carry. And this was not to feed ourselves; we may have tasted a few, but then we threw the rest to the pigs. Our real pleasure was simply in doing something that was not allowed. . . . I became evil for nothing, with no reason for wrongdoing except the wrongdoing itself. The evil was foul, and I loved it; I loved destroying myself; I loved my sin—not the thing for which I had committed the sin, but the sin itself.[3]

Like an imploded star, the sinner is turned in upon himself, corrupting the gifts of his originally good nature—reason, will and right affection—into perverse parodies. Calling evil good and good evil, seeing darkness as light and light as darkness (Is 5:20), the sinner will not, and could not even if he would, turn away from selfishness. As pessimistic as Augustine can seem about fallen human nature, he is equally optimistic about the grace of God. He never tired of emphasizing the grace and power of God in salvation, and thus of praising God for sovereignly changing him. Augustine's deep reflection upon the enslaving power of sin led him to an overwhelming appreciation of God's grace. He was convinced that he did not choose God; God chose him. The helplessness of the sinner and the necessity and sovereignty of grace are perfectly captured in the statement from the *Confessions* that reportedly so angered Pelagius:

> My whole hope is in Thy exceeding great mercy and that alone. Give what Thou commandest and command what Thou wilt. Thou commandest continence from us, and when I knew, as it is said, that no one would be continent unless God gave it to him, even this was a point of wisdom, to know whose gift it was.[4]

---

[3]Augustine *Confessions* 2.4.
[4]Ibid., 10.40.

Pelagius was a British monk who had made something of a name for himself as a champion of monastic moralism against Manichean determinism. When he arrived in Rome in about 405 to take up a teaching post, he was shocked by the apparently low moral state of the Roman church. Reading the *Confessions*, Pelagius was quick to blame the teaching of Augustine for the moral passivity of the church. If Christians believe that abstinence from sin is impossible unless God gives the grace necessary for such abstinence ("continence" in the quotation above), then they will not truly expect to live godly lives and will not pursue holiness. Where Augustine's teaching would center on the inability of the sinner and dependence upon the grace of God, Pelagius's thought moved in the opposite direction. If God demands that we be holy, then the possibility of the moral life lies within us. The debate between Augustine and Pelagius, the Pelagian controversy, raised issues that have resounded throughout the history of the Western church to this day. And several of the issues lie at the very heart of the Calvinist-Arminian debate.

Augustine's mature thinking on sin and salvation began to appear in his anti-Pelagian writings beginning with his treatise *On the Spirit and the Letter* (412 C.E.). Over the next seventeen years he would write a number of treatises dealing with issues arising from his debates with the Pelagians.[5] After the fall of Adam into sin, man became a slave to sin. But he was not created this way. Adam was created good. He was, as Augustine put it: *posse non peccare* ("able not to sin") before the fall. Throughout his writings Augustine repeatedly stressed the original goodness of God's creation and the freedom of Adam and Eve to respond obediently to God. Yet this ability to respond obediently to God should not be thought of as a power inherent within human beings. Even in the Garden, Adam and Eve depended upon God and his fatherly favor for their lives and happiness. For Augustine, grace is the precondition for true freedom, and freedom is neither autonomy nor independence from God. Quite the

---

[5]E.g., *On Nature and Grace* (415 C.E.), *On the Grace of Christ and on Original Sin* (418 C.E.), *On Grace and Free Will* (427 C.E.), *On the Predestination of the Saints* (429 C.E.).

contrary, it is a clinging unto God.

According to Augustine, Adam's original integrity consisted in his ability to respond to God obediently from an unencumbered will. In the sin of the Garden, however, Adam and Eve lost their original freedom and moral integrity. They now became *non posse non peccare* ("not able not to sin").[6] The second consequence of the fall, or the second penalty for the sin of the Garden, was death. Originally Adam had been *posse non mori* ("able not to die"). As fallen he is *non posse non mori* ("not able not to die"). The Adamic rebellion came from a misuse of creaturely freedom, a spirit of autonomous freedom in which Adam and Eve sought to follow their own desires rather than the Word of God. Pushing themselves away from the One who is the source of their true freedom and life, they came under the perverse and perverting powers of sin and death.

Adam's enslavement to sin is such that he now seeks sin, for his sees it as his good. His creational inclination to follow the will of God is replaced by a devilish desire for new sin. Yet Augustine's contention that fallen Adam cannot escape sinning does not entail the complete loss of freedom of choice. Even as a slave, man retains a certain freedom in that he freely does the bidding of sin. "He who is a slave to sin is free to sin."[7] While sin is his master, in choosing sin Adam chooses freely. Thus the fallen will is conditioned by its sinful nature and is oriented toward disobedience. "For he is freely in bondage who does with pleasure the will of his master."[8]

Augustine's notion of the enslaving power of sin becomes more cogent when one grasps his understanding of free will, which is simply doing what one wants to do. He wrote, "In brief, then, I am free with respect to any action (or that action is in my power) to the extent that my wanting and choosing to perform that action are sufficient for my performing it."[9] Augustine can hold that fallen man is free to sin but not free

---

[6]Augustine *The City of God* 14.27.

[7]Augustine *Enchiridion* 30.

[8]Ibid.

[9]Augustine, quoted in T. Kermit Scott, *Augustine: His Thought in Context* (Mahwah, N.J.: Paulist Press, 1995), p. 162.

not to sin, yet still possesses free will, because as a sinner Adam wants to sin. The will is both free and unfree. Hence, Augustine is able to speak of "the captive free will." We might use the analogy of a scale here. One side represents the choice to obey the Word of God, the other the choice to disobey. Fallen Adam is indeed free to choose either side. But the scale is rigged. The choice of disobedience is weighted by the sinful nature. The scale still works, but it is biased toward disobedience. The human free will still exists, but it is biased toward the self, toward rebellion from the will of God, toward sin.

Human beings now have a tendency, a proclivity or urge, to choose for the self and sin rather than God. It is such a strong tendency that Augustine can also speak of the destruction of human free will.

> For it was by the evil use of his free will that man destroyed both it and himself. For as a man who kills himself must, of course, be alive when he kills himself, but after he has killed himself ceases to live, and cannot restore himself to life; so when man by his own free will sinned, then sin being victorious over him, the freedom of his will was lost.[10]

The bias to follow the dictates of the fallen nature is such that sinning is now inevitable.

Since sinning flows naturally from the bias of the fallen heart toward sin, it is not the result of any compulsion external to human nature. The sinner sins not because he must but because he wants to. Yet, because he wants to sin, it is part of his fallen nature to sin; sinning is inevitable for the sinner. We might say then that sinning is inevitable, given our fallen bias toward selfishness, but it is not metaphysically necessary.

The sad tale of our first parents' fall into sin was not an isolated event in the history of humankind. Paul's treatment of Adam in Romans 5 leads Augustine to conclude that Adam was not merely a single individual but the ancestor of all, a representative person who passed on his sinful na-

---

[10]Augustine *Enchiridion* 30-32.

ture to his posterity. Such was the gravity of the Adamic disobedience that it resulted in the ruin of the entire race, a race that became a *massa damnationis* ("a mass of damnation"), a posterity that was itself sinful and capable only of propagating sinners.[11] Thus Adam's sin is imputed to the entire human race, which was represented in him.

This, then, is Augustine's teaching of original sin. Adam's disobedience brought him and us—his posterity—under the enslaving power of sin and death. While we retain free agency, "that is, ability to make and execute one's own decisions," and thus "we are not robots, nor are we programmed by some other mind, as computers or persons under hypnotism are, nor are our actions mere conditioned reflexes like those of Pavlov's dogs,"[12] we are nevertheless creatures who experience that our wills are not free to choose contrary to our natures, natures that are corrupted by sin. Although Augustine's definition of free will might at first strike us as counterintuitive, it is actually far more sophisticated, and closer to the biblical testimony, than our modern notion of free will as the power to choose the contrary. Bernhard Lohse's estimation of the theological and existential power of Augustine's insights regarding original sin should not go unnoticed:

> It is clear that Augustine imparted to the traditional doctrine of sin a profundity which it had not had before. For him sin is not merely this or that wrongful deed, hence sin is not something which can be removed by a mere appeal to the good in man, or through instruction. Sin is, rather, the wrong orientation of all human existence since Adam's fall, an orientation from which no one man can free himself. It is the form of existence in which we, as humans, find ourselves. In insisting upon this, Augustine overcame the moralism which had hitherto dominated the concept of sin.[13]

---

[11]Augustine *On the Grace of Christ and on Original Sin* 17.19.

[12]J. I. Packer, "Free Will," in *The Westminster Handbook to Reformed Theology*, ed. Donald K. McKim (Louisville: Westminster John Knox, 2001), p. 86.

[13]Bernhard Lohse, *A Short History of Christian Doctrine from the First Century to the Present*, rev. ed. (Philadelphia: Fortress, 1985), p. 114.

If original sin is understood as being as radically corrupting and enslaving as Augustine proposed, then sinful man is hopelessly lost and incapable of doing anything to redeem himself or contribute to his salvation. Our help can come only from God's grace in Jesus Christ.

Grace is thoroughly external to us, for it comes from God, and only from God. In short, the resources for salvation are located outside of humanity and human ability. "We are truly free when God orders our lives, that is, forms and creates us . . . as good men, which he is now doing by his grace, that we may indeed be new creatures in Jesus Christ." God's grace in Christ frees the will from its bondage to sin. "It predisposes a man before he wills to prompt his divine aid and aids the will which he has thus prepared."[14] Salvation comes utterly from God's grace. Yet the will of man is not disrespected. While the will cannot of itself seek salvation, the will is repaired and changed by grace so that man can obediently respond to God's call. "For the Almighty sets in motion even in the innermost hearts of men the movement of their will, so that He does through their agency whatsoever He wishes to perform through them."[15] This gracious work of repairing the will is the preceding or prevenient work of grace in the life of the sinner. Even in the acceptance of the gospel call, man is wholly dependent on God's grace.

The fundamental insight that informed all of Augustine's thinking about human beings is the dependence of man upon the goodness of God as his Creator and Redeemer. That dependence is not the determinism of which Augustine has been charged by defenders of libertarian free will, but rather the very ground for true human freedom. As Augustine himself said: "the human will does not attain grace by freedom but rather attains freedom by grace."[16]

There can be little doubt that Augustine "emphasized both the neces-

---

[14]Augustine *Enchiridion* 32.
[15]Augustine *On Grace and Free Will* 41.
[16]Quoted in M. Eugene Osterhaven, *The Faith of the Church: A Reformed Perspective on Its Historical Development* (Grand Rapids: Eerdmans, 1982), p. 78.

sity and work of grace as no one before him, and only a few after him."[17] Yet the consistency with which Augustine emphasized the utter dependence of man upon God alone for salvation and the supremacy of grace to the exclusion of all human contribution has proven a problem for many Christians throughout the centuries, and it still lies at the heart of the Arminian rejection of Calvinism, which was in many ways a sixteenth-century revival of Augustine's teaching on sin and grace. Roger Olson voices something of the Arminian response to Augustine when he writes:

> One of the most vexed questions in the history of theology has been what role, if any, humans play in their own salvation. All Christians have attributed salvation to God's grace and placed Christ and his cross at the center of the gospel as the very basis of forgiveness and transformation. But the debate between Augustine and Pelagius raised the question to new levels of vexation. For the sake of preserving the all-sufficiency of grace, Augustine ended up making salvation such an exclusive work of God that humans play virtually no role at all. If they are saved, it is solely because God chose them and gave them the gift of grace—including faith itself—apart from any decision they might make or action they might undertake.[18]

While there is a hint of complaint in Olson's depiction, the Calvinist would find Augustine's teaching on sin and grace to be an opportunity to praise God for his abounding mercy. Redemption is wholly the work of grace.

Augustine's understanding of redemption is clearly monergistic. The word *monergism* means "coming from a single worker or a single power." Everything in the redemption of man is traceable to the saving grace of God. Redemption is given. It cannot be earned or courted. Perhaps no single biblical text catches the monergistic reality of redemption more

---

[17]Lohse, *Short History of Christian Doctrine*, p. 114.
[18]Roger Olson, *The Story of Christian Theology: Twenty Centuries of Tradition & Reform* (Downers Grove, Ill.: InterVarsity Press, 1999), p. 280.

vividly than our Lord's portrayal of regeneration as a new birth in John 3. Jesus' conversation with Nicodemus about the new birth hinges upon one word, a word that heavily places the accent upon man's inability to reach God. The Greek verb *dynamai* ("to be able" or "to have power") appears five times between John 3:2 and 3:9, and four of those times it appears in the negative. Repeatedly, Nicodemus asks what he can do. To which Jesus responds that when it comes to entering into relationship with God, man can do nothing. The priority of divine power—to the exclusion of human ability—is also emphasized by the image of birth in the passage. Parents are sovereign in the process of reproduction. The parents act; the child receives the action. We are powerless to birth ourselves or contribute to it in any way. Life is a gift. Jesus' message to Nicodemus was that regeneration, the rebirth of fallen man into a child of God, is a gift as well. God does it all by his grace.

Augustine took a rather dim view of the inherent potentialities of fallen human beings. We inherit not only a bias toward sin but also an inability to choose God. God must choose us, and he does so through a gracious and irresistible calling that "not only exhibits truth, but likewise imparts love."[19] But if God must choose man, and he sovereignly and irresistibly calls and redeems sinners by his grace,[20] that grace is obviously not universally bestowed, for all do not believe. Stated differently, if salvation is wholly of God, yet not all are saved, then God does not choose to save all.

Confronted with the same gospel message, some are converted, but others fail to respond. Augustine's explanation here is that God has given his prevenient grace to some—making their unwilling hearts willing—but not all.[21] The grace that alone can save us is always particular; one might even say that it is discriminatory, for it is not given to all. The facts

---

[19]Augustine *Grace of Christ* 13.14. On irresistible grace in Augustine, also see *On Grace and Free Will* 17.30; *Enchiridion* 98; and J. Patout Burns, *The Development of Augustine's Doctrine of Operative Grace* (Paris: Études Augustiniennes, 1980).

[20]"The will of the Omnipotent is always undefeated" (Augustine *Enchiridion* 101).

[21]Augustine *On Predestination* 10.19.

of our experience tell us that not all come to faith, yet biblically we know that if we are to be saved it is wholly the work of divine grace (Eph 2:8-9). Why then does God not save all? Augustine's answer is one of pious ignorance: "The reason why one person is assisted by grace and another is not helped, must be referred to the secret judgments of God."[22] Augustine's reply to those who would push to resolve the mystery was to prefer ignorance to presumption by citing Romans 11:33: "Oh, the depth of the riches of the wisdom and knowledge of God! How unsearchable his judgments, and his paths beyond tracing out!"

While we cannot discern why God lavishes his redemptive grace on one person and withholds it from another, Augustine insisted that the fact that God does not elect all to redemption is not an occasion for our supposing any injustice on God's part. In that all men are the posterity of Adam, they are all "children of wrath" and "bound in a just doom."[23] God is under no compulsion to save anyone. That he should show his mercy by saving one is no injustice to the one not chosen. Indeed, what the one who is not redeemed by God's grace receives is justice.

While Augustine certainly did hold a high view of divine sovereignty, he did not teach a doctrine of double predestination. God does not elect the unregenerate to damnation. He passes them by, leaving them in their unregenerate state, and thus allows them to suffer the destiny that they have earned. But if God is sovereign over all things, and there is sin, then how is it that man rather than God is responsible for sin? Although many have pushed Augustine's thought to the conclusion that ultimately God must be responsible for sin, Augustine himself was reluctant to attribute the cause of sin to God's predestination. Ultimately, the cause of sin must remain mysterious, for sin is the undoing of all reasonability. God does not cause evil, according to Augustine, but in his sovereign governance he has chosen to permit sin and evil. God is the cause of all good, but not the cause of sin. God's elective will is the cause of redemption, but

---

[22]Augustine *On Grace and Free Will* 45.
[23]Augustine *Enchiridion* 33.

not the cause of damnation for the lost. Here we see the basic asymmetry of sin and salvation that will characterize the Augustinian tradition. God is sovereign over all things, and his sovereignty extends even to the sin of man, but in mysterious and noncausal ways.

Throughout his reflection upon sin and redemption, Augustine's concern was to affirm the necessity and sufficiency of grace. He took serious stock of the damage that sin does to man and then asked what are the real resources for restoring man to integrity before God. His answer is that grace alone can save, that if man is to be saved, he will be saved solely by the grace of God. A radical doctrine of sin calls for a radical doctrine of redemption. And Augustine has given us both. Another way to state the point is to suggest that Augustine's concern was to proclaim the centrality and necessity of Christ. If man could obtain some measure of righteous standing before God apart from the work of Christ, then that work is not given the same appreciation and urgency that Scripture affords it. "If, however, Christ did not die in vain, then human nature cannot by any means be justified and redeemed from God's most righteous wrath—in a word, from punishment—except by faith and the sacrament of the blood of Christ."[24]

PELAGIUS

Augustine's understanding of salvation by grace alone is truly good news for every believer who has thought deeply and honestly about the weight and cost of sin. We have done nothing—and can do nothing—to merit the mercy and favor of God. All our righteousness, the performance of the flesh, is as filthy rags (Is 64:6). Harold O. J. Brown has well said that "biblically and theologically Augustine's view that the will is in bondage and distorted and cannot fully choose the good is very persuasive." Brown is also correct, however, when he goes on to say that "morally and emotionally it seems dreadful."[25] Inherent human ability is denied. There is nothing for us to do, nothing we can contribute. The

---

[24]Augustine *On Nature and Grace* 2.
[25]Harold O. J. Brown, *Heresies: The Image of Christ in the Mirror of Heresy and Orthodoxy* (Grand Rapids: Baker, 1984), p. 205.

moralist in each of us is appalled. Certainly, the moralist in Pelagius was offended by Augustine's view of sin and redemption.

Upon reading the *Confessions*, Pelagius was deeply offended by Augustine's contention that sin is inevitable for fallen human beings and that God holds them responsible for behaviors and dispositions that are beyond their control. As an advocate of the rigorous moralism and asceticism of the monasteries, Pelagius was more concerned about Christian conduct than theological questions. All he could see in Augustine's doctrine of grace was license to immorality. Augustine's pessimistic view of sin and human nature could lead only to moral passivity.

The central commitment that shaped Pelagius's response to Augustine was Pelagius's affirmation that human beings possess unconditionally free will as well as moral responsibility. If human beings do not possess the inherent ability to obey the commands of God, then it would be unjust for God to demand obedience and hold people accountable for not obeying. Pelagius's notion of inherent human ability would later be captured in Kant's aphorism: ought implies can.[26] If human beings cannot, by their own natural capacities, do the good, God would be unjust to condemn them for failure. Pelagius would hear nothing of the excuses of those who might wish to blame their sin on the weakness of human nature. Indeed, there is no inherited corruption passed down to us from Adam. His disobedience bears no essential relevance for us. "Evil is not born within us, and we are procreated without fault."[27]

While he was not completely clear or consistent on the issue, Augustine seems to have believed that human nature—including the fallen human nature—is passed on through natural procreation. Thus original sin is bequeathed to posterity in the same way that hair color and baldness are passed on from one generation to the next. Pelagius rejected this view in favor of the notion that each individual person is an immediate and direct creation of God. Since each soul is created immediately by

---

[26]Olson, *Story of Christian Theology*, p. 269.
[27]Pelagius, quoted in Olson, *Story of Christian Theology*, p. 269.

God, then it does not come into the world soiled by the sin of an ancestor. Each human being starts, then, where Adam started: able not to sin. Human beings are created as rational, willing and able creatures. Such is their essential nature, and it cannot be qualified or modified. Sin is never a matter of necessity or inevitability but of free choice. Sin is not located in any necessity of nature, for that would make God its author. Nor is it located in human nature, for the capacity to will the good is constitutional to human nature. Rather, sin is always the free choice to act contrary to the will of God.

Why then do we sin? Pelagius held that people sin freely, without compulsion, without any proclivity toward selfishness. Again, Adam's sin is relevant to us only in so far as it provides us with a bad example and sets into motion a certain historical habit of disobedience. We sin by custom and example. There is no congenital fault in a human being at birth.

> For no other (thing) occasions for us the difficulty of doing good than the lost custom of vices, which has infected us from childhood, and gradually, through many years, corrupted us, and this holds us afterward bound and addicted to itself, so that it seems in some way to have the force of nature.[28]

Gradually, through many years, sin corrupts and holds us bound and addicted to itself—not as some metaphysical force beyond our control but rather as a system of habits and customs. Olson puts it well when he says that "for Pelagius, sin is a social disease, not a genetic one."[29]

Such a different understanding of sin from that of Augustine will necessarily mean that Pelagius will disagree just as radically with Augustine concerning the nature of grace. For Pelagius, grace is most certainly not the decisive act of God that transforms sinful persons into people who will seek the will of God. It does not free them from bondage to sin or

---

[28]Pelagius *ad Demetr.* 8.
[29]Olson, *Story of Christian Theology*, p. 269.

enable them not to sin. Grace is not an internal action of God but rather a purely external aid to obedience. Grace is, first of all, "the necessity of nature," by which Pelagius means the revelation of God's law through reason, the natural human capacity to obey, a capacity that comes from God, "the Author of nature."[30] This "grace of creation" instructs man in his duty toward God and enables him to act according to divine expectation. But since God's original revelation of his will has become somewhat obscured by a history of sinful custom, grace now includes a more explicit declaration of the divine will in the law of Moses and the lived examples of biblical persons, especially Jesus Christ. Sin is avoided and sinful habits are broken through express instruction in the divine law and the presentation of examples of obedience to the law.

First and foremost for Augustine, grace is a gift of redemption, and it is a true gift, something in which there is no possibility of human merit. Grace is the divine action that frees its recipient from the vicious grasp of enslaving sin, a grasp from which only God can free us. "From this Augustine concludes that in relation to grace there is no freedom of the will."[31] Pelagius, on the contrary, saw grace as belonging to the order of creation, a universal endowment of reason and moral ability given to all men. For Augustine, grace is active, irresistible and efficient. For Pelagius, grace is passive and merely persuasive.

Yet as stark as the difference is between Augustine and Pelagius on sin and grace, they shared one thing in common. The structure of each person's understanding of sin and redemption is monergistic. Where Augustine understood redemption as the product of divine grace, grace alone without any merit or contribution from human beings, Pelagius leaned toward a conception of redemption as a humanistic and meritorious enterprise. In the Pelagian conception, it is by earned merit that man is redeemed from sin and advances to holiness.

---

[30]Pelagius, quoted in Jaroslav Pelikan, *The Christian Tradition* (Chicago: University of Chicago Press, 1971), 1:314-15. Cf. Justo L. González, *A History of Christian Thought: From Augustine to the Eve of the Reformation* (Nashville, Tenn.: Abingdon, 1971), 2:32.

[31]Lohse, *Short History of Christian Doctrine*, p. 115.

If Augustine's understanding of redemption can be summarized in the later Reformation era phrase *by grace alone,* Pelagius's can be summarized as *by merit alone.* The purely external and persuasive character of his conception of grace rendered it all but unnecessary for redemption. An unencumbered free will is all that is needed. Pelagius himself pushed his idea of innate human ability to the point of entertaining the notion that human beings have the potential of living sinlessly without the aid of any divine assistance. Again, if God demands perfect holiness, such perfectionism must be at least theoretically possible.

SEMI-PELAGIANISM AND THE SYNOD OF ORANGE

Although Pelagius was condemned by the bishop of Rome in 417 and then after his death by the Council of Ephesus in 431, he certainly did not set out to be a heretic. Bernhard Lohse makes the point that Pelagius's intent was "to elevate the difficult ascetic demands which were then permeating monasticism to a position of a fundamental principle for all Christians."[32] While Pelagius's inordinately low view of sin and grace might—and should—strike us as scandalous and indeed heretical, Lohse does not exaggerate when he notes that "there is hardly an opinion" in Pelagius's teaching on sin and grace "for which some confirmation could not be found among the earlier fathers of the church."[33] Indeed, one could easily argue that it was Augustine, not Pelagius, who was out of step with the tradition of the church.

The generation after Augustine and Pelagius would give birth to the Semi-Pelagian movement. Monks like John Cassian and Vincent of Lérins agreed with Augustine regarding the seriousness of sin, yet they objected to his ideas of the total and disabling bondage of the will to sin, the irresistible power of grace and predestination as predicated upon a particular election. In 434 Vincent of Lérins wrote the *Commonitory,* which contained both a polemic against Augustine's doctrine of grace as

---

[32]Ibid., p. 110.
[33]Ibid.

a dangerous innovation and a description of the Catholic principle of tradition that would become normative for the church. The Augustinian understanding of sin and grace, said Vincent, is contrary to the ancient tradition of the church, "that faith which has been believed everywhere, always, by all. For that is truly and in the strictest sense 'Catholic,' which, as the name itself and the reason of the thing declare, comprehends all universality."[34]

The Semi-Pelagians were convinced that Augustine's monergistic emphasis upon salvation by grace alone represented a significant departure from the traditional teaching of the church. And a survey of the thought of the apostolic fathers shows that the argument is valid.

While affirming the necessity of grace for salvation, early Christian theological reflection tended to be highly moralistic and even legalistic, emphasizing a view of the Christian life that focused more on conduct—often expressed as rigorous prescription—rather than grace, faith or forgiveness. In comparison to Augustine's monergistic doctrine of grace, the teachings of the apostolic fathers tended toward a synergistic view of redemption. For them, salvation is the result of a *working together* of divine grace and human agency. Human beings are fallen such that they need divine help, but that help cooperates with our own striving toward God and the moral life. The synergism in pre-Augustinian thought held that divine grace is necessary for salvation but that our salvation is as much the product of the exercise of human free will and obedience to the law of God as of grace.

The Semi-Pelagian monastics affirmed the free will and ability of human beings. Yet they were far removed from the humanistic monergism of Pelagius. The Semi-Pelagians insisted that human beings cannot be saved apart from the supernatural assisting grace of God. But the fallen human will is not held in bondage to sin; it is not completely disabled by sinful corruption. Human beings can, unaided by grace,

---

[34]Vincent of Lérins *Commonitory for the Antiquity and Universality of the Catholic Faith Against the Profane Novelties of All Heresies* 2.6.

take the first step toward salvation. John Cassian held that human nature is weakened but not disabled by sin; we are fallen but able, fallen enough that we need help, but not so fallen that we cannot contribute to our own recovery. Cassian wrote, "And when He [God] sees in us some beginnings of a good will, He at once enlightens it and strengthens it and urges it on towards salvation, increasing that which He Himself implanted or which He sees to have arisen from our own efforts."[35] In Semi-Pelagian synergism, human beings are the initiators of faith. Grace is responsive to our search for God and the good. *God helps those who help themselves.*

Throughout the fifth and early sixth centuries, the Augustinians and the Semi-Pelagians continued their debate, until the bishops met in 529 at the Synod of Orange to seek a resolution of the controversy. Even a century after his death, Augustine's influence was so great that the synod sought to expunge any lingering strands of Pelagianism within the church. This does not mean, however, that the bishops affirmed Augustine's teaching in its entirety. Somewhat inconsistently, they affirmed the doctrine of original sin and Augustine's teaching on the bondage of the will, but they failed to affirm the doctrine of predestination. They argued that the freedom of the will has been destroyed by sin such that the only thing inherent in fallen humankind is "untruth and sin."[36] Faith is not initiated by human beings and then completed by divine grace so that God's work is dependent upon people. Rather, faith begins in the illuminating work and infused presence of the Holy Spirit, which "precedes" and "enables" human beings' response to grace.[37] Much of the language of the Canons of the Council of Orange was taken directly from the works of Augustine. For example, using a citation from Augustine himself, the canons rejected the Pelagian charge that Augustine's teaching was deterministic: "Men do their own will and not the will of God when they do what displeases

---

[35]Quoted in Olson, *Story of Christian Theology*, p. 283.
[36]*Canons of the Council of Orange*, para. 1-2, 13, 22.
[37]Ibid., para. 3-7, 18.

him; but when they follow their own will and comply with the will of God, however willingly they do so, yet it is his will by which what they will is both prepared and instructed."[38]

Any goodness or righteousness that humankind displays is the result of God's grace working in them. But this should not be taken as evidence that the Synod of Orange affirmed Augustine's gracious monergism. The synod softened the Augustinian teaching into a gracious synergism. First, as stated above, the synod did not endorse predestination. The canons explicitly reject predestination to damnation,[39] but they are completely silent concerning predestination to redemption. Second, while the synod insisted that the initiation of faith begins with the work of grace, it suggested that human agency cooperates with the divine in order to produce redemption. This synergism is subtly but crucially different from that of the Semi-Pelagians. While both see redemption as the product of both divine grace and human effort, the Semi-Pelagians depict redemption as beginning with human agency. The Semi-Augustinian synergism of Orange reversed the sequence. Hence, a person's contribution to salvation is faithful response to the grace of God. Grace is prevenient here in that it precedes human response.

Nevertheless, there is a problem with the conclusions of the synod. If faith is a gift of God in that the seeds of faith are found in a grace that precedes the actual expression of faith in the responsive heart, and if grace must be given to people enabling them to respond (for a person cannot take the first step toward God), how does one account for the fact that not all respond in faith to the gospel? It seems that the bishops at Orange sought to escape having to address this question.

While the synod held that divine grace is necessary unto faith, its refusal to affirm the particularism of Augustine's doctrine of predestination seems to be an implicit affirmation of universal preceding grace. That is, universal repairing and enabling grace is given to all, but each person

---

[38]Ibid., para. 23.
[39]Ibid., para. 25.

must obediently respond to the illuminating work of the Holy Spirit in order to be saved.

WHERE DO CALVINISM AND ARMINIANISM FIT?

The Calvinist understanding of the doctrines of sin and redemption closely conforms to Augustine's gracious monergism. Redemption is utterly the work of grace. Does the antipathy between Calvinism and Arminianism suggest that Pelagius, the arch-opposite of Augustine, is the proper ancestor of Arminianism? Calvinists have often sought to paint Arminianism in Pelagian colors. Associating your opponent with a position that the historic faith has repeatedly judged heretical can only help one's cause. However, the allegation that Arminianism is Pelagian is unfortunate and indeed unwarranted. From Jacob Arminius and the "Remonstrant Articles" on, the Arminian tradition has affirmed the corruption of the will by sin and the necessity of grace for redemption. Arminianism is not Pelagian.

If Arminianism cannot be traced back to Pelagius, perhaps the Semi-Pelagianism of John Cassian and Vincent of Lérins is the ancestor of Arminianism. Both Semi-Pelagianism and Arminianism insist upon a synergistic view of redemption. A person's salvation is the result of two agencies: (1) God's grace and (2) human faith and obedience. But here again, there are important dissimilarities. The Semi-Pelagians thought of salvation as beginning with human beings. We must first seek God; and his grace is a response to that seeking. The Arminians of the seventeenth century, however, held that the human will has been so corrupted by sin that a person cannot seek grace without the enablement of grace. They therefore affirmed the necessity and priority of grace in redemption. Grace must go before a person's response to the gospel. This suggests that Arminianism is closer to Semi-Augustinianism than it is to Semi-Pelagianism or Pelagianism. The word *Pelagian* as a description of Arminians—or Roman Catholics for that matter—does them an injustice because it associates them with a theological tradition that is truly heretical in that Pelagius trivialized grace, and in so doing trivialized the work of

Christ. Both the Semi-Augustinians of the fifth and sixth centuries and the Arminians of the seventeenth century sought understandings of sin and redemption that were qualifications of Augustinianism. Semi-Augustinianism was not a Pelagianism that had moved toward Augustine but rather a softening of Augustinianism that sought to modify or excise elements of Augustine's teaching that were found offensive (particularist election and a doctrine of divine agency that seemed to render human agency irrelevant). As Arminianism began as a reaction to the Augustinian commitments of the Reformed churches and reacted negatively to much the same issues as had the Semi-Augustinians, Arminianism is properly understood as Semi-Augustinianism.

Yet we should appreciate the reality that the four positions sketched here as coming out of the Augustinian-Pelagian controversy of the fifth century do not exhaust the list of possible ways that sin and redemption can be understood or the ways in which divine agency can be thought of as relating to human action and decision making. Yes, Augustinianism (salvation is all of God's grace) and Pelagianism (salvation is the product of human achievement) do seem to mark the polar extremes. But what lies between might be more of a continuum than a few discrete points. Between the two monergistic poles is the admixture, the synergism of dual agency in redemption. The realization of a continuum of beliefs may help us understand something of the diversity of belief within a tradition.

In 529 the Synod of Orange declared Semi-Pelagianism a heresy and declared a form of Augustinianism to be the official teaching of the Roman Church. Yet the emphasis upon the cooperation of human agency in redemption left a space for Semi-Pelagian ideas to flourish in popular belief. Even though the synod did not affirm a doctrine of meritorious works and insisted that God's grace is the sole efficient cause of salvation, a Semi-Pelagian—and often an outright Pelagian—view of human agency would dominate in common folk belief. Indeed, the customs and structures that arose within the medieval Roman Church would lean toward a view of Christianity as a religion of performance, merit and obligatory rite. Something quite similar seems to exist within the Arminian tradition. Popular Arminian writing often tends to be so dismissive of anything that might qualify "libertarian free will" that it gives itself over to a moralist and meritorious doctrine of redemption. Redemption is offered by God, but we must earn it. This is, of course, the very danger that the Calvinist sees in all synergistic understandings of redemption.

But we Calvinists have our own version of popular or folk belief as well. If Arminian popular belief tends toward the overestimation of human ability and the redemptive contribution of human achievement, Calvinist popular belief often seems to overemphasize its redemptive monergism. We seek to out-Augustine Augustine. If a little monergism is good, more is better. As a result, we make God the sole cause of all things, sin as well as grace, unbelief as well as belief. And human beings do become mere pawns or actors walking through the scenery of their lives.

The Augustine-Pelagius controversy is our first monumental historical event. This controversy sets the stage for the following two chapters, which focus on issues keenly debated by Augustine and Pelagius and still disputed today: predestination and the perseverance of the saints.

3

PREDESTINATION

Conditional
or Unconditional?

෨

Arminian theologians have understood the doctrine of predestination in four main ways, each compatible with their understanding of human freedom. First, they have claimed that election in Scripture is corporate and not individual. This is the thesis of William W. Klein's important book *The New Chosen People: A Corporate View of Election.*[1] Second, Arminian writers have argued that when election pertains to individuals in the Bible, it concerns God's choosing them for service, not salvation.[2] Third, Arminianism has maintained that "the election of particular individuals to be the children of God and heirs of eternal life . . . is conditional upon faith in Christ, and including all who believe."[3] That, of course, stands in opposition to the Calvinistic notion of an unconditional election. Fourth, one Arminian theologian taught that election in Scripture has nothing to do with eternal destinies; rather it is "temporal

---

[1]William W. Klein, *The New Chosen People: A Corporate View of Election* (Grand Rapids: Zondervan, 1990), p. 257; cf. H. Orton Wiley, *Christian Theology* (Kansas City, Mo.: Beacon Hill, 1941), 2:339-40; H. Ray Dunning, *Grace, Faith and Holiness: A Wesleyan Systematic Theology* (Kansas City, Mo.: Beacon Hill, 1988), pp. 507-8.

[2]Wiley, *Christian Theology,* 2:339; cf. Richard Rice, "Biblical Support for a New Perspective," in *The Openness of God,* ed. Clark H. Pinnock et al. (Downers Grove, Ill.: InterVarsity Press, 1994), pp. 56-57.

[3]Wiley, *Christian Theology,* 2:340; cf. Dunning, *Grace, Faith and Holiness,* pp. 435-36.

predestination" and "relates only to this life and to the ones who believe. It has to do with God's predecision to bless Christians in various ways."[4]

Although the doctrine of election only comes to full flower in the New Testament, its roots sink deeply into the soil of the Old Testament. We will consider the election of Abraham, Jacob and the nation of Israel.

THE ELECTION OF ABRAHAM

God's choice of Abraham is a striking example of election. In his final address to the Israelites, Joshua provides essential background. "This is what the LORD, the God of Israel, says: 'Long ago your forefathers, including Terah the father of Abraham and Nahor, lived beyond the River and worshiped other gods. But I took your father Abraham from the land beyond the River and led him throughout Canaan and gave him many descendants'" (Josh 24:2-3).

Abraham, the father of the faithful, came from a family of idolaters! And he would have continued the family tradition had not the Lord intervened. But God called Abram, commanding him to leave his people and his father's household and promising to bless him, and through him all people (Gen 12:1-3). Later, God promised that Abram would inherit God himself as his "very great reward" (Gen 15:1). In response to God's promise of countless offspring, "Abram believed the LORD, and he credited it to him as righteousness" (Gen 15:6).

God changed Abram's name ("exalted father") to Abraham ("father of many") and swore, "I will establish my covenant as an everlasting covenant between me and you and your descendants after you for the generations to come, to be your God and the God of your descendants after you" (Gen 17:7).

THE ELECTION OF JACOB

In response to Isaac's prayer, the Lord gave twins to him and his wife

---

[4]J. Kenneth Grider, *A Wesleyan-Holiness Theology* (Kansas City, Mo.: Beacon Hill, 1994), pp. 253-55.

Rebekah (Gen 25:21-22). When the babies moved violently within her womb, she asked the Lord for an explanation. He replied: "Two nations are in your womb, and two peoples from within you will be separated; one people will be stronger than the other, and the older will serve the younger" (Gen 25:23).

Rebekah's two babies were Esau and Jacob. J. Barton Payne regards Jacob as "the most outstanding example of unconditional election to be found in all of Scripture."

> He was chosen before birth. He was one of twins, so humanly equal. He was the younger of the two and, in his personal character, he was an unethical trickster—from his very birth in fact. . . . God even granted him the promise of the testament at the very moment he was fleeing from home as a result of his crimes (Gen 28:15).[5]

Jacob and Esau represented nations, even while within their mother's womb, as the citation of Genesis 25:23 confirms. But God also dealt with the twins as individuals, as Paul explains:

> Rebekah's children had one and the same father, our father Isaac. Yet, before the twins were born or had done anything good or bad—*in order that God's purpose in election might stand:* not by works but by him who calls—she was told, "The older will serve the younger." Just as it is written: "Jacob I loved, but Esau I hated." (Rom 9:10-13, italics added)

God dealt with Jacob and Esau both as individuals and as nations. He chose Jacob as an individual to be a special recipient of his love *and* to be heir of the covenant promises to the nation. Malachi uses the words "Yet I have loved Jacob, but Esau I have hated" to speak of the nations of Israel and Edom, respectively (Mal 1:2-3). Paul uses the same words in Romans 9:13 to refer to Jacob as chosen by God and Esau as rejected. God chose Jacob and rejected Esau before birth "in order that God's

---

[5]J. Barton Payne, *The Theology of the Older Testament* (Grand Rapids: Zondervan, 1962), p. 179.

purpose in election might stand: not by works but by him who calls" (Rom 9:11-12).

THE ELECTION OF THE NATION OF ISRAEL

The Old Testament mentions God's election of individuals, but it says more about his choice of Israel, especially in Deuteronomy 4:37; 7:6-8; 10:14-15; and 14:2.

Deuteronomy 4:37. Moses urges the Israelites to acknowledge the Lord alone as God: "Because he loved your forefathers and chose their descendants after them, he brought you out of Egypt by his Presence and his great strength, to drive out nations greater and stronger than you and to bring you into their land to give it to you for your inheritance, as it is today."

God loved and chose Israel. The bond between God's love and election becomes a pattern, repeated in both testaments. Here Scripture brings together God's election of the nation and his redeeming it from Egyptian bondage. This reflects another biblical pattern—election is the source of redemption.

Deuteronomy 7:6-8. God exhorts Israel to drive the pagan nations out of Canaan:

> For you are a people holy to the LORD your God. The LORD your God has chosen you out of all the peoples on the face of the earth to be his people, his treasured possession.

> The LORD did not set his affection on you and choose you because you were more numerous than other peoples, for you were the fewest of all peoples. But it was because the LORD loved you and kept the oath he swore to your forefathers that he brought you out with a mighty hand and redeemed you from . . . Egypt.

This passage brims with teaching about election. God did not choose Israel because of its great numbers, for it was a small nation (Deut 7:7). This shows that God's choice of Israel was unmerited. God might have chosen a nation with impressive size, accomplishment or prestige, but instead he chose a nation with none of these. The positive reason for God choosing Israel is also given—God's "affection" and "love" (Deut 7:7-8). This is an important principle: God chooses people out of love for them.

God's choice of Israel was exclusive: "The LORD your God has chosen you out of all the peoples on the face of the earth to be his people" (Deut 7:6). God could have chosen more than one nation, or he could have chosen a nation other than Israel. But he chose it alone to be his covenant people.

Deuteronomy 10:14-15. After telling the Israelites to fear, obey, love and serve the Lord whole-heartedly, Moses instructs: "To the LORD your God belong the heavens, even the highest heavens, the earth and everything in it. Yet the LORD set his affection on your forefathers and loved them, and he chose you, their descendants, above all the nations, as it is today."

Although God owns everything already, he still loved and chose Israel. Israel's election, therefore, is a great privilege. Here again God's love and election are joined and his exclusive choice of Israel "above all nations" is taught (Deut 10:15).

Deuteronomy 14:2. This text repeats earlier themes: "Out of all the peoples on the face of the earth, the LORD has chosen you to be his treasured possession."

Conclusion. Both individual and corporate election are taught in the Old Testament. God chose Abraham and Jacob, and also the nation of Israel. It is a mistake, therefore, to pit individual and corporate election against each other.

Several theological principles follow. First, although Arminians have sometimes taught that God elects individuals for service but not salvation, he does both. He chooses Abram for salvation, because God promises that he himself would be his "very great reward" (Gen 15:1) and his God (Gen 17:7). God also chooses Abram for service, commanding him to go to Canaan (Gen 12:1) and to sacrifice Isaac (Gen 22:2), to cite two examples.

It is the same for Jacob. God chooses him before birth (Gen 25:23;

Rom 9:11-12) to be the heir of the promises made to Abraham and Isaac both for service and salvation. Consequently, in the Old Testament, God's declaration "Jacob I loved" speaks of the service of the nation Israel that God would bring from Jacob (Mal 1:2). In the New Testament, the same declaration speaks of God's electing love for Jacob as an individual (Rom 9:11-13).

A second theological principle follows: God does not elect Abraham and Jacob based on foreseen merit or even foreseen faith. Rather, the basis of their election is God's love and will. "The Lord chooses Abram the same way God determines to create the heavens and earth, out of the sheer freedom that comes from being the unique, all-sufficient, self-contained God."[6] We know that because Abram is an idolater when God chooses him (Josh 24:2-3).

If someone were seeking an example of God's choosing individuals based on foreseen faith or holiness, Jacob would make a poor choice. "God's grace selects this terribly imperfect man and not because of merit on his part."[7] Jacob's sins surface repeatedly in the Old Testament story, including his scheming (Gen 25:31-33), deceit (Gen 27:19, 24, 35; 31:20) and cowardice (Gen 26:7; 31:31; 33:3, 8). God's choice of Jacob is not based on faith or holiness, but God's choice produces faith and holiness. Indeed, it was not until Jacob's return to Bethel (Gen 35:9-15) that he wholeheartedly committed himself to the God who over twenty years before had graciously committed himself to Jacob.

The paramount example of election in the Old Testament is God's choice of the nation of Israel. There are four important points. First, the story of Abraham demonstrates the compatibility of individual and corporate election. God chose Abram as an individual, from Abraham God brought the elect nation of Israel, and from Israel he brought the Christ through whom the promise to Abram was fulfilled: "All peoples on earth will be blessed through you" (Gen 12:3; Gal 3:8).

---

[6]Paul R. House, *Old Testament Theology* (Downers Grove, Ill.: InterVarsity Press, 1998), p. 73.
[7]Ibid., p. 78.

Second is the reason for Israel's election. God did not choose Israel because of its great size; it was a small nation (Deut 7:7). Rather, three times we read that God loved Israel and chose it (Deut 4:37; 7:7, 8; 10:15). The idea that God chose Israel because he saw something (present or future) in it does not fit the Old Testament picture, which consistently presents Israel as a stubborn and stiff-necked people, whom God loves in spite of its rebellion. Israel's election is based not on foreseen faith but on God's free grace.

Third is the particularity of God's election of Israel. Three times we read that God chose Israel out of all the nations (Deut 7:6; 10:15; 14:2). God did not choose every nation in Old Testament times; he chose Israel alone. Although some would consider this unfair, the Old Testament does not.

Fourth, at times Arminian writers have labeled the Calvinist understanding of election arbitrary and lacking reason. But as we saw in Deuteronomy, God's choosing of Israel alone to be his covenant people is not arbitrary; it lies in his love and will. If we search for reasons behind God's love and will for why God chose Israel, we find that Scripture is silent. We must trust God's character in revealing to us what he wanted us to know and leave "the secret things . . . to the LORD our God" (Deut 29:29). Beyond that it is not wise for us to inquire.

ELECTION IN THE SYNOPTIC GOSPELS

The first three gospels advance the biblical story and introduce election in the New Testament. Jesus' eschatological discourse in Mark 13 (and its parallel in Mt 24:22, 24, 31) contains several references to persons chosen for salvation. He warns of horrendous days. "If the Lord had not cut short those days, no one would survive. But for the sake of the elect, whom he has chosen, he has shortened them" (Mk 13:20). The Lord has chosen people and will shorten the terrible days that are coming, so that they will survive.

Jesus says that false Christs will appear and perform miracles "to deceive the elect—if that were possible" (Mk 13:22). God has chosen people and will protect them spiritually from being duped by the miracles of the false Christs who will come.

Jesus urges spiritual preparedness in light of the Second Coming. At that time, he will return "with great power and glory. And he will send his angels and gather his elect from the . . . ends of the earth" (Mk 13:26-27). There are people chosen for salvation—"the elect." Their election is for salvation because the returning Son of Man will gather them to share in his kingdom.

There is development from the Old Testament to the gospels. "The election motif is an important element in the theology of Jesus and transforms the corporate identity of Israel's view to the individual thrust of Jesus' view."[8] That is correct as long as we note that there were instances of individual election in the Old Testament. Furthermore, Jesus teaches that God chooses certain Israelites and Gentiles for salvation. God will protect them during the difficult times ahead, guard them from spiritual deception and usher them into his kingdom.

ELECTION IN THE GOSPEL OF JOHN

The fourth gospel paints three pictures that pertain to election: the Father giving people to the Son, the prior identity of God's people and Jesus choosing people for salvation.

John 6:35-45. After multiplying the loaves and fish (Jn 6:1-15), Jesus proclaims that he is the Bread of Life who satisfies eternally the spiritual appetite of those who believe in him (Jn 6:25-59). The Jews have seen him and do not believe (Jn 6:36). By contrast, Jesus says, "All that the Father gives me will come to me" (Jn 6:37). John 6:35 illumines the meaning of "coming" to Jesus. "I am the bread of life. He who *comes* to me will never go hungry, and he who *believes* in me will never be thirsty" (italics added). "To come" to Jesus means to believe in him. Consequently, Jesus teaches that all whom the Father gives him will believe in (come to) him.

---

[8]Grant Osborne, "Soteriology in the Epistle to the Hebrews," in *Grace Unlimited,* ed. Clark H. Pinnock (Minneapolis: Bethany Fellowship, 1975), p. 168. There are also hints of election in Mt 22:14 and Lk 18:7-8.

The Father's giving people to the Son is a picture of election. In addition, the Father's giving people to the Son precedes their believing in him for salvation. Election is not based on foreseen faith; it precedes faith and results in faith. "All that the Father gives me will come to me" (Jn 6:37).

John 10:26-30. Jesus, the Good Shepherd, says to his hearers who reject him despite his miracles, "You do not believe because you are not my sheep." By contrast, "My sheep listen to my voice; I know them, and they follow me" (Jn 10:25-27).

Jesus' words divide his hearers into two categories: sheep and those who are not sheep (we'll call them goats). People have one of these two identities, and Jesus implies that they are sheep or goats *before* they respond to him. Their response of belief or unbelief doesn't cause them to become either sheep or goats. Instead, their responses *reveal* their prior identities. Listen carefully to Jesus' words, "But you do not believe because you are not my sheep. My sheep listen to my voice" (Jn 10:26-27). Jesus does not say that they are goats because they don't believe, but the opposite: they don't believe because they are goats. Jesus here teaches predestination: people are sheep or goats before they believe or reject Jesus, and their faith or unbelief manifests their prior identity.

John 15:14-19. After giving the analogy of the vine and the branches, Jesus assures his eleven disciples (Judas has already left to betray him), "You did not choose me, but I chose you and appointed you to go and bear" lasting fruit (Jn 15:16). The implication is that the fruitful branches spoken of earlier in this chapter are those whom Jesus has chosen. They bear fruit because he has chosen and appointed them to that end.

Someone will say that Jesus' choice is a choice of persons to be his disciples and not a choice to eternal life. Jesus speaks of such a choice in John 6:70, "Have I not chosen you, the Twelve? Yet one of you is a devil!" But Jesus' choice of the eleven in John 15:16 differs from his choice of the Twelve in John 6:70. Here Jesus warns the disciples that the world will hate them because it has hated him first. Then he says: "If you belonged to the world, it would love you as its own. As it is, you do not belong to the world, but I have chosen you out of the world. That is why the world hates you" (Jn 15:18-19). The choice of John 6:70 was Jesus' choice of twelve men to be his disciples. The choice of John 15:16, 19 was a choice of the eleven disciples "out of the world" that results in their belonging no longer to the world, but to Jesus.

Despite the Arminian claim that election is not for salvation but for service, this passage reveals that it is for both. Jesus chose the eleven out of the world so that they would belong to him (Jn 15:19; salvation) and also so that they would bear lasting fruit (Jn 15:16; service).

John 17:2, 6, 9-10, 24. Jesus prays in anticipation of the cross and his return to the Father. The Son's mission of salvation is governed by the Father's prior election of people. Although the Father has "granted" the Son "authority over all people," the Son only gives "eternal life to all those" the Father has "given him" (Jn 17:2). The Son is thus sovereign over all people but only grants the gift of eternal life to the elect. Furthermore, Jesus explains his mission, "I have revealed you to those you gave me out of the world" (Jn 17:6). As a result, they accept the divine message and believe in the Son (Jn 17:7-8).

Jesus' prayers likewise reflect a prior divine discrimination. "I pray for them. I am not praying for the world, but for those you have given me, for they are yours" (Jn 17:9). Jesus uses the word *world* to refer to those not given to him by the Father. Envisioning his cross work as completed, Jesus prays that the elect will join him in heaven: "Father, I want those you have given me to be with me where I am, and to see my glory" (Jn 17:24).

In this famous passage, John portrays election as the Father's having given people to the Son. They first belonged to the Father, and he gave them to Jesus (Jn 17:6). Jesus gives eternal life and reveals the Father to them alone; he prays for them alone and specifically asks the Father to take them to heaven (Jn 17:2, 6, 9-10, 24).

Conclusions. Arminian views of election do not fare well in light of the Gospel of John. The idea that election is for service and not salvation is incorrect because John's gospel specifically relates election to salvation. For example, Jesus prays, "Father, . . . you granted him [the Son] authority over all people that he might give eternal life to all those you have given him" (Jn 17:1-2; see also 6:37-40; 10:27-29; 15:19; 17:6, 9-10, 24).

Furthermore, the fourth Gospel clashes with the Arminian view that God chooses on the basis of foreseen faith. Instead, because faith is the result of election, the basis of election resides in God's action and not in people's. To cite one example: Jesus said, "All that the Father gives me will come to me" (Jn 6:37; see also 10:27; 15:19; 17:2, 6, 9, 24). Election is not based on faith; faith is the result of the Father's prior election.

ELECTION IN ACTS

In light of Luke's emphasis on God's sovereignty in both his Gospel and the Acts, we will investigate statements concerning predestination in Acts 13:48 and 18:9-10.[9]

Acts 13:48. Paul and Barnabas's ministry in Pisidian Antioch on the first missionary journey is met alternatively by faith in their message (Acts 13:42-44, 47-49) and persecution (Acts 13:45-46, 50-51). As a result the apostles are up (Acts 13:42-44), down (Acts 13:45-46), up (Acts 13:47-49) and down (Acts 13:50-51). In the midst of the vacillating responses, the Gentiles turn to the Lord. "When the Gentiles heard this, they were glad and honored the word of the Lord; and all who were appointed for eternal life believed" (Acts 13:48).

Luke presents a divine classification or appointment to eternal life. And that appointment to eternal life precedes faith on the part of the believers—"all who were appointed for eternal life believed." William W. Klein attempts to harmonize Acts 13:48 with an Arminian view of predestination by reversing Luke's order: "The Gentiles believed and entered the category of the appointed ones."[10] On the contrary, there is a category of appointed ones (known only to God), and when Paul preached, appointed Gentiles believed the message.

Acts 18:9-10. In Corinth on his second missionary journey, Paul, discour-

---

[9]See I. Howard Marshall, *Luke: Historian and Theologian* (Grand Rapids: Zondervan, 1970), pp. 104, 106-7; Donald Guthrie, *New Testament Theology* (Downers Grove, Ill.: InterVarsity Press, 1981), p. 618.

[10]Klein, *New Chosen People,* p. 121; cf. pp. 109-10.

aged by Jewish opposition, stops preaching in the synagogue and turns to the Gentiles (Acts 18:5-8). The Lord speaks to Paul in a vision one night telling him to continue preaching the gospel (Acts 18:9). God promises the apostle, "I have many people in this city" (Acts 18:10). Paul obediently stays on in Corinth for eighteen months ministering the Word of God (Acts 18:11).

Luke teaches that people in Corinth belonged to God even before they believed the Gospel. Again we see God's election of people to salvation. Interestingly, although some claim that an emphasis on God's sovereignty in salvation hinders evangelism, that emphasis encouraged Paul to continue preaching.

Conclusions. In at least two passages in Acts, then, there are indications of a divine choice to salvation. Contrary to the Arminian notion that election is corporate and not individual, in Acts it is both. Acts 13:48 and 18:9-10 teach that God chose individuals for salvation. These individuals, of course, make up the church. In addition, the Arminian idea of election based on God's foreseeing of faith clashes with Acts 13:48, where faith is the consequence (not the cause) of election.

ELECTION IN REVELATION

A theme from Revelation that pertains to the doctrine of election is "the book of life" (Rev 3:5; 17:8; 20:12, 15) or "the Lamb's book of life" (Rev 13:8; 21:27). This book serves as the census register of the city of God. The names of the saints were enrolled "in the book of life from the creation of the world" (Rev 17:8). The chief use of that book is to assure those listed therein of God's spiritual protection (Rev 3:5; 13:8; 17:8; 20:15; 21:27). Although Arminians sometimes claim that predestination does not result in salvation, the passages mentioning the book of life disprove that claim. That is because those whose names are written in the book from creation (Rev 17:8) will be spared the lake of fire (Rev 20:15) and will enter the New Jerusalem (Rev 21:27).[11]

---

[11]See G. K. Beale, *The Book of Revelation*, New International Greek Testament Commentary (Grand Rapids: Eerdmans, 1999), pp. 281-82.

ELECTION IN PAUL'S EPISTLES

All agree that the apostle Paul is the main theologian of predestination in Scripture. Although he mentions the idea of predestination in many texts, he discusses its meaning in Romans 8:29-30; Ephesians 1:4-5, 11 and Romans 9:6-24.

Romans 8:28-30. Paul writes, "And we know that in all things God works for the good of those who love him, who have been called according to his purpose" (Rom 8:28). Paul means that even in present sufferings believers can be sure that God is working for their ultimate good. Why? Paul answers, "For those God foreknew he also predestined to be conformed to the likeness of his Son, that he might be the firstborn among many brothers. And those he predestined, he also called; those he called, he also justified; those he justified, he also glorified" (Rom 8:29-30). Christians are assured that God will work all for their good because he has accomplished the greatest good for them—he planned and brought about their salvation from beginning to end.

Paul uses five verbs in the past tense to describe what God has done. He foreknew, predestined, called, justified and glorified "those who love him" (Rom 8:28). It is important to note that God is the subject of those verbs and that the verbs have the same object—believers. We will briefly define the verbs in reverse order. God glorifies people when he causes them to behold Christ's glory and be transformed by it. He justifies believers by declaring them righteous because of Christ's righteousness. He calls them by effectively summoning them to himself in the gospel. He predestines them by marking them out beforehand for salvation. Foreknowledge is controversial and deserves special treatment.

Arminians and Calvinists understand foreknowledge differently. Arminians hold that God foresees who will believe in him and chooses people for salvation on that basis. This is called conditional election because God's choice is conditioned upon foreseen human belief or unbelief. Calvinists disagree and usually maintain that God's foreknowledge in Romans 8:29 and related passages means his choosing of people for salvation. Arminians rightly protest that if this is true then Paul teaches that those whom God chose ("foreknew") he also chose ("predestined").

The apostle is not merely reiterating the same idea. The key to under-standing the biblical idea of foreknowledge in election passages lies in carefully noting the combination of words.

As we pointed out above, "foreknew" in Romans 8:29 has God as sub-ject and his people as object. The words *know* and *foreknow* have a broad range of meaning in Scripture, and sometimes *foreknow* means knowing facts beforehand. But that is not its meaning in Romans 8:29. Paul does not say that God foreknows certain facts (which of course he does; he knows all facts); instead he says that he foreknows certain people. This is parallel to other Scriptures that speak of God or Christ knowing hu-man beings in a personal saving relationship. Consider Jesus' strong words to hypocrites: "I never knew you. Away from me, you evildoers!" (Mt 7:23). Jesus is not claiming ignorance of facts; he is saying that he did not know the hypocrites with a saving knowledge. Likewise, Jesus proclaims, "I am the good shepherd; I know my sheep and my sheep know me" (Jn 10:14). If he were speaking of facts, he would know both sheep and goats perfectly. But he speaks of the knowledge of saving re-lationship. Paul's words also fit that pattern: "Formerly, when you did not know God, you were slaves to those who by nature are not gods. But now that you know God—or rather are known by God—how is it that you are turning back to those weak and miserable principles?" (Gal 4:8-9). Paul doesn't speak of the knowledge of facts; he speaks of the knowledge of a person—God.

When Paul says, "God foreknew" people in Romans 8:29, therefore, he means that God planned to enter into a saving personal relationship with them, to set his love upon them. Scripture teaches that God did this "before the creation of the world" (Eph 1:4) and "before the beginning of time" (2 Tim 1:9). "For those God foreknew he also predestined," means that "God predestines us on the basis of his gracious commitment to us before the world was."[12] Because those foreknown are the same

---

[12]S. M. Baugh, "The Meaning of Foreknowledge," in *Still Sovereign*, ed. Thomas R. Schreiner and Bruce A. Ware (Grand Rapids: Baker, 2000), p. 194.

ones who are predestined, called, justified and glorified and because Scripture teaches that not everyone will be finally glorified, it follows that not everyone is foreknown or loved beforehand.

Though some Arminian thinkers have neglected this passage entirely,[13] and others have given it scant attention,[14] Ken Grider treats it in his systematic theology: "This passage states that 'those God foreknew,' meaning surely those He foreknew would believe, 'he also predestined to be conformed to the likeness of his Son.'"[15] Grider merely assumes the Arminian understanding of foreknowledge without offering argument or proof.

Grider understands Paul's words to speak of "temporal predestination." "Predestination does not have to do with a pre-decision of God regarding the eternal destiny of people, but . . . it has to do with what God graciously decides for believers temporally,"[16] even their being conformed to Christ's likeness. But conformity to Christ *is* the eternal destiny of Christians. So, when Paul says, "Those God foreknew he also predestined to be conformed to the likeness of his Son" (Rom 8:29), he teaches that predestination is unto the eternal destiny of conformity to Christ.

Ephesians 1:4-5, 11. The theological context for the study of election in Ephesians 1 is praise directed to the Trinity for a grand salvation (Eph 1:6, 12, 14). Here Paul teaches at least four truths about God's election: its timing, basis and results and the fact that it was "in Christ."

For the first time Scripture gives the timing of election. God "chose us in him [Christ] before the creation of the world" (Eph 1:4). The Father chose his people before creation. Why does Paul write that? For the same reason that he introduces a time element in Romans 9:11, "Yet, *before the twins were born or had done anything good or bad*—in order that God's purpose in election might stand: not by works but by him who calls—she was told, 'The older will serve the younger'" (italics added). Paul high-

---

[13]Wiley, *Christian Theology*, 2:335-40.
[14]Dunning, *Grace, Faith and Holiness*, p. 508.
[15]Grider, *Wesleyan-Holiness Theology*, p. 250.
[16]Ibid., p. 249.

lights the fact that God chose Jacob for this purpose before he and Esau were born to establish God's electing purpose.

Similarly, when Paul says that God chose us before creation, he underlines God's purpose in election. We didn't exist before the foundation of the world and therefore could contribute nothing to election. Paul teaches the same truth in 2 Timothy 1:9 when he writes that God's grace "was given us in Christ Jesus before the beginning of time."

As clearly as anywhere in the Bible, Ephesians 1 teaches that God chose his people for salvation because of his love and sovereign will. God's love, his grace, is the basis of election. "*In love* he predestined us to be adopted as his sons through Jesus Christ . . . to the praise of *his glorious grace*" (Eph 1:4-5; italics added). Because the Father set his affection upon a multitude of human beings, he chose to adopt them as his children.

God's sovereign will also is the basis of election. That is affirmed at the end of verse 5: "In love he predestined us to be adopted as his sons through Jesus Christ, in accordance with his pleasure and will" (Eph 1:4-5). Ephesians 1:11 reinforces that truth: "In him we were also chosen, having been predestined according to the plan of him who works out everything in conformity with the purpose of his will." The apostle could not say more emphatically that God causes everything to conform to his sovereign will, including his free choice of his people.

The basis of God's election is God's love and good pleasure, his grace and plan, his mercy and the purpose of his will. It is best to combine the two aspects into one expression, using an adjective for one aspect and a noun for the other—predestination finally rests on God's sovereign mercy, free grace, loving choice, gracious will. This cuts across the grain of Arminian teaching because election is based not on foreseen human faith but on God's love and will (Eph 1:3-4, 11).

Election produces results, namely salvation. The Father "chose us . . . to be holy and blameless in his sight" (Eph 1:4). That is, election results in sanctification. "In love he predestined us to be adopted as his sons through Jesus Christ" (Eph 1:4-5). That is, predestination results in adoption. Sanctification and adoption are two ways of speaking of salvation applied. Election, then, results in salvation. Consequently, Arminian teaching errs when it says that election pertains to service not salvation.

What does Paul mean when he says that God "chose us in him" (Eph 1:4), that "in him we were also chosen" (Eph 1:11)? Jack Cottrell summarizes the Arminian view: "[God] foreknows whether an individual will meet the *conditions* for salvation which he has sovereignly imposed. . . . This is the import of Eph. 1:4, which says that 'He chose us in Him'—in Christ."[17] Is this correct?

Paul often (not always) uses "in Christ" and "in him" to signify union with Christ. At least six times in Ephesians 1, for example, this is the case: in Ephesians 1:1, 3, 6, 7, 9 and 13. And, when Paul twice says God chose us "in him" (Eph 1: 4, 11), "in him" refers to union with Christ. What is the difference between Paul's regular use of "in Christ" and his use of it to refer to election? The difference lies in the time factor. When speaking of election, Paul says God chose us in Christ *before creation* (Eph 1:4). The other times that Paul uses this phrase he speaks of God actually joining people to Christ in history.

God's choosing us "in him before the creation of the world" (Eph 1:4, 11) refers to union with Christ before creation. The words cannot speak of actual union with Christ because we didn't exist before we were created. Rather, they speak of God's planning to join us to Christ. The meaning of the whole expression God "chose us in him before the creation of the world" is that God not only elected a people for himself; he also planned the means by which they would be saved; he planned to join them to his Son and his saving benefits.

Paul's words "He chose us in him before . . . creation" do not describe a condition that sinners must meet in order to be chosen by God. The words do not speak of people's response at all; they speak of God's plan. And it is the same for Ephesians 1:11. Paul does not speak of human beings but of God's sovereign will when he says, "In him we were also cho-

---

[17]Jack Cottrell, "Conditional Election," in *Grace Unlimited*, ed. Clark H. Pinnock (Minneapolis: Bethany Fellowship, 1975), p. 61 (italics in original).

sen, having been predestined according to the plan of him who works out everything in conformity with the purpose of his will."

Paul uses plural and not singular pronouns to depict those chosen by God in Ephesians 1. Does that fact prove the Arminian view that election to salvation is corporate and not individual? No. Ephesians was not written to an individual; it was written to a church or churches. So, of course, Paul employs plural pronouns. With regard to election being individual or corporate, it is a matter not of either/or but of both/and. God chooses individuals for sanctification and adoption (Eph 1:3-4), individuals who constitute the church. God elected Jews ("we who were the first to hope in Christ," Eph 1:12) and Gentiles ("you also," Eph 1:13) to compose the Christian church.

Romans 9:6-24. Paul's discussion of the weak and strong believers at Rome gets to the heart of the historical context of Romans 9:6-24. The weak believers were Jewish Christians who ate kosher (Rom 14:2, 14) and observed Jewish religious days (Rom 14:5). The Gentiles could eat anything and did not feel compelled to observe Jewish festivals. Paul exhorts both factions in the church at Rome: "Let us therefore make every effort to do what leads to peace and to mutual edification. . . . Accept one another, then, just as Christ accepted you, in order to bring praise to God" (Rom 14:19; 15:7).

This background helps readers appreciate Paul's references to "the Jew(s) and the Gentile(s)" (Rom 1:16; 2:9, 10; 3: 9, 29; 9:24; 10:12). One purpose of Romans is to foster unity in a church that is divided along ethnic lines, between Jews and Gentiles. Romans 9—11 is the section of Romans most directly aimed at healing the breach in the congregation.

The Jewish Christians in Rome were among the pilgrims in Jerusalem at Pentecost when the New Testament church began (Acts 2:10-11). Their congregation at the first was Jewish Christian. But by the time Romans was written the Jewish Christians in Rome were in the minority (Rom 11:13), and their Gentiles brothers had been disrespectful (14:1, 4, 10, 13, 15, 19). Consequently, the Jewish Christians were struggling with this question: Have God's promises to Israel failed?

After rehearsing the blessings that God showered upon Israel, Paul answers that question, "It is not as though God's word had failed" (Rom 9:6). In fact, Paul addresses that question in three chapters. First, he says that God's word hasn't failed but God fulfilled his sovereign plan (Rom 9:6-29). Second, he answers in terms of human accountability: God's word hasn't failed; rather, Israel reaped rejection from God because it sowed unbelief (Rom 9:30-10:21). Third, Paul answers in light of God's commitment to his promises to the patriarchs: God will yet bring a Jewish remnant to himself (Rom 11:1-32).

God's promise to Israel hasn't failed, Paul asserts (Rom 9:6), and as evidence he offers a lesson in redemptive history. From the first generation, God sovereignly has fulfilled his word to Israel, in spite of its unbelief and disobedience.

God executes his plan in providing an heir for Abraham and Sarah (Rom 9:6-9). Mere physical descent from Abraham is insufficient to establish membership in Israel. Rather, the line passes through Abraham and Sarah's son Isaac. "It is not the natural children who are God's children, but it is the children of *the promise* who are regarded as Abraham's offspring" (Rom 9:8; italics added). Arminians might claim that "the promise" here points to human freedom in responding to the gospel, but the next verse specifies: "For this was how the promise was stated: 'At the appointed time I will return, and Sarah will have a son'" (Rom 9:9). God gave his sovereign word, promising an infertile couple that they would have a son. Abraham and Sarah had tried to fulfill God's promise on their own using the handmaid Hagar to produce Ishmael. But that would not be God's way; instead, he would produce a child from a man whose "body was as good as dead" and his wife whose "womb was also dead" (Rom 4:19). God sovereignly fulfills his word contrary to all human ability and expectation.

God's rule also shines in the next generation of Israel's history (Rom 9:10-13). Although the twin boys had the same father, Isaac, and although Esau, not Jacob, was the firstborn, God chose Jacob and rejected Esau. Indeed, "Before the twins were born or had done anything good or bad—in order that God's purpose in election might stand: not by works but by him who calls—she [their mother Rebekah] was told, 'The older will serve the younger.' Just as it is written: 'Jacob I loved, but Esau I hated'" (Rom 9:11-13). Plainly, the outcome was not of human devising, but divine. God chose the second son, Jacob, to magnify his "purpose in election" (Rom 9:11).

The protest lodged in Romans 9:14 confirms our interpretation of Romans 9:6-13. "What then shall we say? Is God unjust?" If election involved God's foreknowing and ratifying human responses to the gospel, Paul would answer, "You misunderstand me. I don't mean that God is as sovereign in human affairs as your objection implies. He doesn't choose us, but only confirms our choice of him." Instead, Paul writes, "Not at all! For he says to Moses, 'I will have mercy on whom I have mercy, and I will have compassion on whom I have compassion'" (Rom 9:14-15). Paul does not back away from the idea of sovereignty implied in the objection; rather, he reinforces it. God is free in his mercy to show compassion to whomever he wills. It is God's will, not ours, that is ultimately determinative in matters pertaining to salvation.

The next verse is particularly difficult for Arminianism. "It does not, therefore, depend on man's desire or effort, but on God's mercy" (Rom 9:16). Paul explicitly excludes human desire (literally, "willing") or effort (literally, "running") as the determining factor in salvation. The determining factor is God, not human beings and their responses to God.

This is confirmed by God's dealings with Pharaoh. Paul teaches that God raised up Pharaoh to display God's power and glory in the ancient Near East (Rom 9:17). Paul's conclusion to the redemptive history lesson begun in Romans 9:6 devastates theologies based on free will. "Therefore God has mercy on whom he wants to have mercy, and he hardens whom he wants to harden" (Rom 9:18).

In Romans 9:19, as in 9:14, Paul raises an objection to his strong monergistic teaching. "Then why does God still blame us? For who resists his will?" Paul's reply confirms the correctness of our exposition. He does not tone down his emphasis on sovereignty and say, "God is not absolutely in control, as your protest misunderstands me to teach. Instead, God grants us free will and makes his choice based upon our response to the gospel." Rather than qualifying his teaching, Paul protests against the protest. "But who are you, O man, to talk back to God? 'Shall what is formed say to him who formed it, "Why did you make me like this?"'" (Rom 9:20).

Paul continues his response to the objector, "Does not the potter have the right to make out of the same lump of clay some pottery for noble purposes and some for common use?" (Rom 9:21). Paul expects a positive answer to his question, as the Greek implies.[18] God, the divine Potter, has the right to do as he pleases with the pots that he fashions from a lump of clay.

Next Paul uses the form of a question to give the strongest teaching on predestination found in Scripture. "What if God, choosing to show his wrath and make his power known, bore with great patience the objects of his wrath—prepared for destruction? What if he did this to make the riches of his glory known to the objects of his mercy, whom he prepared in advance for glory?" (Rom 9:22-23). Paul teaches that God stands behind the fate of every human being, whether for glory or wrath.

Arminians handle Romans 9:6-23 in three main ways. First, sometimes they ignore these verses in their treatment of predestination. This is the case for the standard systematic theologies of Orton Wiley, Ray Dunning and Ken Grider. Second, Arminians have held that when Paul speaks of "objects of wrath" and "objects of mercy," he refers to Jews and Gentiles, respectively. He is speaking not of the eternal destinies of individuals but of the fates of those two groups. Third, Arminians have maintained that Paul's questions in Romans 9:22-23 (one big question in Greek) are hypothetical. Paul asks, "What if God . . . ?" He doesn't say that God actually chooses some persons and rejects others; he merely states a hypothesis. We know from other Scriptures, the Arminian argument continues, that God does no such thing.

---

[18]He uses the negative particle οὐ in the question.

Romans 9:24 shows the inadequacy of these Arminian approaches to Romans 9:22-23. "What if he did this to make the riches of his glory known to the objects of his mercy, whom he prepared in advance for glory—*even us, whom he also called, not only from the Jews but also from the Gentiles?*" (Rom 9:23-24; italics added). Paul identifies first-century Jews and Gentiles as among "the objects of his mercy." That means that the questions in Romans 9:22-23 are not hypothetical but rhetorical. Paul commonly uses rhetorical questions as teaching devices to drive home points.

Furthermore, because Paul identifies "the objects of his mercy" with Jews and Gentiles, the Arminian corporate interpretation is also incorrect. "The objects of his wrath" and "the objects of his mercy" cannot be Jews and Gentiles, respectively, because Paul says that the latter category includes both Jews and Gentiles. Paul teaches that God as the Creator has the rights over his creatures. "The objects of his wrath" are human beings whom God has passed over and appointed for judgment; "the objects of his mercy" are human beings whom God has chosen in advance for glory.

Arminian teaching on predestination founders, therefore, on the classic passage of Romans 9:6-24. Election here is not corporate rather than individual; it is both individual and corporate. God chooses Jacob and hardens Pharaoh (Rom 9:10-13). And he chooses individuals to make up the corporate entity of the church (Rom 9:19-24). The Arminian claim that election is for service and not salvation is not corroborated by Romans 9. God's choice results in people receiving God's mercy (Rom 9:15-16, 18, 23) and glory (Rom 9:23).

The Arminian view that predestination is based on God's foreseeing faith is incompatible with Romans 9, for, Paul writes, "It does not, therefore, depend on man's desire or effort, but on God's mercy" (Rom 9:16). Moreover, the apostle gives the positive basis of election: God's love (Rom 9:13), mercy (Rom 9:15, 16, 18, 23), compassion (Rom 9:15) and sovereign will (Rom 9:19-24). It is no wonder, then, that Arminian scholars commonly skip Romans 9 when discussing election, because it contradicts their theory at several points.

Although Romans 9 gives a true answer to the question of whether God's word has failed, it does not give an exhaustive answer. Romans 9 answers: God's word has not failed, but God did what he sovereignly ordained. Romans 10 gives a complementary answer: God's word has not failed, but unbelieving Israel reaped what it deserved for its unbelief—God's judgment. Paul thus sets God's absolute sovereignty (Romans 9) side by side with genuine human freedom (Romans 10). Notice that sovereignty and freedom don't cancel each other out. The fact that God is in control (Romans 9) doesn't mean that we are puppets. Neither does human freedom (Romans 10) mean that God has relinquished control. Rather, in a way that we cannot fully comprehend, God is absolutely in control, and we are genuinely responsible. Of course, both perspectives cannot be equally ultimate. God alone is Lord, and his sovereignty is the ultimate cause of all things. But human freedom, although not ultimate, is significant and considerable.

CONCLUSION

First, although Arminians hold to corporate rather than individual election, the Bible teaches both. God elects individuals: Abraham (Josh 24:2-3), Jacob (Rom 9:10-13) and New Testament saints (Jn 6:37-40; Acts 13:48; Rom 8:29; 9:22-24; Eph 1:4-5). God also elects corporate entities: Israel (Gen 12:3; Deut 4:37; 7:6-8; 10:14-15) and the church (Acts 13:48; Rom 9:22-24; Eph 1:11-13). Arminianism, then, makes a false distinction between individual and corporate election.

Second, Arminians hold that election has to do with service and not salvation. Scripture, however, presents election as having to do with both salvation (Acts 13:48; Eph 1:4-5; Jas 2:5) and service (Jn 15:16; 2 Pet 1:10). Therefore, when Arminianism pits salvation and service against each other, it again forges a false choice.

Third, and most important, Arminianism maintains that individual election to salvation is based on foreseen faith. But that is not taught by a single passage of Scripture. Instead, Scripture denies it (Rom 9:16) and repeatedly teaches that election to salvation is based on God's sovereign will (Jn 6:37; 10:28; 17:2, 6, 9, 24; Acts 13:48; Rom 8:29; 9:19-24; Eph 1:4, 5, 11; 2 Tim 1:8-9) and grace (Deut 7:7, 8; Rom 8:29; 9:13, 15, 16, 18, 23; Eph 1:4-5; 2 Tim 1:8-9).

Fourth, Grider denies that election pertains to eternal destinies and holds that it is "temporal predestination" of Christians to various temporal blessings.[19] But he errs, because when Scripture speaks of God's purpose in predestination, it uses synonyms for salvation, including calling (Rom 9:24), adoption (Eph 1:5), sanctification (Eph 1:4), resurrection (Jn 6:39), conformity to Christ (Rom 8:29) and glorification (Rom 8:30).

How do people know that they are chosen for salvation? Not by trying to discern the eternal counsels of the Almighty, for he has not revealed them to us. Rather, it is when people turn to Christ in faith that they know God has chosen them for salvation. "For we know, brothers loved by God, that he has chosen you, because our gospel came to you not simply with words, but also with power, with the Holy Spirit and with deep conviction" (1 Thess 1:4-5).

What are the purposes of predestination? That God might be praised for lavishing grace on us (Eph 1:4-6). That believers might be moved to thank God for choosing people for salvation (2 Thess 2:13). That Christians might be strengthened in assurance (Rom 8:29-30; Rev 13:8; 17:8; 20:15; 21:27). That we might be motivated to serve the Lord with all of our strength, knowing that he guarantees results (Acts 18:9-11; 2 Tim 2:10).

Arminians sometimes reject the Calvinistic understanding of election as arbitrary or random. Consider Wiley's words: "Nothing is more grievous in the predestination theory than the way in which it shadows the love of God. Between love as a nature or disposition, and an arbitrary choice of its beneficiaries, there is an irreconcilable antithesis."[20] But why must God's sovereign decision to love some be considered arbitrary? All deserve his wrath; none deserve his grace. He freely chooses to

---

[19]Grider, *Wesleyan-Holiness Theology*, pp. 253-55.
[20]Wiley, *Christian Theology*, 2:339.

bestow saving grace on billions of undeserving sinners. That is not arbitrary; the Bible itself teaches that election is the result of God's love and will. His gracious choosing ultimately transcends our reason, but it is not arbitrary.

4

PERSEVERANCE

Uncertain or Certain?

ᑲ

Clark Pinnock begins the story of why he abandoned Calvinism for Arminianism by citing the incompatibility of the doctrine of the perseverance of the saints with the apostasy passages in Hebrews.[1] This chapter will address questions raised by Pinnock and more.

SCRIPTURE AFFIRMS THAT GOD PRESERVES
HIS PEOPLE FOR FINAL SALVATION

Scripture affirms that God keeps to the end those he has saved. This work of God in keeping believers is called preservation. We will investigate nine passages that teach God's preservation of his saints.

Luke 22:31-32. After the last supper, Jesus tells Simon Peter that Satan has requested to sift the disciples as wheat, that is, to harm them. The shift in pronoun from *you* plural ("to sift you," all) to *you* singular ("I prayed for you," Simon Peter) specifies Peter as Satan's special target. Indeed, in spite of Peter's protests, Jesus' prediction comes true—Peter denies Christ three times (Lk 22:33-34; cf. vv. 54-62).

Although Satan would mount a fierce attack, Christ tells Peter, "I have prayed for you . . . that your faith may not fail" (Lk 22:32). At first it ap-

---

[1]Clark H. Pinnock, ed., *The Grace of God, the Will of Man* (Grand Rapids: Zondervan, 1989), p. 17.

pears that Peter's faith has failed three times. But further reflection reveals that Jesus means "utterly fail," as his next words imply: "And when you have turned back, strengthen your brothers." Peter would stumble badly, but not fall away completely. Why? Because the same one from whom Satan asked permission to harm Peter—Jesus Christ—had prayed on his behalf. Because of Christ's effective prayer, although Peter's faith flickered, it did not go out.

"Holy Father, protect them by the power of your name. . . . My prayer is not that you take them out of the world but that you protect them from the evil one" (Jn 17: 11, 15). Our risen, glorious Lord continues to intercede for us before the throne of God (Rom 8:34; Heb 7:25). Christ's present ministry of intercession, therefore, preserves the children of God in their faith, even as his prayer for Peter kept him from falling away.

John 6:37, 39-40, 44. The Father and Son work harmoniously in salvation. The Father gives people to the Son and draws them to him. As a result they come to the Son (that is, they believe in him; cf. Jn 6:35) and receive eternal life. The Son doesn't drive them away or lose them, but keeps them and will raise them at the last day.

The harmonious efforts of the Father and Son result in continuity of the people they save. The Father gives and draws certain people to the Son; the Son in turn promises to preserve these same people to eternal life. Two devices stress divine preservation. First, John uses "never" and "none": "I will never drive away . . . I shall lose none" (Jn 6:37, 39). Second, John uses repetition: three times the passage says that the Son will raise believers from the dead (Jn 6:39, 40, 44). The result is a ringing affirmation of the safety of God's children in the Son's care.

John 10:27-30. Jesus gives the gift of eternal life to his sheep and promises, in a strong negative, "They shall *never* perish" (Jn 10:28; italics added).[2] Jesus states categorically that he will never revoke his gift of eternal life. And he adds that "no one can snatch" (Jn 10:29) the sheep from

---

[2]οὐ μή with the aorist subjunctive often shows emphatic negation. See Friedrich Blass and Albert Debrunner, *A Greek Grammar of the New Testament and Other Early Christian Literature,* trans. Robert Funk, rev. ed. (Chicago: University of Chicago Press, 1961), para. 365.

his hand or that of the great Father, where *hand* stands for power.[3] The sheep are secure in the sovereign protection of the Son and his Father.

The Arminian protest, "But it doesn't say that we can't take ourselves out of his hands," is not strong. How could Jesus make his preservation of us any clearer than to say categorically we will never perish and to promise us the protection of himself and the Father? Because each of us is "someone," each is included in the "no one" who cannot snatch us away from salvation. We would have to be more powerful than God himself to undo his gift of salvation.

Romans 5:9-10. Paul teaches that God keeps those he saves by drawing two pictures of salvation: justification and reconciliation. First, Paul argues in terms of justification. He provides the result clause but omits the conditional clause, intending for readers to imply it from the preceding context (Rom 5:6, 8). Here is Paul's full argument with the implied "if" clause supplied: "[If when we were guilty, God justified us through Christ's death,] since we have now been justified by his blood, how much more shall we be saved from God's wrath through him!" (Rom 5:9).

Paul argues that if God did the harder thing—acquitting guilty sinners through Christ—he will surely do the easier thing—keeping us acquitted, sparing us God's wrath through Christ. Next, the apostle argues in terms of reconciliation: "For if, when we were God's enemies, we were reconciled to him through the death of his Son, how much more, having been reconciled, shall we be saved though his life!" (Rom 5:10). Paul reasons this way: if God did the more difficult thing—made peace with his enemies through Christ's death—God can be counted on to do the easier thing—continue to save those who have been reconciled through Christ's resurrection.

Romans 8:28-39. Paul marshals four arguments to show that God keeps his people saved to the end. First, Paul argues on the basis of God's plan. Paul uses five verbs in the simple past tense to speak of God's saving

---

[3]According to W. Bauer et al., *A Greek-English Lexicon of the New Testament and Other Early Christian Literature,* ed. Frederick Danker, 2nd ed. (Chicago: University of Chicago Press, 1979), p. 880.

work from the beginning to the end. The same people God foreknew (foreloved), he predestined, called, justified and glorified (Rom 8:29-30). It is amazing that future salvation (glorification) is spoken of in the past tense! The final salvation of God's people is viewed as already accomplished because they are safe in his care.[4]

Second, Paul argues for preservation based on God's power: "If God is for us, who can be against us?" (Rom 8:31). If God himself is on our side, who could defeat us? No one could, of course, but how do we know that God is in fact on our side? Paul answers, "He who did not spare his own Son, but gave him up for us all—how will he not also, along with him, graciously give us all things?" (Rom 8:32). The greatest demonstration that God is on our side is his sending his Son to be our Savior. Will he not, therefore, give his justified children all they need for a successful journey home?

Third, Paul argues for preservation on the basis of God's justice. "Who will bring any charge against those whom God has chosen?" (Rom 8:33). Who can bring an accusation against us and make it stick? No one, because the supreme Judge in the universe already has declared us righteous—"It is God who justifies" (Rom 8:33). Paul rehearses this argument when he asks, "Who is he that condemns?" (Rom 8:34). The Bible's answer is that the Trinity is the Judge, especially the Father and Son. Here the Son is in view, but he will not condemn us because it is he who "died—more than that . . . was raised to life—is at the right hand of God and is also interceding for us" (Rom 8:34). Jesus, who will condemn the wicked (cf. Mt 7:23; 25:41), will not condemn us because he died for us, was raised, ascended to God's right hand and now intercedes for us to keep us saved!

Fourth, Paul argues for preservation based on God's love. "Who shall separate us from the love of Christ?" (Rom 8:35). Paul lists formidable foes, including death ("sword"), but concludes that nothing "will be able

---

[4]So C. E. B. Cranfield, *A Critical and Exegetical Commentary on the Epistle to the Romans,* International Critical Commentary (Edinburgh: T & T Clark, 1975), p. 433.

to separate us from the love of God that is in Christ Jesus our Lord" (Rom 8:39). Paul's affirmation of our security in Christ is "utterly comprehensive."[5] He says that "neither death nor life, neither angels nor demons, neither the present nor the future, nor any powers, neither height nor depth, nor anything else in all creation" will separate us from God's love (Rom 8:38-39). Our entire existence is summed up by "life" and "death." Assuming that past sins are forgiven, everything is included in "the present" and "the future." Paul assures us that not even demons will take us away from God's love. Finally, the apostle adds "nor anything else in all creation" to the list of things that can't separate us from God's love. Lest someone protest that we could remove ourselves from God's love, we need only note that we are part of "all creation" and therefore *not,* according to Paul, able to do so.

Ephesians 1:13-14. God the Father seals believers with the Holy Spirit in union with Christ: "you were marked in him [Christ] with a seal, the promised Holy Spirit" (Eph 1:13; cf. 2 Cor 1:21-22). Paul highlights the fact that the Spirit seals our salvation when he speaks of "the Holy Spirit of God, with whom you were sealed for the day of redemption" (Eph 4:30). God gives us the Spirit as his seal on our lives for the day of final salvation. The apostle conveys the same idea when he views the Spirit as a "deposit guaranteeing our inheritance until the redemption of those who are God's possession" (Eph 1:14; cf. 2 Cor 1:22).

Hebrews 6:17-20. One of the sternest warning passages in Scripture (in Heb 6:1-12) is immediately followed by a strong preservation passage. Remarkably, when God made promises to Abraham, God swore by himself, "I will surely bless you and give you many descendants" (Heb 6:14).

The writer cites the practice of taking oaths for confirmation in human affairs and says, "Because God wanted to make the unchanging nature of his purpose very clear to the heirs of what was promised, he con-

---

[5]Judith M. Gundry Volf, *Paul and Perseverance* (Louisville, Ky.: Westminster John Knox, 1990), p. 57.

firmed it with an oath" (Heb 6:17). God's condescension is astounding. Although he always speaks the truth, he stoops to confirm his promises to Abraham and his heirs with an oath! And what did God promise "Abraham's descendants" (Heb 2:16)? He promised final salvation to all who believe in Jesus Christ and become Abraham's seed (Heb 2:16; 9:15; cf. Gal 3:6-9).

God went to great lengths to assure Abraham's spiritual children: "Because God wanted to make the unchanging nature of his purpose very clear to the heirs of what was promised, he confirmed it with an oath. God did this so that, by two unchangeable things in which it is impossible for God to lie, we who have fled to take hold of the hope offered to us may be greatly encouraged" (Heb 6:17-18). God gave believers "two unchangeable things"—his promise and his oath—to confirm "the unchanging nature of his purpose" and thereby strengthen their hope of eternal life.

Again the writer bolsters our assurance: "We have this hope as an anchor for the soul, firm and secure. It enters the inner sanctuary behind the curtain, where Jesus, who went before us, has entered on our behalf" (Heb 6:19-20). He compares our hope of eternal life to "an anchor for the soul." As anchors provide stability amidst shifting seas and winds, so the hope that God grants is "firm and secure." The writer mixes maritime and priestly metaphors to good effect when he announces that Jesus has planted the anchor of our hope in the most holy place, even the very presence of God in heaven. He means that our hope is sure; we have already gone to heaven, so to speak.

Hebrews 7:23-25. The Old Testament priesthood was characterized by big numbers, because when a high priest died, his son would take his place to continue the priestly duties. This had to continue generation after generation or the priesthood would have ceased and with it God's provision for atonement. By contrast, because Jesus arose from the dead and lives forever, his priesthood is perpetual. And, therefore, "he is able to save completely those who come to God through him" (Heb 7:25). As Philip Hughes notes, the expression translated "completely" (*eis to pan-*

teles) combines "the notions of perpetuity . . . and of completeness."[6]
Jesus saves "completely"—forever and in any other way that salvation
can be conceived. For that reason, believers are safe in his care "because
he always lives to intercede for them" (Heb 7:25). That is, we are saved
forever because Jesus perpetually presents his perfect sacrifice in the Father's
presence in heaven on our behalf.

1 Peter 1:3-5. Peter praises God the Father's mercy that moved him
to regenerate us, welcome us into his family and grant us an inheritance.
Peter describes this inheritance—it "is imperishable, undefiled, and un-
fading, kept in heaven for you" (1 Pet 1:4 ESV). Because our inheritance is
"kept," already reserved in heaven, it is secure and cannot be lost.

Furthermore God's heirs are those "who through faith are shielded by
God's power until the coming of the salvation that is ready to be revealed
in the last time" (1 Pet 1:5). God's might protects his children and preserves their heavenly inheritance. How does God mediate this salvation
to his people? Through the instrumentality of faith. Faith is not here (as
it is elsewhere) presented as a condition of attaining final salvation;
rather, it is the means that God uses to keep his people saved.

Conclusion. We could have discussed more passages,[7] but these nine
are sufficient to illustrate the abundant biblical testimony to believers'
security due to God's faithfulness.

Each member of the Trinity plays a role in preservation. The Father
preserves his people by willing that Christ not lose any of the elect
(Jn 6:37), holding them secure in his almighty hand (Jn 10:29), pledging
to keep saved those whom he reconciled and justified (Rom 5:9-10), regarding their glorification as a *fait accompli* (Rom 8:30), defeating their
enemies for them (Rom 8:31-32), justifying them (Rom 8:33), allowing
nothing to separate them from his love (Rom 8:35-39), swearing to grant
them an eternal inheritance (Heb 6:13-18), planting the anchor of their
salvation in the most holy place (Heb 6:19-20), reserving their heavenly

---

[6] Philip E. Hughes, *A Commentary on the Epistle to the Hebrews* (Grand Rapids: Eerdmans, 1977), p. 269 n. 35.
[7] Among other passages, Jn 5:24; 1 Cor 11:29-34; Phil 1:6; 2 Tim 1:12 teach preservation.

inheritance for them (1 Pet 1:4) and shielding them for final salvation (1 Pet 1:5).

The Son preserves Christians by interceding for them (Luke 22:31-32; Rom 8:34; Heb 7:25), promising to keep them (Jn 6:37, 39) and raise them for final salvation (Jn 6:39-40, 44), categorically stating that they will never perish (Jn 10:28), keeping them in his hand (Jn 10:28), and saving them completely by virtue of his resurrection life and permanent priesthood (Heb 7:24-25).

The Holy Spirit preserves believers as the Father's seal of their union with Christ (Eph 1:14) "for the day of redemption" (Eph 4:30) and as "a deposit guaranteeing" their "inheritance" (Eph 1:14).

Arminian responses. Arminians sometimes ignore this overwhelming biblical testimony to God's keeping his saints, even as Calvinists sometimes ignore apostasy passages. I. Howard Marshall and Grant R. Osborne are to be commended for rejecting the simplistic answers of former interpreters who committed linguistic and logical fallacies in attempts to counter Calvinistic treatments of the preservation texts.[8] But although Marshall and Osborne each devote more than twenty pages to the doctrine of salvation as expressed in Hebrews, they neglect the two preservation passages in Hebrews 6:17-20 and 7:23-25.[9]

When Arminians address the preservation passages, they tend to take two approaches. First, they appeal to features within the passages in an attempt to qualify the accent on preservation. Concerning Romans 8:28-30, Marshall argues that Paul in verse 28 makes salvation dependent on "God's purpose and call and upon human response to that call." Looking at the five simple past-tense verbs in verses 29-30, he writes, "But the continuation of this process requires a human response. . . . The comple-

---

[8]E.g., Robert Shank's *Life in the Son: A Study of the Doctrine of Perseverance* (Springfield, Mo.: Westcott, 1960).

[9]I. Howard Marshall, *Kept by the Power of God: A Study of Perseverance and Falling Away* (Minneapolis: Bethany House, 1969), pp. 137-57, 247-50; Grant R. Osborne, "Soteriology in the Epistle to the Hebrews," in *Grace Unlimited,* ed. Clark H. Pinnock (Minneapolis: Bethany House, 1975), pp. 144-66.

tion of the whole chain of blessings is dependent upon faith."[10] Concerning verse 29, he urges that predestination is not unto salvation but unto conformity to Christ. And foreknowledge (in v. 29) "refers to God's loving knowledge which God already has of His people. It does not refer to the separation of the elect and consequent rejection of the reprobate, a thought which is not present in the context."[11] Osborne agrees and adds the idea that God's foreknowledge takes human response into account.[12]

We will respond to each of these arguments in turn. Marshall errs when he claims that Paul's reference to those "who have been called" in Romans 8:28 makes salvation contingent upon human response to God's call. Indeed, as C. K. Barrett points out, "Paul cannot allow himself to leave the impression that men may exercise an initiative which properly belongs to God alone. Those who love God are more searchingly defined as 'those who are called in accordance with his purpose.'"[13]

Marshall's claim that the continuation of the process of salvation in Romans 8:29-30 hinges on human response cuts across the grain of the text. The passage speaks of salvation in terms of God's working from beginning to end. It is God who foreknows, predestines, calls, justifies and glorifies his people. The completion of the chain of blessings depends upon divine faithfulness not human.

Marshall is correct in asserting that the goal of predestination in Romans 8:29 is conformity to Christ, but he is wrong in pitting that idea against salvation, because conformity to Christ is one way of speaking about salvation! Marshall's attempt to separate foreknowledge and salvation fares no better. All five of the verbs ("foreknew," "predestined," "called," "justified" and "glorified") in Romans 8:29-30 speak of salvation. When Paul says, "Those God foreknew," he means, "Those God

---

[10]Marshall, *Kept by the Power of God*, pp. 102-3.
[11]Ibid., p. 102.
[12]Grant R. Osborne, "Exegetical Notes on Calvinist Texts," in *Grace Unlimited*, ed. Clark H. Pinnock (Minneapolis: Bethany House, 1975), p. 178.
[13]C. K. Barrett, *The Epistle to the Romans*, Harper's New Testament Commentaries (New York: Harper & Row, 1967), p. 169.

loved beforehand," as is apparent from a study of God as knower and his people as known.[14] Moreover, Osborne errs when he interprets God's foreknowing here as God's foresight of human decision, because when Paul writes, "Those God foreknew," he speaks of *whom* and not *what* God foreknew. Paul's words speak of God foreknowing people, not their responses, when he predestines them. Therefore, the Arminian case against Calvinism based upon features in the preservation texts fails.

A second way that Arminians have responded to the preservation texts is to appeal to systematic theology (that is, drawing on the whole of Scripture). This second argument is more successful precisely because it moves away from these strong texts. Consider the way Arminians treat Ephesians 1:13-14, where Paul says that believers "were marked in him with a seal, the promised Holy Spirit, who is a deposit guaranteeing our inheritance until . . . redemption." Osborne speaks for Marshall when he writes, "There is a very real security in this passage. However, we must ask if this is an unconditional, final security. Personal responsibility parallels divine protection in [Ephesians] 4:30, where the Christian is warned not to 'grieve' the Spirit."[15]

It is true that both Ephesians 4:30 and 1:13 speak of the sealing with the Spirit. And 4:30 does warn believers not to "grieve the Holy Spirit of God." But that text says nothing about the loss of salvation. Rather, Paul teaches preservation when he says, "And do not grieve the Holy Spirit of God, with whom you were sealed for the day of redemption" (Eph 4:30). Rather than teaching the conditional security that Arminians espouse, Paul in Ephesians 4:30 appeals to godliness based on God's keeping his people.

We applaud the frankness of Marshall, when he writes of John 10:28-29, "Nowhere else in the New Testament is the fact of divine preservation of the disciples of Jesus so clearly presented as here, and no theology of perseverance and apostasy must fail to give these verses their full

---

[14]See the explanation on pages 54-56 of this book.
[15]Osborne, "Exegetical Notes," p. 181. Marshall agrees. See *Kept by the Power of God,* p. 108.

value."[16] But later Marshall qualifies his words and asserts that Jesus' promise to keep the disciples saved is true only for those who continue to believe; those who fail to abide risk being cast away as fruitless branches. Osborne agrees.[17]

It is legitimate for Arminians, as well as Calvinists, to work with difficult passages by appealing to systematic theology. Nevertheless, Arminians have not done justice to the passages we discussed in this section, including John 10:28-29, Romans 8:28-30 and Ephesians 1:13-14. They have not dealt adequately with the comprehensiveness of the teaching of Jesus and Paul. Jesus categorically says his sheep will never perish. Marshall and Osborne say that is true, if they continue in the faith. Paul says that those whom God foreknew he glorified. Marshall's and Osborne's attempts to blunt the apostle's words are not convincing. Paul says we are sealed with the Spirit for final redemption. Marshall and Osborne say that is true, as long as we don't grieve the Spirit.

We ask: What could the biblical writers have said to make our safety in God's care any clearer? The Arminian rejection of the doctrine of preservation is not due to any lack of clarity in the scriptural witness but is due to a prior commitment to the freedom of the human will in matters pertaining to salvation.

SCRIPTURE ALSO AFFIRMS THE NECESSITY
AND INEVITABILITY OF THE SAINTS' PERSEVERANCE

Scripture teaches a complementary truth to God's keeping of his saints—the necessity of their perseverance. Arminians and Calvinists agree that professed Christians must continue to the end in three areas if they are to be saved: believing the gospel, loving Christ and other believers, and living godly lives.

Scripture affirms the necessity of the saints' perseverance.

Perseverance in faith: Colossians 1:21-23. First, it is necessary for pro-

---

[16]Marshall, *Kept by the Power of God*, p. 181. In fairness to Marshall, we acknowledge that he emphasizes preservation and regards falling away as possible but unlikely.

[17]Ibid., pp. 185-86. Cf. Osborne, "Exegetical Notes," pp. 172-73.

fessed believers to persevere in faith. After extolling Christ as cosmic Reconciler (Col 1:19-20), Paul applies Christ's reconciliation to the Colossians. God reconciled them through Christ's atonement with a goal in mind—their final and perfect sanctification (Col 1:22). Then, Paul adds a condition that the Colossians must meet in order to attain final salvation: God will "present you holy in his sight, without blemish and free from accusation—*if you continue in your faith, established and firm, not moved from the hope held out in the gospel*" (Col 1:22-23; italics added).

Paul wants his readers not to waver but to be solidly anchored in the gospel, so he calls them to persevere in faith (Col 1:23). The professed Colossian Christians will attain to final salvation if they believe the gospel to the end. Other passages teach the same truth, including John 15:7; Hebrews 3:14; 6:11-12; 10:35-39.

Perseverance in love: John 15:9, 12, 17. Second, it is necessary for professed believers to persevere in love of Christ and their neighbors if they are to be finally saved. Using the analogy of the vine and the branches, Jesus repeatedly exhorts the disciples to remain in him (John 15:4-9). He helps us understand what it means to remain in him when he tells them, "Remain in my love" (Jn 15:9). To remain in Jesus is to remain in his love, to continue enjoying his love and to love him in return.

John's summons for the disciples to remain in Christ's love and to love one another is addressed to ordinary Christians and not to supersaints. We say this for three reasons. (1) His most basic distinction in the passage is between disciples who bear no fruit and those who bear fruit (Jn 15:2). Consistently in Scripture, bearing no fruit indicates an absence of salvation. Because disciples cannot bear fruit without abiding in Christ, abiding is the way to bear fruit and is evidence of salvation (Jn 15:4-5). (2) Jesus threatens those branches that do not abide in him with being cut off from him (Jn 15:2), being thrown into the fire and being burned (Jn 15:6). This speaks not of the loss of rewards but of hell. Thus abiding is not optional but is necessary for salvation. (3) The way people show that they are true disciples is by abiding in Christ and bearing fruit: "This is to my Father's glory, that you bear much fruit, showing yourselves to be my disciples" (Jn 15:8). Those who bear no fruit, by contrast, reveal that they are not Jesus' disciples.

Thus love for Christ and for fellow Christians is necessary for salvation, as other passages also affirm, including 1 John 2:9-11; 3:11-18; 4:7-21.

Perseverance in holiness: Hebrews 12:14. Third, it is necessary for professed believers to persevere in holiness. The writer to the Hebrews issues a double command. (1) He commands his readers to actively pursue peace: "Make every effort to live in peace with all men." (2) He also commands, "Make every effort . . . to be holy" (Heb 12:14). The writer enjoins his readers to pursue holiness. Notice the important qualification: "without holiness no one will see the Lord." The predictive future "will see" points to the outcome of salvation, the vision of God that fills the beholders with joy. Put simply, perseverance in holiness is essential for Christians to reach heaven, a truth reinforced by other passages, including John 15:10, 14; Hebrews 3:13; 1 John 2:3-6, 29; 3:3-10.

Scripture affirms the inevitability of the saints' perseverance. Arminians and Calvinists agree that the Bible teaches the necessity of the saints' perseverance in faith (Col 1:21-23), love (Jn 15:9, 12, 17) and holiness (Heb 12:14) if they are to attain final salvation. But Arminians part company with Calvinists when the latter maintain that Scripture teaches not only that perseverance is necessary but also that it is inevitable. We will examine three passages that teach that the saints not only *must* persevere but *will* persevere because of God's grace.

John 15:16. Previously we saw from John 15 that believers must continue in love to be saved. Now we return to the same text to show that God's sovereignty (specifically Christ's) is compatible with the saints' responsibility.

After telling the disciples repeatedly of their need to abide in him to bear fruit, Jesus tells them that ultimately they did not choose him but vice versa. This choosing is not simply his choice of them to be among the twelve disciples, which he spoke about in John 6:70: "Have I not chosen you, the Twelve? Yet one of you is a devil!" Jesus' choosing of the Twelve is a choice that results in their being disciples; it is not a choice that necessarily results in salvation, as the case of Judas bears out (Jn 6:71). Jesus' choice of the Eleven in John 15:16 is different from his choice of the Twelve in John 6:66. The choice in John 15 is a choice that results in salvation, as Jesus' words make clear, "If you belonged to the world, it would love you as its own. As it is, you do not belong to the world, but I have chosen you out of the world. That is why the world hates you" (Jn 15:19).

We can now understand Jesus' words in John 15:16, "You did not choose me, but I chose you." Of course, on one level they did choose him; they chose to follow him. But on a deeper level, that of salvation, they did not choose him; he chose them.

Hebrews 3:14. The writer to the Hebrews warns his readers of the danger of apostasy: "See to it, brothers, that none of you has a sinful, unbelieving heart that turns away from the living God" (Heb 3:12). We might conclude from this that Christians can fall away from the faith. To prevent readers from reaching that conclusion, however, the writer adds: "We have come to share in Christ if we hold firmly till the end the confidence we had at first" (Heb 3:14). "The confidence we had at first" refers to belief in the gospel. This passage teaches the necessity of perseverance in faith (in Heb 3:6, 12). It also teaches the certainty of perseverance when it says, "We have come to share in Christ." These words in the perfect tense indicate completed action with ongoing results. Professed believers have come to share in Christ in time past if they continue to believe the gospel "till the end." And if they don't believe to the end, they have not come to share in Christ. This indicates not a loss of salvation but a demonstration that the professed Christians had not really been united to Christ in the first place. In other words, the fires of trial separate true believers from false ones. Those who have been united savingly to Christ show it by persevering in faith to the end.

1 John 2:19. John identifies as "antichrists" false teachers who hurt the churches to whom he writes. When they were unable to persuade the churches to accept their false teaching, these teachers abandoned them.

John describes the apostasy of the false teachers: "They went out from us, but they did not really belong to us" (1 Jn 2:19). Are we correct, then, to interpret their leaving as a forfeiture of salvation, as a falling from grace? No, John insists. Rather, their departure reveals that they were not genuine children of God; it shows "they did not really belong to us."

John underscores this point: "For if they had belonged to us, they would have remained with us; but their going showed that none of them belonged to us" (1 Jn 2:19). John's use of the Greek second-class condition (contrary to fact) is significant. He means, "If they had belonged to us, they would have stayed, but they didn't and that is why they left." The false teachers' apostasy revealed their unsaved status. Perseverance is thus both necessary and certain.

Conclusion. Christians must continue to believe the gospel (Col 1:21-22), love God and other believers (Jn 15:9, 12, 17), and live godly lives (Heb 12:14) to be finally saved. Easy believism, the view that persons are to be regarded as Christians who have made professions of faith but whose lives are unchanged, is incompatible with biblical teaching. On this point Arminians and Calvinists agree.

Differences emerge, however, when Calvinists claim that perseverance is certain as well as necessary. Arminians take issue with that conclusion, for it challenges their notion of the freedom of the will: by a free act of the will (enabled by prevenient grace) one believes the gospel; by a free act of the will one can stop believing the gospel and forfeit salvation. The Arminian teaching that Christians can fall from grace is contradicted by Scripture's teaching on the inevitability of perseverance.

Scripture warns of apostasy. So far we have demonstrated that God saves and keeps his people, that they must persevere to be finally saved, and that, by God's grace, it is certain that they will do so. It is time to bring another factor into the equation—apostasy. Apostasy is the abandonment of the Christian faith by someone who formerly professed it. There is virtual agreement among scholars that Hebrews contains five warnings of apostasy: Hebrews 2:1-4; 3:7—4:11; 5:11—6:12; 10:26-39; and 12:14-29.

We admit that some Calvinist treatments of these passages are inadequate. The view that the warnings are hypothetical is wrongheaded and, in the words of Roger Nicole, "tends to artificiality."[18] Plainly, some of the original readers of Hebrews were in danger. Contrary to Thomas Kem Oberholtzer, these passages were not written to warn Christians of possible loss of rewards in the millennium;[19] rather, they warn of hell (cf. Heb 10:27, 29, 31, 39). Scot McKnight has shown that V. D. Verbrugge's view that the passages warn not individuals but the covenant community clashes with the text's concern for each reader (cf. Heb 6:11).[20]

We turn to the two most difficult of the five warning passages for Calvinism: Hebrews 5:11—6:12 and 10:26-39.

Hebrews 5:11—6:12. In Hebrews 5:11—6:3 the writer rebukes his readers for their spiritual sluggishness. Although sufficient time has elapsed since their profession of faith for them to teach others God's truth, they themselves need to be taught the first principles of the spiritual life (Heb 5:12). And by God's grace, they will grow (Heb 6:3).

"It is impossible for those who have once been enlightened, who have tasted the heavenly gift, who have shared in the Holy Spirit, who have tasted the goodness of the word of God and the powers of the coming age, if they fall away, to be brought back to repentance" (Heb 6:4-6). This passage explains the impossibility of bringing back to repentance persons who have experienced the blessings mentioned and who then commit apostasy.

---

[18]Roger Nicole, "Some Comments on Hebrews 6:4-6 and the Doctrine of the Perseverance of God with the Saints," in *Current Issues in Biblical and Patristic Interpretation,* ed. G. F. Hawthorne (Grand Rapids: Eerdmans, 1975), p. 356, lists advocates of this view and refutes them.

[19]Thomas Kem Oberholtzer set forth this view in a series of articles in *Bibliotheca sacra*: "The Eschatological Salvation of Hebrews 1:5-2:5" (145 [1988]: 83-97); "The Kingdom Rest in Hebrews 3:1-4:13" (145 [1988]: 185-96); "The Thorn-Infested Ground in Hebrews 6:4-12" (145 [1988]: 319-28); "The Danger of Willful Sin in Hebrews 10:26-39" (145 [1988]: 410-19); and "The Failure to Heed His Speaking in Hebrews 12:25-29" (146 [1989]: 67-75).

[20]Scot McKnight, "The Warning Passages of Hebrews: A Formal Analysis and Theological Conclusions," *Trinity Journal* 13 n.s. (1992): 53-54; V. D. Verbrugge, "Towards a New Interpretation of Hebrews 6:4-6," *Calvin Theological Journal* 15 (1980): 61-73.

The following description apparently depicts believers in Christ. "Those who have once been enlightened" (Heb 6:4) are those who have understood the way of salvation. Those "who have tasted the heavenly gift" are persons who have experienced spiritual blessings. Calvinist attempts to interpret "tasted" (here and in the next verse) and "shared" (in the Spirit, in the next expression) as speaking of less then full participation are misguided.[21] Those "who have shared in the Holy Spirit" (Heb 6:4) are those who have participated in the Spirit of God. The description "who have tasted the goodness of the word of God and the powers of the coming age" (Heb 6:5) refers to the readers' personal experience of the Word and miracles.

The burden of proof rests with those claiming that the description in Hebrews 6:4-5 does not portray Christians. Before pursuing the question of the spiritual status of the readers, we note that Arminian interpreters have difficulties with this passage. On an Arminian reading, when the text says "It is impossible for those . . . if they fall away, to be brought back to repentance," it speaks of believers committing apostasy and losing their salvation. If that is true, then the passage also teaches that these lapsed believers cannot be saved again. Although some Arminian interpreters accept this implication,[22] most are uncomfortable with it. And it will not do to attempt to solve the problem by softening the meaning of "impossible" (*adynaton*) in Hebrews 6:4, as Philip Hughes shows.[23]

We now assume the burden of proof mentioned above. Because the description of the apostates in Hebrews 6:4-6 seems so strong, there would have to be clear contextual indicators for one to deny that the passage speaks of saved persons. The writer gives just such clear indicators in order to teach that if any of his readers apostatize, they thereby reveal their unsaved condition. The apostates have known the truth of the gospel, en-

---

[21]So Nicole, "Some Comments," pp. 360, 361.
[22]So McKnight, "Warning Passages of Hebrews," pp. 34-35.
[23]Philip E. Hughes, "Hebrews 6:4-6 and the Peril of Apostasy," *Westminster Theological Journal* 35 (1973): 144-45.

joyed God's blessings, participated in the Spirit and seen miracles. Nevertheless, the writer uses an agricultural illustration and encouraging words to distinguish the majority of his readers from the potential apostates.

These words immediately follow the warning of Hebrews 6:4-6: "Land that drinks in the rain often falling on it and that produces a crop useful to those for whom it is farmed receives the blessing of God. But land that produces thorns and thistles is worthless and is in danger of being cursed. In the end it will be burned" (Heb 6:7-8). This illustration sheds light on the preceding verses. The writer describes two types of land, both of which receive rain. One type of land produces useful vegetation and reaps God's blessing; the other yields only thorns and thistles and is close to being cursed by God and burned. With this illustration the writer describes both believers and unbelievers who have been exposed to the things of God, for both types of land receive rain. But only the good land yields fruit; the bad land produces only weeds. The fruit and weeds stand for the good deeds of believers and the sinful deeds of unbelievers (especially apostasy), respectively. God's blessing and cursing stand for eternal life and death, respectively, as the burning of the bad land suggests.

The writer invites us to identify the apostates of Hebrews 6:4-6 with the unfruitful land. They have had great contact with spiritual things but have not persevered in their professed faith. Their departure is "thorns and thistles" that reveal their unsaved status. And the judgment of God awaits them. Calvinist exegesis fares better here than does Arminian. The writer does not want us to regard the fruitless land as formerly fruit bearing. The apostates are not lapsed Christians but persons who were never saved. By contrast, the fruitful soil stands for the majority of readers, who have worked hard and displayed genuine Christian love (Heb 6:10).

The key to understanding this passage, in our estimation, lies in Hebrew 6:9: "Even though we speak like this, dear friends, we are confident of better things in your case—things that accompany salvation." Although he speaks of apostasy in Hebrews 6:4-6 and of fruitless and worthless land in Hebrews 6:8, he is convinced of better things than these concerning most of his readers. He is convinced that they are good soil, true believers. This is underlined by the change from third person (in Heb 6:4-6) to second (in Heb 6:9-12). Even his form of address is designed to encourage them, for here alone in the epistle does he call them "dear friends." He is confident that the majority of his readers are not barren land fit for judgment; they are not apostates.

He elaborates concerning the "better things." They are "things that accompany salvation." After the warning of Hebrews 6:4-6, he assures the believers among his readers that they are fruitful land that receives God's blessing.

The writer issues a real warning to a minority of his readers whom he fears may not know Christ and may show it by committing apostasy. At the same time, he encourages the majority, whom he is convinced are saved, to persevere and thereby grow in their faith and be strengthened in their assurance.

Hebrews 10:26-39. This warning passage also presents a problem for Calvinism. Having "received the knowledge of the truth" (Heb 10:26) signifies at least a profession of faith. Because of the severity of the rest of this verse, we understand sinning "deliberately" as indicating a deliberate renunciation of one's faith rather than speaking generally of intentional sin. For those who profess Christ and then apostatize, there is no atonement because they have rejected the only God-given means of forgiveness. Instead of forgiveness, they will know only God's wrath because they have joined ranks with God's foes.

"Anyone who rejected the law of Moses died without mercy on the testimony of two or three witnesses" (Heb 10:28). Violators of the Mosaic Covenant, convicted by the evidence of two or more witnesses, paid a severe penalty. The Old Testament background speaks of the sin of idolatry when it condemns any Israelite who "in violation of his covenant . . . has worshiped other gods" (Deut 17:2-3). Apostates who exchanged the worship of Yahweh for that of other gods suffered capital punishment.

"How much more severely do you think a man deserves to be punished who has trampled the Son of God under foot, who has treated as an unholy thing the blood of the covenant that sanctified him, and who has insulted the Spirit of grace?" (Heb 10:29). The writer's argument advances from the Old Covenant to the New. If transgressors of the Old Covenant were punished by death, how terrible the fate of violators of the New Covenant! The three expressions "trampled . . . treated as an unholy thing . . . [and] insulted" are three ways of saying "despised the New Covenant." Those in danger of apostatizing had professed allegiance to the Son of God and his cleansing blood and had come into the church, the sphere of the Holy Spirit's special influence.

"The blood of the covenant that sanctified him" would appear to refer to a true believer but does not necessarily do so. It could refer to a covenantal sanctification in which persons are set apart as part of God's covenant community, the church, but are not necessarily saved. Examples include unbelieving children of Christian parents and persons who have made an insincere profession of faith. The idea of covenantal but not saving "sanctification" appears in Hebrews 9:13 and 1 Corinthians 7:14. In view of the contrast here between the Old and New Covenants, we interpret "sanctified" to mean set apart by virtue of the covenant as belonging to God.[24]

"For we know him who said, 'It is mine to avenge; I will repay,' and again, 'The Lord will judge his people.' It is a dreadful thing to fall into the hands of the living God" (Heb 10:30-31). These Old Testament quotations (from Deut 32:35, 36) refer to God's delivering Israel by inflicting judgment on its enemies. By quoting the Old Testament the writer reminds his readers that the living God knows how to judge his covenant people in order to separate the true from the false. Those who fail the test will "fall into" his "hands," that is, feel his wrath.

In Hebrews 10:32-34 the writer reminds his readers of their past diligence in the face of persecution in order to motivate them to con-

---

[24]We reject as contrived John Owen's idea, accepted by Roger Nicole and others, that *en hō hēgiasthē* refers to Christ. See Nicole, "Some Comments," p. 356 n. 1.

tinue to persevere during present trials. Our thesis is that the warnings are addressed to professed believers in the congregation who have come short of faith and may be tempted to apostatize. The encouragements are addressed to the believing (although struggling) majority.

He next ties confidence of salvation to perseverance. They started well; they need to finish well to enjoy the full assurance of faith. "So do not throw away your confidence; it will be richly rewarded. You need to persevere so that when you have done the will of God, you will receive what he has promised" (Heb 10:35-36).

"For in just a very little while, 'He who is coming will come and will not delay. But my righteous one will live by faith. And if he shrinks back, I will not be pleased with him'" (Heb 10:37-38). The writer uses the emphatic language of Habakkuk 2:3-4 (LXX) to remind his readers that their reward is as close as the Lord's impending return. Once again he provides impetus for them to persevere. God's people will persevere in faith. But those who do not persevere reject their covenant Lord and will reap his wrath.

"But we are not of those who shrink back and are destroyed, but of those who believe and are saved" (Heb 10:39). The writer assures his readers that he is confident of their faith in Christ. By shifting to the first person ("we"), he includes himself with them among those who persevere in faith unto final salvation. We take these words to refer to the majority of the readers, as we did the reassuring words of Hebrews 6:9-12.

Conclusion. We have tackled the two most difficult apostasy passages, Hebrews 5:11—6:12 and 10:26-39, interpreting each in its literary and historical contexts.

The audience of Hebrews is crucial. If the recipients are only believers, then the Arminian position that Christians may fall from grace seems correct. We contend, however, that the audience includes unbelievers. This is not Calvinist special pleading for Hebrews. Our analysis of the audience of the rest of the epistles is the same—they are written to professing Christians, some of whom may be unsaved.

This is easily understood by any pastor. As a pastor, you regard your flock as largely composed of believers, but you are not sure of the spiritual status of every person, and from time to time in preaching and in personal work you exhort them to examine their spiritual condition, to come to Christ, and so on. The writings of the New Testament do the same.[25]

The writer to the Hebrews repeatedly warns a group of professing Christians not to depart from Christ. We saw this in Hebrews 6:4-8 and 10:26-31, 35-38. He fears that some might commit apostasy. But he periodically assures the majority of his readers of his confidence that they are believers who will demonstrate it by persevering. We saw this in Hebrews 6:9-12 and 10:32-34, 39. Philip Hughes agrees: "The confidence expressed in 6:9 and 10:39 arises from the assurance that a true work of God has taken place in their midst; but this does not exclude the possibility that some of their number are rebellious at heart and on the road to irremediable apostasy."[26]

Scot McKnight's article on the warning passages in Hebrews deserves special mention. He does meticulous exegesis, displays exceptional scholarship, and writes in an irenic spirit. His synthetic approach—studying all of the warning passages together—is sound. We agree with his conclusions that the writer exhorts his readers to persevere in faithfulness to Christ, that he warns them of the danger of apostasy, and that the result of committing that sin is eternal damnation.[27] We disagree, however, when he concludes that the sin of apostasy can separate believers from their final salvation.[28]

We must criticize McKnight's inconsistent employment of his own synthetic method. He excludes the very component of the warning passages that forms the basis of our argument for a divided audience: "the

---

[25]Examples are found in Mt 7:21-23; 2 Cor 13:5; Jas 2:14-26; 2 Pet 1:5-9; 1 Jn 5:13.

[26]Philip E. Hughes, "Hebrews 6:4-6 and the Peril of Apostasy," *Westminster Theological Journal* 35 (1973): 144.

[27]McKnight, "Warning Passages of Hebrews," p. 54.

[28]Ibid., pp. 58-59.

pastoral encouragement . . . found at 6:9 and 10:39" (italics his).[29] He thereby omits data unfavorable to his thesis. A synthetic study should consider all of the evidence from the warning passages.

CONCLUSION

This chapter treated preservation, perseverance and apostasy. To conclude, we want to consider them in relation to one another and draw practical implications. First, we sampled the abundant biblical testimony to God's preservation of his saints. Preservation relates to perseverance as cause to effect. Because God preserves his saints, they will persevere and not fall from grace. God's power and faithfulness in preservation preclude true believers from committing final apostasy.

We respect the godly concerns of Arminians that "the eternal security doctrine" will lead to license. With sorrow we admit that some have indeed presumed on God's grace and used this teaching as an excuse for not repenting of their sins. But the abuse of a doctrine does not disprove that doctrine. The Bible not only plainly and repeatedly teaches preservation; it also presents the doctrine as a source of great comfort and blessing to the saints.

God's preservation is the cause of believers praising him; his keeping us "until the redemption of those who are God's possession" is "to the praise of his glory" (Eph 1:14). Preservation brings encouragement, as God's dealings with Abraham's spiritual descendants demonstrate. God gave us a promise and an oath so that "we who have fled to take hold of the hope offered to us may be greatly encouraged" (Heb 6:18). God's promise to keep us is a great comfort during persecution.

Furthermore, God uses his promises to keep us saved (1 Pet 1:3-5) to motivate believers to "be holy in all you do," to live our "lives as strangers here in reverent fear" and to "love one another deeply from the heart" (1 Pet 1:15, 17, 22). God intends for his gracious promises of preservation to have a profound impact on the way his people live for him.

---

[29]Ibid., p. 28.

In God's Word, perseverance is just as plainly taught as preservation. Scripture clearly and frequently affirms the obligation of those who profess Christ to continue believing the gospel (Col 1:21-23), loving God and other Christians (Jn 15:9, 12, 17), and living holy lives (Heb 12:14). For people to profess faith in Christ is necessary but not sufficient.

To put it that way without qualification, however, is misleading. It is God who changes the lives of his people, causing them to conform to the image of his Son (Rom 8:29). Scripture combines believers' responsibility and God's sovereignty in the same sentence: "Continue to work out your salvation with fear and trembling, for it is God who works in you to will and to act according to his good purpose" (Phil 2:12-13). Notice that we don't work *for* our salvation; rather, we work *out* what God has freely given. Also notice that God's sovereign grace does not lead us to inactivity. Instead, God's willing and acting are the basis of our working out our salvation!

We saw that Scripture not only teaches the necessity of perseverance but also implies its certainty: in John 15:16, Hebrews 3:14 and 1 John 2:19. Those implications include Jesus' teaching that his appointment stands behind our fruit bearing (Jn 15:16). Likewise, they include the epistles' teaching that continuance in faith is proof of union with Christ (Heb 3:14) and that those who belong to the body of Christ do not apostatize (1 Jn 2:19). When Scripture affirms the inevitability of perseverance, it reinforces its teaching of preservation.

Scripture warns church members of the danger of apostasy. Jesus' reply at the Last Judgment to some who called him Lord and performed miracles in his name is chilling: "I never knew you. Away from me, you evildoers!" (Mt 7:23). Note that he does not say, "You have lost your salvation"; he says, "I never knew you." Their persistence in doing evil, despite their Christian profession, revealed that they had never been saved.

Why does Scripture warn of apostasy if believers cannot commit it? The answer is suggested by the famous warning passages in Hebrews. The audience of Hebrews includes many immature persons who are not applying the Christian truth that they know (Heb 5:11-14). It is difficult for pastors to know whether such parishioners are Christians. So, in light of persecutions, the writer issues solemn warnings of apostasy in Hebrews 6:4-6 and 10:26-31. He is fearful that some in his audience might indeed turn away from Christ. But with his qualifying words in Hebrews 6:9 and 10:39 he expresses confidence that the majority of his readers are truly saved and will persevere to prove it. And God uses the warnings in his Word to goad his people to maturity.

Further evidence of the impossibility of believers committing apostasy is provided by the presence of preservation texts in Hebrews 6:13-20 and 7:23-25. In the very book where the sternest warnings against apostasy appear are some of the sweetest affirmations of believers' security in Christ.

5

ARMINIUS AND
THE SYNOD OF DORT

എ

Following in the Augustinian tradition of Martin Luther and John
Calvin, the Reformed churches of the early seventeenth century would
accept the following loose syllogism as being both experientially and
biblically true:

> Sin so debilitates the sinner that if we are to be saved, God must
> do it.
> Not all are saved.
> Therefore, God only intends to save some.

Yet this redemptive discrimination—some are sovereignly saved
while others are not—did not sit any better with many believers in
the late sixteenth and early seventeenth centuries than it had in the
early fifth century, when Pelagius attacked Augustine's emphasis on
the necessity and sovereignty of divine grace. In the Dutch context of
the early seventeenth century, the debate between Augustinian mon-
ergists and Semi-Augustinian synergists would erupt into the Arminian controversy and would come to public expression in the Dutch
National Synod of 1618-1619, the Synod of Dort, and the canons
produced by that synod. Any consideration of the Calvinist-Arminian debate must take stock of the Synod of Dort and the persons and
events that led up to it, for it was this synod, and especially the "Re-

monstrant Articles" to which the Canons of Dort were a response, that would frame the discussion for succeeding generations and give us the famous "five points."

We must begin our narrative well before the "Remonstrant Articles" and the Synod of Dort. We must begin even before Jacob Arminius, who died the year before the publication of the "Remonstrant Articles." Because Arminianism represents a response to Calvinism, we begin with the Calvinism with which Arminius was familiar, the Calvinism that he rejected. Rejection of the Calvinism of his time led him toward other ways of understanding God's relation to man in salvation.

THEODORE BEZA AND CALVINIST DECRETAL THEOLOGY

Supralapsarianism. Upon Calvin's death in 1564, the leadership of the Geneva Academy fell upon his son-in-law, Theodore Beza. Beza would head the Academy for almost half a century, until his own death in 1605, and most of the participants in the Arminian controversy—including Jacob Arminius—would be trained at Geneva under his tutelage. Therefore, it is fitting that we begin our narrative with a brief look at Beza.

Where the first generation of reformers equated theology with biblical exposition, the successors of Luther and Calvin moved toward the development of theological systems. They sought to organize, fill out and defend the thought of the reformers. And, as was the case more often than not among the systematizers, Beza employed medieval scholasticism and its methodological concerns in his presentation of Calvin's theological insights. The revival of scholasticism introduced into Reformed theology a greater emphasis upon philosophical and metaphysical concerns than Calvin entertained.

The highly metaphysical thought of scholasticism was oriented toward the creation of a sharp distinction between eternity and time, the preceding will of God and the execution of the divine plan in history, with the focus falling upon God's determining eternal decree or plan for whatever occurs in history. Thus, "the decisive action occurs in a prior eternity, and history effects what God has already caused."[1] Even Richard Muller, whose own project has been committed to rehabilitating the flagging reputation of Reformed scholasticism and showing the development-within-continuity between Calvin and his seventeenth-century successors, admits that the product of the turn toward scholasticism in the second generation of the Reformation was a revived interest in "a speculative formulation of the will of God"[2] in which reflection upon the ways of God came to be dominated by the concept of divine will, and divine goodness and justice became correspondingly less important.[3]

For our purposes, the term *scholasticism* need only mean the elevation of rational conceptualization over historical action and logical relationships over personal relationships for the sake of the creation of a rational theological system. A scholastic approach toward theology flourished during the Middle Ages, and in one way or another typified the work of such thinkers as Anselm, Abelard, Bonaventure, Thomas Aquinas, Duns Scotus and William of Ockham. While both Luther and Calvin were highly critical of scholastic approaches to theology, the successors of both men would employ scholastic method in their theological construction.[4] The return to pre-Reformation scholastic theological method enabled a more precise definition and more central place given to the notion of divine decrees and the doctrine of predestination

---

[1]Philip C. Holtrop, "Decree(s) of God," in *The Westminster Handbook to Reformed Theology,* ed. Donald K. McKim (Louisville: Westminster John Knox, 2001), p. 55.

[2]Richard A. Muller, *Christ and the Decree: Christology and Predestination in Reformed Theology from Calvin to Perkins* (Grand Rapids: Baker, 1986), p. 11; Richard A. Muller, *God, Creation, and Providence in the Thought of Jacob Arminius: Sources and Directions of Scholastic Protestantism in the Era of Early Orthodoxy* (Grand Rapids: Baker, 1991), pp. 27-32.

[3]Muller, *Christ and the Decree,* 189.

[4]William Placher comments that "Beza's relation to Calvin interestingly parallels Melanchthon's to Luther. In both cases, the younger theologian tried to make his mentor's work more systematic and to fit it into an overall philosophical context, using Aristotelian categories. When scriptural evidence was ambiguous and nothing central to Christian piety was at stake, Calvin . . . was willing to leave questions unanswered. Beza often was not. For example, Calvin left it unclear whether God had predestined some to damnation from the beginning or only after the fact of original sin. Beza unambiguously favored the 'supralapsarian' position—even before the Fall (*super lapsum*) God had determined to abandon

in the thought of such Reformed theologians as Beza, Vermigli and Zanchi than they had enjoyed in Calvin's more exegetically driven theology. Beza held that the beginning of all meditation on God and his works is that "the created order stands totally under the divine decree" because "since God is eternal and immutable, all he does regarding man is ordained from eternity."[5] Since God is in eternity, not time, God's ordained plan for history is extratemporal, in effect outside time. According to Beza, "God is immutable in his counsels, and cannot be wrong in them, or impeded in any manner from executing them, from which it follows that all that happens to men has been eternally ordained by God, according to what we have said regarding providence."[6]

As Beza sought to move Reformed theology toward greater scholastic consistency, he also brought all things, including the affairs of men, under the eternal decree of God. Nothing falls outside of the divine will. Even human sin, which is contrary to God's will, is encompassed by his decree. Being eternal, God's sovereign decree is not contingent upon human activity or decision. The will of God is never reactive, but always prior to and determinative for human affairs. God predetermines all events and all human destinies by his eternal will, his decree.[7]

Augustine's asymmetric understanding of predestination, in which God causes belief in the elect but does not cause the unbelief of the unregenerate, is replaced by a doctrine of double predestination. The decree of God relates to belief and unbelief in the same manner. Even though Beza sought to soften the harshness of the doctrine of double predestination by emphasizing the role of secondary causes, human responsibility for sin, and the notion of divine permission in relation to

---

some to perdition. Calvin gave no clear answer on whether Christ died for all or only for the elect. Beza insisted on limited atonement—Christ died only for the elect" (William C. Placher, *The Domestication of Transcendence: How Modern Thinking About God Went Wrong* [Louisville: Westminster John Knox, 1996], pp. 152-53).

[5]Ibid., pp. 84, 87.

[6]Theodore Beza, *Confession de la foy chrestienne* (1563), quoted in Justo L. González, *A History of Christian Thought* (Nashville: Abingdon, 1987), 3:271.

[7]Muller, *Christ and the Decree,* pp. 86-87.

human sin and unbelief, it is difficult to imagine how God escapes cul-
pability for human sin in his thought. Within our temporally bound
glance we can see no further than our own sins. Yet behind and before
us lies the decretive will of God. Beza insisted that reprobation justly refers to man's own wickedness and unbelief. Yet his conception of the all-
determining will of God has led many commentators to conclude that he
was incapable of denying that God is ultimately responsible for the existence of sin and unbelief. Even the fall of Adam and Eve took place in
conformity to the predetermining will of God. Prior to all things and all
other causes, and in accordance with his immutable decree, God ordains
some to salvation out of sheer grace, but others according to his justice
he reprobates to wrath. Election and reprobation are equally ultimate in
relation to the divine decree. They differ in that election to salvation ev-
idences the mercy and justice of God, while reprobation proceeds out of
the divine justice.

Beza subjects even the first sin, the disobedience of the garden, to the
divine decree. The Adamic fall into sin was ordained by the divine will.
Man was created to sin. Beza's doctrine of the decree became known as
supralapsarianism, meaning "before the Fall." The elective work of God
precedes the fall into sin within the eternal counsel of God. As decretal
theology developed in Reformed circles in the late sixteenth century, the
eternal will of God was analytically divided into a sequence of moments
or a series of decrees. Since the decree takes place in eternity rather than
in time, the sequence was envisioned as logical rather than temporal, but
in truth it is difficult not to assign some temporal value to it. According
to the supralapsarian order of decrees, God's first decree is to glorify himself through the election of some to salvation and the reprobation of others to damnation. The second decree is God's decision to create the universe. Third, God decrees the fall into sin. The fourth decree is God's
decision to provide a savior for the elect in the mediatorial work of
Christ. God's decretive will begins with predestination. As prior to God's
decree to create, election and reprobation are God's primary work. As
one can see following the sequence, the second through fourth decrees

are means toward the realization of the first. Creation is for the sake of salvation and damnation. The fall serves God's elective purpose. Subsuming all history to the doctrine of predestination suggests, as Harold O. J. Brown has pointed out, that "some human beings are created for the express purpose of being damned forever," and thus "supralapsarianism implies that God is responsible for the fall."[8]

Infralapsarianism. While the Arminians will argue that supralapsarianism is representative of the Calvinist position relative to the divine decree, such was not the case. A somewhat less strident form of Calvinist decretal thought arose alongside Beza's supralapsarianism and would become the dominant confessional position among Reformed churches. *Infralapsarianism* (subsequent to the Fall) held that God's elective decree presupposes or is logically subsequent to man's fall into sin. The infralapsarian order of decrees follows the historical sequence of creation, fall and salvation that we see in Scripture. Here God's first decree is his decision to create the world. The decree to create is followed by God's decision to allow man to fall into sin through his own self-determination. Third, God decrees to elect some to salvation in Jesus Christ. And finally God determines to pass by and leave the nonelect to their just fate and condemnation.

While the infralapsarian doctrine of decrees agrees with the supralapsarian that all things come to pass in accordance with God's eternal plan, the infralapsarians objected to the supralapsarian notion of the fall as "an upward step in fulfilling God's redemptive purposes," thus compromising the evil of sin.[9] In the supralapsarian scheme, election and reprobation pertain to man as created; one might even say that humankind is created for the sake of election and reprobation—God created in order to save and condemn. Sin becomes a necessary means toward the fulfillment of

---

[8]Harold O. J. Brown, *Heresies: The Image of Christ in the Mirror of Heresy and Orthodoxy* (Grand Rapids: Baker, 1984), pp. 356-57.

[9]John M. Frame, "Infralapsarianism," in *The Westminster Handbook of Reformed Theology*, ed. Donald K. McKim (Louisville: Westminster John Knox, 2001), p. 121; John Frame, *The Doctrine of God: A Theology of Lordship* (Phillipsburg, N.J.: P & R, 2002), p. 339.

God's plan. Creation and the fall serve predestination. According to infralapsarianism, however, election and condemnation pertain to man as sinner. Further, God's intention was that he would glorify himself through his creation. Thus redemption serves the order of creation.

We should note two further distinctive elements within the infralapsarian scheme of decrees. First, infralapsarianism represents a return to Augustinian passive reprobation. The infralapsarian order of decrees presents an asymmetric relationship between the plan of God and election, which is viewed as unconditional, and the plan of God and condemnation, which is viewed as conditional upon human sinfulness and unbelief.[10] Second, infralapsarianism posits a much closer relationship between Christ and election than is presented in the supralapsarian model. As Brown states the problem of supralapsarianism, "the Christian's standing with God does not depend primarily on his relationship with Christ, but on God's decree."[11] By grounding election in its first decree and placing it before creation and the fall, supralapsarianism abstracts election from its biblical heart, namely, that the people of God are chosen in Christ (Eph 1:4; 2 Tim 1:9). "Supralapsarian theology removes the attention of the believer from the historical person of Christ and his work, and centers it on the eternal decree of God, cold and intellectual, before all time."[12]

JACOB ARMINIUS

Born in 1559, the same year that Calvin published the final edition of the *Institutes of the Christian Religion*, Jacob Arminius entered the Geneva

---

[10]Muller, *Christ and the Decree*, p. 215.

[11]Brown, *Heresies*, p. 357.

[12]Ibid. Ultimately both infralapsarianism and supralapsarianism are unsatisfying. As John Frame has observed, the entire discussion of an order of decrees was engaged in a speculation that the Bible simply does not underwrite. One must "try to picture the process of God's thinking before he created the world." But "Scripture warns us against trying to read God's mind. His thoughts are not our thoughts (Isa. 55:8). This discussion runs great risks of engaging in speculation into matters God has kept secret" (*Doctrine of God*, pp. 335-37).

Academy as a student in 1581. Even though Beza's supralapsarian doctrine never appealed to Arminius, the unusually gifted young man enjoyed a good relationship with Theodore Beza, who was both the head of the school and the professor of New Testament. But the young scholar did imbibe the scholastic methodology he was taught at Geneva. Although he struggled with Beza's idea of a divine decree that preceded all contingent causes, Arminius would use medieval scholasticism to develop a synergistic doctrine of conditional divine decrees.[13]

Upon completing his education, Arminius returned to Amsterdam in 1587 to take a pastorate in the Reformed church. While he was an effective and beloved pastor, throughout the 1590s his preaching and teaching incurred the increasing suspicion of the strict Calvinists in and around Amsterdam who judged him as placing too much emphasis on human freedom in the process of belief and repentance. Between 1591 and 1596 Arminius presented his developing views on human free will and predestination in a series of sermons on Romans 7 and 9. He argued that Isaac and Ishmael, and Jacob and Esau, are not represented as individual persons by Paul in Romans 9; rather, Paul presented them as typological characters. God predestines not individuals but classes of persons, that is to say, those who will believe the gospel and those who will not.[14] Although his preaching earned him the displeasure of a number of other pastors, Arminius remained on good terms with his own congregation throughout his Amsterdam pastorate.

In October 1602 a plague swept through the city of Leiden, claiming the lives of scores of people, including both professors of theology at the University of Leiden. Franciscus Gomarus (1563-1641), a rather strict former student of Beza and a confirmed supralapsarian, was subsequently appointed to fill one of the vacant posts. The second appointment went to Arminius, who began teaching in 1603. Contro-

---

[13]Muller, *God, Creation, and Providence,* pp. 10-13.
[14]Richard A. Muller, "Grace, Election, and Contingent Choice: Arminius's Gambit and the Reformed Response," in *The Grace of God, the Bondage of the Will,* ed. Thomas R. Schreiner and Bruce A. Ware (Grand Rapids: Baker, 1995), 2:255.

versy began almost at once, as Gomarus showed an immediate hostility toward the views Arminius was presenting to the students at Leiden. It was not long before Gomarus publicly accused Arminius of doctrinal error.

But the tensions within the University of Leiden soon overflowed throughout the Reformed church as other teachers, pastors and interested laypeople aligned themselves with one or the other of the two feuding professors. From the beginning, Gomarus took the offensive, accusing Arminius of deviation from the confessional standards of the Reformed church, the Belgic Confession (1561) and the Heidelberg Catechism (1563).[15]

Arminius presented his defense against the charge of confessional infidelity in his "Declaration of Sentiments" in 1608. The work also contained a broadside against Calvinist decretal theology and Arminius's most complete discussion of his own views. As to the charge of confessional deviance, Arminius noted that the doctrine of predestination was nowhere affirmed by any of the ecumenical creeds of the ancient church, and the confessions of the Reformed churches either omitted explicit reference to predestination or were sufficiently oblique that they allowed for a number of interpretations, including Arminius's own.[16] This suggests that Arminius favored a broad toleration of opinion within the church, and that was so. Yet he admitted that he found supralapsarianism intolerable, and he put forth twenty objections to the doctrine. Olson summarizes the gist of Arminius's argument:

---

[15]The issue of confessional allegiance was a significant one for both sides of the controversy. The Calvinists argued that a Reformed church is a confessional church. Hence they pleaded for the maintenance of particular confessional standards. Following in the tradition of Erasmus of Rotterdam, however, the Arminians championed the idea of the liberty of individual conscience relative to doctrinal standards. While the debate is tangential to the soteriological issues of the Arminian controversy, we should note that the question of ecclesiastical authority and the integrity of the church as a confessional body was an intense point of contention for both sides in the struggle between the Calvinists and the Arminians within the Dutch church.

[16]Carl Bangs, *Arminius: A Study in the Dutch Reformation,* 2d ed. (Grand Rapids: Zondervan, 1985), pp. 309-10.

He argued that it is contrary to the nature of the gospel itself since it treats people as being saved or not saved completely apart from their being sinners or believers. They are saved or damned first (in God's first decree) and only then made believers or sinners. He also argued that this doctrine is a novelty in the history of theology because it had never been heard before Gomarus and his immediate predecessors (e.g., Beza). Furthermore, it is repugnant to God's nature as love and to human nature as free. Perhaps Arminius's strongest objection was that supralapsarianism (and, by extension, any doctrine of unconditional election) is "injurious to the glory of God" because "from these premises we deduce, as a further conclusion, that God really sins . . . that God is the only sinner . . . that sin is not sin." Arminius never tired of arguing that the strong Calvinist doctrine of predestination cannot help making God the author of sin, and if God is the author of sin, then sin is not sin because whatever God authors is good.[17]

Arminius judged supralapsarianism as placing so much emphasis upon sovereign omnipotence as the head and cause of all things that it necessarily lessened the gracious love of God. The effects of supralapsarian doctrine, he argued, are devastating to the exercise of religion. Any doctrine which says that some are predestined to salvation and others to damnation without reference to their faith

---

[17]Roger Olson, *The Story of Christian Theology: Twenty Centuries of Tradition & Reform* (Downers Grove, Ill.: InterVarsity Press, 1999), p. 467. Cf. Bangs, *Arminius,* pp. 308-10. Beza has often played the part of historical whipping boy for both Calvinists and Arminians. As we will see, the Arminians will repeatedly portray Beza's supralapsarianism as the typical Calvinist position, a habit often continued to this day. Reformed Christians often seek to distance themselves from Beza by depicting him as a hyper-Calvinist, a man whose theology revolved around the single concern of divine sovereignty. For each, he is the arch unilateral decretalist, a purveyor of an inhumane view of history in which human beings are but pawns in a predetermined historical drama that glorifies God in all things, whether good or bad. We suspect that history has not been totally fair to Beza. See Muller, *Christ and the Decree,* pp. 79-96, for a more sympathetic reading of Beza's contribution to Calvinist theology.

prevents . . . godly sorrow for sins . . . removes all pious solicitude about being converted . . . restrains all zeal and studious regard for good works . . . extinguishes the zeal for prayer . . . takes away all that most salutary fear and trembling with which we are commanded to work out our own salvation . . . [and] produces within men a despair both of performing that which their duty requires and of obtaining that toward which their desires are directed.[18]

As Olson hints above, Arminius also rejected infralapsarianism. Indeed, "all of Arminius's writings on predestination and related topics manifest dissent from the teaching of his Reformed contemporaries, whether infra- or supralapsarian."[19] Again Olson captures the substance of Arminius's objection:

> When he turned to examining infralapsarianism, Arminius was not much more generous than with supralapsarianism. Even though it does not place God's decree of election and reprobation prior to creation and the Fall, it still nevertheless makes the fall of humanity necessary and God its author. In the final analysis, according to Arminius, any monergistic doctrine of salvation makes God the author of sin and thus a hypocrite "because it imputes hypocrisy to God, as if, in His exhortation to faith addressed to such, He requires them to believe in Christ, whom, however, He has not set forth as a Savior to them."[20]

So, like supralapsarianism, infralapsarianism for Arminius also makes God responsible for sin. Both of the Calvinist approaches toward the decree envision God as "above human law and notions of fairness. Everything that God does is right because it glorifies God."[21] Again, divine love and justice are subordinated to and relativized by

---

[18]Jacob Arminius, "Declaration of Sentiments," in *The Writings of James Arminius*, trans. James Nichols and William Nichols (Grand Rapids: Baker, 1956), 1:230-31.
[19]Muller, *God, Creation, and Providence*, p. 10.
[20]Olson, *Story of Christian Theology*, p. 467.
[21]Ibid., p. 459.

omnipotence. Arminius insisted that any unconditional redemptive decision or action necessarily coerces the human will and therefore is a violation of human freedom. Thus both Calvinist decretal schemes are deterministic and differ only in degree.

Arminius's criticisms of Calvinist decretal theology were aimed at what he perceived as a unilateral agency, an emphasis upon sovereign divine action that gave no consideration to contingent causes. But this does not mean that he was averse to the idea of divine decrees. Indeed, while Arminius took positions that were often at the antipodes of those affirmed by Theodore Beza, and while the two men worked from decidedly different theological presuppositions, Arminius and Beza used the same methodological tools for doing theology. Arminius posited in the mind of God a series of decretal moments that proceeded on a distinction between antecedent and consequent or absolute and conditional aspects of the divine will.

God's first decree, according to Arminius, was his decision to be gracious toward sinful human beings by providing a Savior in Jesus Christ. In his appointment as Redeemer, Jesus Christ would die for sin and thus provide salvation for sinners. This first decree is not directed toward the salvation of particular persons; rather it is a general decree applied to a class of persons, sinners. The second decree also pertains to classes rather than particular persons, and it presumes the first decree. God decrees to accept those who repent and believe in Christ, but to leave the unrepentant and unbelieving in their sin and to hold them over to the wrath of damnation. This decree is the preface to Arminius's doctrine of the divine prescience of human choice, to which we will turn shortly. The third decree provides for the means toward the fulfillment of the first two decrees by the appointment of the proclamation of the gospel and whatever means are necessary to that end, namely, the institution of the church. Like the first two decrees, the third also refers to the antecedent will of God without reference to specific human beings.

Thus in Arminius's thinking, God predestines all who will believe in

Christ to be saved and all who reject the gospel to be damned. This general predestination of classes does not pertain to any particular historical persons. The first three decrees pertain to the preparation of causes and conditions for salvation antecedent to historical contingency, that is, the agency of human beings.[22] In his fourth and final decree, however, Arminius moves toward the application of salvation and reprobation to particular persons. Arminius wrote:

> To these succeeds the FOURTH decree, by which God decreed to save and damn certain particular persons. This decree has its foundation in the foreknowledge of God, by which he knew from all eternity those individuals who *would,* through his preventing grace, *believe,* and, through his subsequent grace *would persevere,* according to the before described administration of those means which are suitable and proper for conversion and faith; and, by which foreknowledge, he likewise knew those *who would not believe and persevere.*[23]

For Arminius neither election nor reprobation is causal in any way. The decree is conditioned by contingent causes, that is, determined by human choices. While the predestination of classes is unconditional, the predestination of particular persons is conditional, being based on God's prescience of human choices. God knows from all eternity those particular persons who will believe, and on the basis of that prescience he elects them to salvation. Likewise, from all eternity he knows those persons who will reject the gospel, and from that prior knowledge he condemns them to damnation. Putting this all together, we begin to see a scheme in which divine election is purely cognitive, a matter of simple prescience, and this prescience is fundamentally passive and non-

---

[22]Muller comments that Arminius's first three decrees "could have been construed in a favorable relationship to the doctrine of the Reformed confessions. In the fourth decree, Arminius points more clearly toward his divergence from the Reformed" ("Grace, Election, and Contingent Choice," p. 259).

[23]Arminius, "Declaration of Sentiments," 1.653-54 (italics in original).

determining (Arminians often refer to this prescience as "simple fore-knowledge"). Predestination, on the other hand, is God acting upon his knowledge of future contingents. Between the two—prescience and predestination—stands the free will of contingent agents and the choices they make.

Carl Bangs, an Arminian, ends his discussion of Arminius's doctrine of the divine decree by regretting what he takes as the "highly speculative element" which "intrudes into the fourth decree." How can prescience not cause that which it foresees? "To speak of future things *that shall be* is either a contradiction in terms or a statement of a divine predestination of those things, which would be another kind of contradiction in terms."[24] In other words, if God knows in the past how I will respond to the gospel, is it not unavoidable that my response to the gospel is determined by that knowledge? What God knows will happen, must happen. The specter of determinism that accompanies any notion of divine prescience has led many Arminians to question whether a belief in God's ability to know the future is compatible with the doctrine of free will. Unfortunately, this leads them to re-examine not the idea of free will but instead the idea of divine prescience. William Hasker, for example, writes:

> There are serious questions concerning the logical compatibility of comprehensive divine foreknowledge and libertarian free will. The idea, roughly, is this: If God knows already what will happen in the future, then God's knowing this is part of the past and is now fixed, impossible to change. . . . If God knows that a person is going to perform [some action], then it is impossible that the person fail to perform it, so one does not have a free choice whether or not to perform it.[25]

Hasker's resolution to the problem that "it is logically impossible that

---

[24]Bangs, *Arminius*, p. 354 (italics in original).
[25]William Hasker, "A Philosophical Perspective," in *The Openness of God: A Biblical Challenge to the Traditional Understanding of God*, ed. Clark Pinnock et al. (Downers Grove, Ill.: InterVarsity Press, 1994), p. 147.

God should have foreknowledge of a genuinely free action"[26] is not to reconsider human free will—it is the one unassailable dogma—but to reject the doctrine of divine prescience. God cannot know in the past what is yet to be decided by free agents.

How did Arminius himself resolve the problem of divine prescience and free human agency? The Calvinist Richard Muller picks up on Arminius where Bangs left off. Muller traces Arminius's conception of the relationship between the divine decree and future contingents to the contemporary Roman Catholic speculation regarding middle knowledge, especially the thought of Luis de Molina (1535-1600) and Francisco Suárez (1548-1617). Although Arminius nowhere cites either thinker, "his argument is quite similar to, and probably based upon, Molina's hypothesis of a divine middle knowledge or *scientia media*: here God provides the conditions for the future contingent acts of individual human beings."[27] Like the Molinists, Arminius sought to bring together a doctrine of divine decree with an affirmation of human freedom through the construct of a cognitive, noncausal divine prescience: God elects or reprobates on the basis of a prior knowledge of human response to sin and the gospel.

Arminius held that "a thing does not come to pass because it is foreknown or foretold; but it is foreknown or foretold because it is yet to be."[28] In other words, God's knowledge of the future does not determine the future if God knows the future as contingent, that is to say, as dependent upon the choices or actions of other agents. Prescience does not determine future contingents if God knows them as contingent. Indeed, "what he knows as contingent is, therefore, established with certainty as contingent."[29] Thus God can foreknow the future, yet human beings

---

[26]Ibid., p. 148.

[27]Muller, "Grace, Election, and Contingent Choice," p. 258. Cf. Muller, *God, Creation, and Providence*, pp. 21, 155, 161-63.

[28]Arminius, *Private Disputations*, 28.16, quoted in Muller, *God, Creation, and Providence*, p. 161.

[29]Muller, "Grace, Election, and Contingent Choice," p. 264.

can also possess true freedom only if God's knowledge of the future is noncausal. If this were not the case, either God's knowledge of the future would deny all contingency or true contingency would limit or annul the possibility of God's knowledge of the future. The solution for Arminius, as it had been for the Molinists, was to deny that divine knowing is causal. True contingent events lie outside of divine causality; events that are not the effects of God's knowing them but rather are themselves the cause of God's knowing.

Muller shows that Arminius employed medieval Thomism in order to argue his position. First, Arminius accepted Aquinas's priority of the intellect over the will, although, unlike Aquinas, he envisioned divine knowledge as passive or merely cognitive rather than determining. Second, Arminius also took from Aquinas the Aristotelian distinction between potency and actuality. God's knowledge precedes his will. He passively or noncausally foresees future conditional events. Yet the events, being caused by agents other than God, cause his knowledge of them. All of this is prior to the decree. One might say that the free decisions of other beings cause or actualize God's knowledge. Once God's knowledge of future potentialities is actualized by free human choice, God's decree makes it certain that foreseen human free choices will take place.

Both for the Molinists and for Arminius the divine will to save particular persons rests upon God's knowledge of the future free choices of human beings. "Indeed," writes Muller, "it is only by the device of [middle knowledge] that Arminius can argue a genuinely universal will to save, resting on a knowledge of possibility and also argue, subsequently, a genuine specific will to save believers only."[30] Like Molina before him, Arminius began by assuming the free choices and actions of human beings and then sought to explain a divine prescience that does not limit human freedom. Rather, it is human freedom that limits the divine knowledge and will. That which is willed by divine decree is, according

---

[30]Ibid., p. 164.

to Arminius, a knowledge of "things which depend on the liberty of created choice or pleasure."[31] Thus, God's will in saving any particular person is responsive to human choice, even if it is a choice conditioned by gracious enablement. In Arminius's decretal scheme the work of God enables salvation but falls short of bringing it about. The metaphysics of middle knowledge suggest that it is our free acceptance of the gospel that effects salvation.

Arminius softens the suggestion of the human-centered view of salvation implied in his predestination-through-prescience doctrine by insisting that belief is a response to God's prevenient grace. "I confess," he wrote, "that the mind of . . . a natural and carnal man is obscure and dark, that his affections are corrupt and inordinate, that his will is stubborn and disobedient, and that man himself is dead in sins."[32] Arminius accepted the Augustinian doctrine of human moral depravity and spiritual inability:

> The free will of man toward the true good is not only wounded, maimed, infirm, bent, and weakened; but it is also imprisoned, destroyed, and lost. And its powers are not only debilitated and useless unless they be assisted by grace, but it has no powers whatsoever except such as are excited by divine grace. For Christ has said, "Without me ye can do nothing."[33]

For fallen sinners, in bondage to sin and death, God's gracious initiation is absolutely necessary for belief and salvation. "Grace is simply and absolutely necessary for the illumination of the mind, the due ordering of the affections, and the inclination of the will to that which is good,"

---

[31]Arminius, *Private Disputations,* 17.12, quoted in Muller, "Grace, Election, and Contingent Choice," p. 265. As Arminianism seeks to preserve an unqualified human freedom and defines the knowledge and will of God in terms of that freedom, it is not surprising that Muller writes that "middle knowledge is the heart and soul of the original Arminian position" (ibid.).

[32]Arminius, "A Letter Addressed to Hippolytus a Collibus," in *The Works of James Arminius,* trans. James Nichols and William Nichols (Grand Rapids: Baker, 1999), 2:700.

[33]Arminius, "Declaration of Sentiments," 1:526.

for "Free Will is unable to begin or to perfect any true spiritual good, without Grace."[34] This grace is given to all human beings, and enables the response of faith. God's preceding grace "goes before, accompanies, and follows; . . . excites [and] assists" the sinner, and in doing so effectively removes the slavery produced by the fall so that a person can repent of his sin and turn to Christ. The bondage of the will is canceled such that the sinner is free to believe if he so will.

Yet God will not impose this grace upon man. Grace does not coerce or annul the free will. Grace allows the sinner to hear the call to believe the gospel free from the shackles of sin's binding and blinding effects. Thus the sinner is enabled to freely accept the gospel. While the ability to believe is made possible by grace,[35] salvation is dependent upon the free choice of the sinner empowered by preceding grace.

Arminius insisted that he was not a Pelagian.[36] He consistently affirmed that the initiative in salvation is God's, that salvation is a response to God's preceding grace, and that salvation is by grace alone through faith alone. Yet the faith that saves (the "instrumental cause" of justification) properly belongs to human beings.[37] Between the universal love of God for the world and the application of salvation to particular persons stands the active faith of the sinner as the essential determining cause of salvation, for God "does not lead" people "to life or to death, except after certain precedent actions of theirs."[38] The elect are saved because, through the exercise of faith, they cooperate with God's prevenient grace. H. Orton Wiley speaks of this synergism between divine grace and hu-

---

[34]Arminius, "Letter Addressed to Hippolytus a Collibus," 2:700.

[35]Roger Olson observes that "Arminius was always cautious to attribute all of salvation to grace and none of it to good works" (*Story of Christian Theology*, p. 470). Likewise, Bangs comments that "all response of man to the divine vocation is the work of grace. The entire process of believing—from 'initial fear' to 'illumination, renovation, and confirmation'— is of grace" (*Arminius*, p. 341).

[36]Arminius, "Letter Addressed to Hippolytus a Collibus," 2:700-701.

[37]Bangs, *Arminius*, p. 342.

[38]Arminius, "Examination of the Theses of Dr. F. Gamaurs Respecting Predestination," in *The Works of James Arminius*, trans. James Nichols and William Nichols (Grand Rapids: Baker, 1999), 3:560.

man will as a "basic truth of the Arminian system."[39]

"The grace sufficient for salvation is conferred on the Elect, and on the Non-Elect," wrote Arminius, "that, if they will, they may believe or not believe, may be saved or not be saved."[40] The difference between the elect and the nonelect lies in the use that each makes of the grace offered to all men. Those who believe accept the gospel through the agency of their free will, and those who remain in their sins resist the gracious call of the gospel through the same renewed will by which the redeemed come to faith. "I believe according to the Scriptures that many persons resist the Holy Spirit and reject the grace that is offered."[41] Hence, the enabling that God gives to the sinner through prevenient grace may be resisted by the free will of the sinner. But we should note that this will is not that of a blindly recalcitrant rebel. No such person is possible according to Arminius, for all people are sufficiently enabled to accept the gospel, if they so will. Thus it is not sin that impedes the acceptance of the gospel but the free and unencumbered human will. People who do not come to Christ do so simply because they choose not to, a choice that is—thanks to the ministry of prevenient grace—not enslaved to the debilitating powers of sin. Arminius is pushed into this box by his contention of a universal prevenient grace and an antecedent divine will that wishes the salvation of all people. God intends the rescue of all sinners. But each sinner must freely accept the offered grace, and each is sufficiently enabled to do so by a will that is liberated from the power of sin. The only thing that prevents God from realizing his intention to save all people is the exercise of human free will.

---

[39]H. Orton Wiley, *Christian Theology* (Kansas City, Mo.: Beacon Hill, 1941), 2:355. Also see John Miley, *Systematic Theology* (New York: Eaton and Mains, 1892-94; reprint, Peabody, Mass.: Hendrickson, 1989), 2:336-37. Carl Bangs, however, cautions that the word *synergism* might suggest some natural capacity in man to cooperate with grace, a capacity that Bangs finds alluded to in the work of both Wiley and Miley. Bangs wants it clearly understood that Arminius entertained no such notions of inherent human ability to cooperate with divine prevenient grace. The ability to cooperate with the grace of God is itself a product of grace (*Arminius*, pp. 342, 358).

[40]Arminius, "Apology Against Thirty-One Theological Articles," in *The Works of James Arminius*, trans. James Nichols and William Nichols (Grand Rapids: Baker, 1999), 2:53.

[41]Ibid., 1:664.

Arminius rejected the Calvinist belief in meticulous providence and absolute predestination in which God's sovereign plan superintends and orders all things. In its place he elevates human free will to an unqualified dictum of his theology. Where the Calvinists affirmed a human freedom that is enveloped by and subordinate to the sovereign will of God, Arminius would affirm an unqualified human freedom and then define divine sovereignty such that it enables but does not conflict with human freedom. The will of God cannot, according to Arminius, circumscribe human choices such that any particular choice is metaphysically necessary. Divine determination of any degree or stripe is a violation of the integrity of the human free will. To be free, the will must be free from all coercion. The integrity of the autonomous creature is the one irreducible theological principle of Arminius's thought. God's power and will are unabashedly circumscribed by the principle of human autonomy. If it is appropriate to speak of a doctrine of sovereignty here, it appears that it can only be the sovereignty of the human will. In arminius's thinking, God can get his way only if he happens to be traveling in the same direction that we are.

THE REMONSTRANTS

Simon Episcopus, a man whose theological convictions followed lines similar to those of Arminius, was appointed to succeed Arminius at the University of Leiden upon Arminius's death in 1609. Instead of abating, the controversy over Arminius's views on predestination intensified as Gomarus and his followers stepped up their accusations of heresy against the Arminians. The widespread suspicion and caricature that typified the followers of both Gomarus and Arminius were exacerbated by the Erastian relationship between the government and the Reformed church in the Netherlands. Since the Reformed church was the state church of the Netherlands, civil magistrates exercised considerable power in the determining of policy, and even doctrine, in the church. University professorships and pastorates were filled by civil appointment. Men with theological sentiments similar to those of Arminius filled a number of the pastorates in and around Amsterdam by 1610. Yet, if the members of the church of an Arminian pastor were unhappy with him, they were largely unable to oust him from office. Churches began putting pressure upon the government to get rid of the Arminian pastors.

Forty-six advocates of Arminius's theology met in the city of Gouda in 1610 under the leadership of Hans Uytenbogaert (a pastor) and Simon Episcopus. Seeking to solicit the protection of the state from consistories or congregations that sought their dismissal, the assembled company drafted a short remonstrance (a complaint or protest) against the Calvinists. The Remonstrance was a defense meant to answer the charges of heresy against the pastors.

The document of just under one thousand words, set in the form of a confession of faith, was divided into five points and thus has often been referred to as The Five Arminian Articles. The first article deals with predestination. Far from denying it, the Remonstrants affirmed it:

> That God by an eternal and immutable decree has in Jesus Christ his Son determined before the foundation of the world to save out of the fallen sinful human race those in Christ, for Christ's sake, and through Christ who by the grace of the Holy Spirit shall believe in this his Son Jesus Christ and persevere in this faith and obedience of faith to the end; and on the other hand to leave the incorrigible and unbelieving in sin and under wrath and condemn [them] as alienate from Christ, according to the word of the holy gospel in John 3:36, "He that believeth on the Son hath eternal life, and whosoever is disobedient to the Son shall not see life, but the wrath of God abideth on him," and also other passages of the Scriptures.[42]

Following the lead of Arminius, the Remonstrant view of predestination

---

[42]The Remonstrance can be found in Peter Y. De Jong, *Crisis in the Reformed Churches: Essays in Commemoration of the Great Synod of Dort, 1618-1619* (Grand Rapids: Reformed Fellowship, 1968), pp. 207-9. An English translation, together with the Dutch and Latin versions, appears in Philip Schaff, *The Creeds of Christendom* (Grand Rapids: Baker, 1931), 3:545-49.

is predicated upon a foreseen faith. The synergistic and conditional intention of the first article is found in the words "who by the grace of the Holy Spirit shall believe." Election takes place by the prescient knowledge by which God foresees who will respond positively to the gospel, and on the basis of that prescience of human decision he elects.

One immediately notices the strong association of election with Christ. This is due in part to the fact that Arminius began his decretal scheme in the same way, election is "in Christ." But the first article also takes the shape that it does because of the prevailing Arminian criticism of supralapsarianism. A popular Arminian complaint was that supralapsarianism diverted the believer's attention and religious devotion from Christ and his redeeming work by finding the true cause and fount of election in an eternal decree. After all, within the supralapsarian model, Christ can appear to function merely as the executor of a decree already made by the Father. Thus election finds its ultimate origin and cause in something other than the work of Christ. The picture, according to the Arminians, is that according to the Calvinists it is not Christ and his historical work that saves, but rather salvation is the product of an impersonal decree lost in the mists of eternity.

The first article affirms the notion that God elects those who believe in the gospel of Christ and "persevere in this faith and obedience of faith to the end." God chooses us because he foresees that we will choose him. Arminians insist that the faith that God foresees in us is not meritorious. It should not be thought of as a work, an earning of salvation in some way, for it is enabled by grace and is a response to grace. While the intention here is to reject any notion of salvation by works, a salvation by merit, Arminius's doctrine of election through foreseen faith, cannot fully escape the allegation that merit is intrinsic to his understanding of salvation. John Frame states the Calvinist analysis here most succinctly: "The Arminian wants to have it both ways. He wants to say that faith has no merit, but he also wants to say that our faith somehow motivates God to save us, that God chooses us on the basis of our choosing him. But if faith motivates God to save us, then it must have merit in his eyes."[43]

The second article is aimed at the Calvinist doctrine of particular atonement, the notion that Christ died for the elect. While the Calvinists had always held that the work of Christ was sufficient for the sins of every sinner, it is efficient only for those whom God has predestined to be his children "in Christ." The Remonstrance seeks to speak of the work of Christ, however, not in terms of the particularity of the Calvinist understanding (which allows me to say that Christ died for me) but in conformity with Arminius's notion of a general decree of redemption (which compels me to say only that Christ died for sins):

> that in agreement with this Jesus Christ the Savior of the world died for all men and every man, so that he merited reconciliation and forgiveness of sin for all through the death of the cross; yet so that no one actually enjoys this forgiveness of sins except the believer—also according to the word of the gospel of John 3:16, "God so loved the world that he gave his only-begotten Son that whosoever believeth in him shall not perish but have eternal life." And in the first epistle of John 2:2, "He is the propitiation for our sins; and not only for ours, but also for the sins of the whole world."[44]

In the third article the Remonstrance seems to agree with the Calvinists on the seriousness of the fall. As fallen, the natural human being is impotent, dead in sin and blind to the things of God:

> that man does not have saving faith of himself nor by the power of his own free will, since he in the state of apostasy and sin cannot of and through himself think, will or do any good which is truly good (such as is especially saving faith); but that it is nec-

---

[43]John M. Frame, *No Other God: A Response to Open Theism* (Phillipsburg, N.J.: P & R, 2001), p. 76. Frame also comments here regarding Arminius's view that election is a response to human faith: "On this view, our choice is the cause, and God's choice is the effect. We are the first cause, and God is the second."
[44]The Remonstrance in De Jong, *Crisis in the Reformed Churches*, pp. 207-9.

essary that he be regenerated by God, in Christ, through his Holy Spirit, and renewed in understanding, affections or will, and all powers, in order that he may rightly understand, meditate upon, will, and perform that which is truly good, according to the word of Christ, John 13:5 [sic], "Without me ye can do nothing."[45]

This is a strong statement of the pervasive depravity of the natural man. The mind, heart and will of the sinner are in bondage to sin such that the work of salvation must begin from some point external to the sinner. God must initiate redemption. The fall of Adam brought both himself and his posterity under the reign of sin and death. The main point, for both Arminius and the Remonstrants after him, was that "the recipient of evangelical grace is a sinner in desperate straits, involved and caught in the consequences of Adam's sin. His acts of sin are not mere free choices in imitation of bad example but the result of the predicament of man in the fall."[46]

But how does this third article fit with Arminius's optimistic view of human free will and his synergistic view of redemption, which insisted that man's acceptance of the gospel is a necessary condition for regeneration? The Remonstrant solution comes in the next article, and it is there that we see the real meaning of the Arminian doctrine of sin:

that this grace of God is the commencement, progression, and completion of all good, also in so far that regenerate man cannot, apart from this prevenient or assisting, awakening, consequent and cooperating grace, think, will or do the good or resist any temptation to evil; so that all good works or activities which can be conceived must be ascribed to the grace of God in Christ. But with respect to the mode of this grace, it is not irresistible, since it is

---

[45]Ibid. The correct reference is Jn 15:5.
[46]Bangs, *Arminius,* pp. 340-41. Cf. Arminius, "Public Disputation 7.15," in *The Works of James Arminius,* trans. James Nichols and William Nichols (Grand Rapids: Baker, 1999), 2:156-57.

written concerning many that they resisted the Holy Spirit. Acts 7 and elsewhere in many places.[47]

At the end of the article, we read that grace can be resisted by the recalcitrant human will. Grace is not efficacious as in the Augustinian and Calvinist sense that by God's power his grace effects its goal, namely, the redemption of sinners such that their redemption comes by no power of their own but is the result solely of the power and work of the triune God. The Calvinist unabashedly confesses that grace *causes* redemption. The only reason anyone believes the gospel and comes into saving relationship with Jesus Christ is because grace brings the sinner into the company of the redeemed. God does not merely *initiate* redemption; he effects the entirety of it. Here in the Remonstrance, however, grace is merely persuasive. Grace is not causal but rather persuasive in nature. And such a notion of grace is demanded by Arminius's doctrine of the free human will. God cannot coerce belief. The call of the gospel is not *you will* but rather *you should*. And because the final determinant is the will of man, the call of grace is resistible. The sinner, should he or she so choose, is free to reject the gospel.

But the real center of the Remonstrance and the lynchpin of the Arminian approach to salvation is found in the phrase "this prevenient or assisting, awakening, consequent and cooperating grace." This phrase places the Arminian articles firmly in the synergistic tradition of the Semi-Augustinians. Salvation is a matter of both God and the sinner doing their part. God begins by giving each sinner sufficient repairing grace that he or she is enabled to freely accept or reject the gospel. Human beings, who were formerly unable to contribute the slightest to their own redemption, who were depraved by and enslaved to sin, are sufficiently restored by God's gift of prevenient grace so that they are able to choose for or against the work of Christ. Grace nullifies the moral, affective and intellectual effects of the fall. Rather than being predisposed toward the self, rather than seeing evil as good, under prevenient grace, the will is restored so that sin does not impede the will's response to the gospel.

---

[47]The Remonstrance, in De Jong, *Crisis in the Reformed Churches,* pp. 208-9.

Where the Calvinist claims that grace causes salvation, the Arminian can only say that grace causes the freedom of the will. The Arminian claim asserts both too much and too little. The Arminian notion of prevenient grace is barely gracious at all. Its goal is the restoration of the free will, a will that the vast majority of people will then employ to reject Christ and his work. From a Calvinist perspective, such grace is decidedly underwhelming, for it suggests a view of God whose primary interest is not redemption but rather the restoration and protection of human free will. And what is this *free will* anyway? Repeatedly—and shockingly—Arminian writers define free will as *the ability to choose the contrary* or its equivalent.[48] This view is often called the libertarian view of the will, the idea being that the will is free only when it is uncoerced. One can pick X or not pick X as one will; the choice is neutral. While such a notion might be justified by my choice of Cheerios rather than Frosted Flakes this morning, does it fit the entire tenor of my life choices? And equally, if not more importantly, does it fit the biblical picture of things? We believe that the Arminian notion of libertarian free will is false both experientially and biblically. It enshrines an almost idolatrous doctrine of the autonomous human being that is in fact closer to a biblical description of sin than true humanity.

Yet if the Arminian notion of prevenient grace makes too little of the grace of God, it also asserts too much. As a universal enabling that liberates the free will, the Arminian doctrine of prevenient grace de facto nullifies the doctrine of depravity that was affirmed in the last article. The spiritual inability spoken of in the third article becomes an empty shell, a purely hypothetical notion. If all people have sufficient free will that they are able to respond believingly to the gospel, then when or where is anyone who lives under the conditions described in the article on the

---

[48]This definition of free will is implied in Wiley, *Christian Theology,* 2:355-57, and Grider, *Wesleyan-Holiness Theology,* pp. 244-46, and made explicit by recent writers such as William Hasker: "An agent is free with respect to a given action at a given time if at that time it is within the agent's power to perform the action and also in the agent's power to refrain from the action" (*Openness of God,* pp. 136-37).

fall as devoid of "the power of his own free will" and "in the state of apostasy and sin"? What was lost in the third article—the freedom of the will—is reinstated in the fourth.

Not surprisingly, Calvinists have been less than fully convinced by Arminian affirmations of the spiritual inability of the natural man and have often described the Arminian position on the fall and original sin as a partial depravity view.[49] Whether that evaluation is fair or not, the net effect of articles three and four is that every human being retains (or regains) a will that is able to cooperate with the redemptive activity of God.

Something of the real-world effects of the Arminian emphasis upon a synergistic redemption in which the will of man is the deciding factor is to be seen in the final article:

> that those who are incorporated into Jesus Christ and thereby become partakers of his life-giving Spirit have abundant strength to strive against satan, sin, the world, and their own flesh and to obtain the victory; it being well understood [that this is] through the assistance of the grace of the Holy Spirit, and that Jesus Christ assists them through his Spirit in all temptations, extends the hand, and—if only they are prepared for warfare and desire his help and are not negligent—keeps them standing, so that by no cunning or power of satan can they be led astray or plucked out of Christ's hands, according to the word of Christ, John 10, "No one shall pluck them out of my hands." But whether they can through negligence fall away from the first principle of their life in Christ, again embrace the present world, depart from the pure doctrine once given to them, lose the good conscience, and neglect grace, must first be more carefully determined from the Holy Scriptures before we shall be able to teach this with the full persuasion of our heart.[50]

Although not quite denying the Calvinist doctrine of the perseverance of

---

[49]Klooster, "Doctrinal Deliverances of Dort," in De Jong, *Crisis in the Reformed Churches,* p. 60.

[50]The Remonstrance, in De Jong, *Crisis in the Reformed Churches,* p. 209.

the saints—that the redeemed are kept by the same gracious and efficacious divine power that saved them—the fifth article leans heavily in the
direction of conditional perseverance—that staying saved is contingent
not only upon the grace of God but also human effort. This final article
is as unsurprising as it is disconcerting to the redeemed. It is expected
because it fits the Arminian dictum of the sovereignty of the human free
will. Human choice—even a choice that consists of negligence in the
things of God—is determinative. Free will trumps all else, even the grace
of God. When man has veto power over the redemptive work of God,
the power of determination is always in the hands of man and never in
God's. The hand of God can hold us only as tightly as we allow. Perseverance in the faith may be enabled by grace, but is finally dependent
upon our own achievements and strivings.

The Calvinist response to the Arminian controversy would eventually
lead to the publication of the Canons of Dort in 1619, a document often
credited with producing the so-called five points of Calvinism. But the five
points do not belong to Calvinism, nor were they forged at Dort. The meet-
ing of the Synod of Dort was a reaction to the Arminian articles of 1610.
The Dortian order is different, but it follows the five points of Arminianism
set down in the Remonstrance. The five points, then, actually belong to the
Arminians. Thus it is worth our time to briefly summarize them.

The first article affirms election. But in light of the emphasis placed
upon a person's free will and the synergistic conception of redemption
that pervade the Remonstrance, the first article may be titled *conditional
election*. As in Arminius, God's election of any particular person to salvation is subsequent to God's prescience of that person's believing response
to the gospel. Hence, election is conditional upon the faith of the sinner.
The second article affirms the idea that Christ died potentially for all sinners. He did not die for particular people. What we have here, then, is
universal atonement. As we noted, the third article looks like an Augustinian statement of the bondage of the will under the power of sin. But
this affirmation must be balanced—if not denied—by the idea of universal prevenient grace mentioned in article four. Thus we must title this

third article *total depravity/prevenient grace.* The fourth article explicitly denies that grace is irresistible. By the power of the free will the sinner can reject the call of the gospel. It is an affirmation, then, of *resistible grace.* The fifth article suggests that perseverance, like election, is conditional upon the freely chosen decisions and life paths of those who accept the gospel. As salvation is wrought synergistically, it is kept by the same compound agency. We are kept by a *conditional perseverance.* Here then are the five points of Arminianism:

1. Conditional election
2. Universal atonement
3. Total depravity/prevenient grace
4. Resistible grace
5. Conditional perseverance

Unfortunately, these five points, or rather the rejection of them at Dort, would come to define the Reformed faith for many Christians over the succeeding centuries. But the five points do not sufficiently define Calvinism, and certainly do not say all there is to be said about the Reformed faith. In the popular mind, Calvinists are those Christians who believe in total depravity and predestination. But why have predestination and Calvinism become virtual synonyms for most people? Calvin did not invent the doctrine of predestination. He was not the first person to talk about reprobation or the absolute sovereignty of God. As we have previously seen, the spiritual inability of the sinner and monergistic redemption characterized Augustine's teaching on salvation. Medieval theologians like Anselm of Canterbury and Thomas Aquinas were every bit as predestinarian in their writings as Calvinists are. And Martin Luther championed the doctrines of the bondage of the will and meticulous providence before Calvin did. We are not protesting the association of Calvinism with these doctrines, only the reduction of Calvinism to them. Elucidating the issues of contention between the Calvinists and the Arminians in five points, begun in the Arminian articles of 1610, often has encouraged a particular belligerence around these five points among

Calvinist believers, as if holding a certain view of them constitutes an essential definition of what it means to be a Calvinist, or even a Reformed believer. We assume that a similar phenomenon exists among Arminians.

We affirm and teach a Calvinist understanding of these contested five points of soteriology. But we also want our students to be exposed to a Reformed understanding of the church and the sacraments, the particularly Reformed contribution to Christian reflection on the covenant and the kingdom of God, and the church as the people of God called to seek a cultural life in the world that is typified by justice, mercy and a transformational vision for individual vocational life and the social existence of humankind. And we teach many other things that we suspect our Arminian brothers and sisters also teach: an orthodox view of the Bible as the authoritative and trustworthy Word of God, the triune nature of God, the bodily resurrection of our Lord Jesus Christ from the dead and the blessed hope of Christ's second coming, to name just a few. We urge readers not to imagine that the five points over which Arminians and Calvinists argued give a full picture of either tradition. Certainly they distinguish us from one another, but there is more to each tradition than the five points of contention.

After the publication of the Remonstrance, at the urging of Prince Maurice of Orange, six representatives of both parties met at a conference in the Hague in 1611. The proceedings of the almost two-and-a-half-month long conference were published the next year. The primary contribution of the 440-page proceedings was the Counter Remonstrance, a document prepared by the Calvinist representatives to the Hague conference. While the Counter Remonstrance touched upon the question of the extent of the atonement,[51] depravity and perseverance, the chief concern of the Calvinists was to affirm unconditional election. The issue of debate was not the philosophical problem of determinism but whether God has the right to

---

[51]"Although the suffering of Christ as that of the only-begotten and unique Son of God is sufficient unto the atonement of the sins of all men, nevertheless the same, according to the counsel and decree of God, has its efficacy unto reconciliation and forgiveness of sins only in the elect and true believer" (from "The Counter Remonstrance, 4" in De Jong, *Crisis in the Reformed Churches*, pp. 211-13).

elect whom he will to salvation and to do so by sheer grace alone apart from the condition of any foreseen faith on the part of the chosen.

> that God in his election has not looked to the faith or conversion of his elect, not to the right use of his gifts, as the grounds of election; but on the contrary He in his eternal and immutable counsel has purposed and decreed to bestow faith and perseverance in godliness and thus to save those whom He according to his good pleasure has chosen to salvation.[52]

More than once during the Hague conference the Calvinists challenged the Arminian depiction of Calvinist belief. The Calvinists insisted that supralapsarianism did not represent all of Calvinism, yet the Arminians had continually treated the two as virtually the same thing. The Arminians alleged that the Calvinists held that "those who are predestined unto perdition (being by far the majority) must be damned necessarily and unavoidably, and they cannot be saved."[53] The Calvinists rejected as a caricature of their position the notion that God causes unbelief and reprobation. The issue was not reprobation at all.[54] The Calvinists perceived their infralapsarian view of reprobation to be not all that different from the view entertained by the Arminians, yet the latter continued to portray the supralapsarian view as the Calvinist position. Consequently, the Calvinists declared "that they would have left the Arminians free in their view of reprobation, if only they had been willing to confess that God out of mere grace, according to his good pleasure, had elected some to eternal life, without any regard to their faith as a preceding condition."[55] And at the close of the conference the Calvinists repeated the point: the issue was unconditionalism versus conditionalism, election by grace alone (monergism) or election by grace conditioned by foreseen faith (synergism).

---

[52]Ibid., art. 3.

[53]Runia, "Recent Criticisms of the Canons" in De Jong, *Crisis in the Reformed Churches*, p. 174.

[54]As if to emphasize this point, the Counter Remonstrance is silent on reprobation.

[55]A. D. R. Polman, quoted in Runia, "Recent Criticisms of the Canons," p. 174.

THE CANONS OF DORT

The conference at the Hague brought no resolution to the Arminian controversy. A war of words and pamphlets tore at the fabric of the Reformed church until a national synod was held in the city of Dordrecht in 1618-1619. Unlike the Hague conference, the Synod of Dort was not a doctrinal conference in which equals could air their theological views, but rather an ecclesiastical decision-making assembly, and the judicial and doctrinal machinery of the synod was controlled by the Calvinists. Thirteen Arminian leaders were summoned to attend so that the synod could examine and pass judgment upon their views. Regional synods had elected two Arminian representatives to attend the national synod, but the two men would soon join the thirteen other Arminian defendants. The Remonstrance and other Arminian writings were cited as evidence that the teachings affirmed by the defendants were in deviation from the confessional standards of the church. After some four months of deliberation, the fifteen were found guilty of heresy. The defendants, along with some two hundred other Arminian pastors, were deposed from their ecclesiastical posts and excommunicated.

By 1618 the five-point presentation set out in the Remonstrance of 1610 had become the standard form for addressing the contested doctrinal issues between the Calvinists and the Arminians. The "Opinions of the Remonstrants," a document prepared by the defendants summoned to the synod, followed the five points of the Arminian articles. The decision of the synod, commonly called the Canons of Dort, would also follow the order of the Remonstrance. The salient point here is that the canons were not a piece of doctrinal construction but were essentially reactionary to the five points of Arminianism. The synod's decision was a judicial and doctrinal response to the five points. This can be seen in the full title of the canons: *The Decision of the Synod of Dort on the Five Main Points of Doctrine in Dispute in the Netherlands.* In so far as Dort can be legitimately associated with the five points first put forth by the Remonstrance, it must be said that Dort was first and foremost a repudiation of the Arminian articles, a rejection of the five points.

The line of thought within the canons begins with the plight of sinful humanity, the doctrine of spiritual inability. Indeed, the First Head of Doctrine in the Canons of Dort begins with a reference to humankind's fall into sin and need for the gospel. The doctrine of election does not appear until article six of the First Head of Doctrine. Thus the Arminian third article is thematically the first in the Dortian presentation. And this fits with the decretal position taken by the Calvinists at Dort. While the Arminian articles follow an order of presentation that generally conforms to supralapsarianism, the canons are decidedly infralapsarian in outlook.

The Canons of Dort, intended as a condemnation of Arminianism and the five articles of the Remonstrance, also seek to set out a positive affirmation relative to each of the five points. Our concern here is the affirmative declaration of the canons, for they provide the context for the Dortian rejection of Arminianism.[56]

Far from the common Arminian depiction of the Canons of Dort—and Calvinism generally—the canons do not begin in eternity past with an all-determining decree; rather they begin with humankind's historical predicament of sin. As the biblical story of redemption begins with Adam's disobedience in the garden, so too do the canons. Sin came into the world through Adam's rebellion, and since then all humanity has suffered under the regime of sin. All are enslaved, and all come under the curse of corruption and death (Rom 5:12; Eph 2:1, 5). The rejection of God and his word and the corruption of his creational gifts are second nature to the race of Adam. We do not simply ape the misbehaviors and attitudes of peers and elders. The inclination to selfishness and stubbornness is born within us.

The canons do not use the phrase *total depravity*. Indeed, the term and

---

[56]Donald Sinnema suggests that the condemnation of the Arminian articles, "the Rejection of Errors," was the original goal of the synod and was written first, but the resulting document was thoroughly negative. Once this was noted, the committee of nine writers who drafted the Rejection of Errors also wrote a contextualizing statement for each of the points of rejection (Donald Sinnema, taped lectures on the Synod of Dort).

its association with Dort is unfortunate, for it gives the impression that Calvinists are misanthropes, that they believe that unregenerate people are utterly bad, incapable of knowing and doing good. But the Canons of Dort do not teach that, given the choice between loving his children and hating them, my unregenerate neighbor must hate them. Rather, the point of the doctrine of the depravity of sin is that the sinful inclination inherited from Adam pervasively corrupts every area of our lives and bends every faculty toward the self and away from God. It is not that we are rotten through and through but that all our inclinations and acts, even our best ones, are marred by our addiction to sin.

But just how far have we fallen? While the canons do affirm a common grace through which "a certain light of nature" remains within us so that we retain "some notions about God, natural things, and the difference between what is moral and immoral," they immediately add that the light of nature does not bring us to a saving knowledge of God.[57] Common grace belongs to the order of creation. It is God's upholding the goodness of his creation, in spite of the sinfulness of man. And that good creation order imposes itself upon the darkness of the fallen human soul such that even though we are sinners we retain some sense of the good. But common grace (*creational grace* might actually be the better term) is not redemptive grace. The light of nature cannot save us. And regarding the saving work of God the natural man is blind as a mole and enslaved to sin. Even though the law written upon the heart and the creaturely conscience that still retains a sense for its creator restrain us from absolute evil, in our unconverted state we are still "prone to sin."

Paul graphically states the plight of the fallen human being in 2 Corinthians 4:4: "The god of this age has blinded the minds of unbelievers, so that they cannot see the light of the gospel of the glory of Christ, who is the image of God." And in 1 Corinthians 2:14 he describes

---

[57]The Canons of Dort 3/4.4.4, in *Ecumenical Creeds & Reformed Confessions* (Grand Rapids: Christian Reformed Church, 1988).

the same reality in different terms: "The man without the Spirit does not accept the things that come from the Spirit of God, for they are foolishness to him, and he cannot understand them, because they are spiritually discerned." Following Paul, the Canons of Dort conclude that the unregenerate are "incapable of saving good." As fallen, we are "neither able nor willing to return to God."[58]

God could have left Adam and his posterity in their sin. Indeed, "God would have done no one an injustice if it had been his will to leave the entire human race in sin and under the curse, and to condemn them on account of their sin."[59] But in his fierce determination to be gracious, God sent his own Son into the world to reclaim the lost. In Christ, God has chosen a people to believe in his Son and receive eternal life. That God has predestined some people to faith does not mean, according to the teaching of the canons, that God has predetermined all things such that human choice and responsibility are removed. Rather, God's sovereign work repairs the enslaved will and the corrupted heart of the sinner. The fall into sin constituted, in part, a loss of true free will. Man became a slave to sin; and what remains of the will is incapable of breaking the bonds of sin, and thus cannot be said to be free in any true sense. Yet some semblance of man's original integrity remains. Though the Canons of Dort insist upon the radical corruption of human nature as a result of the fall, sinners are not regarded as "blocks and stones." In falling, "man did not cease to be man, endowed with intellect and will." Though sin has pervasively spread through all our members, it "did not abolish the nature of the human race but distorted and spiritually killed it."[60]

The Canons of Dort are often associated with an emphasis upon the sovereign grace of God in the salvation of humanity, and that is appropriate. But the representatives at Dort did not believe it necessary to denigrate human agency in order to confess the sovereignty of God. Fred Klooster notes that "human responsibility pervades the canons. Without

---

[58]Ibid., 3/4.4.3.
[59]Ibid., 1.1.
[60]Ibid., 3/4.16.

wishing to minimize Dort's emphasis on divine sovereignty, one will nevertheless discover that in terms of space the Canons devote more attention to human responsibility than they do to divine sovereignty."[61] While God's election is "the fountain and cause of faith and good works," grace does not "abolish the will and its properties or coerce a reluctant will by force." Rather, grace repairs and liberates the will. Grace "revives, heals, reforms, and—in a manner at once pleasing and powerful—bends it back."[62] But the grace that repairs rather than coerces is not merely an assistance to inherent human powers or faculties. Faith is not a human act that God enables. The Canons of Dort insist that the beginning of the redeemed life is solely the work of God, for God graciously "produces in man both the will to believe and the belief itself."[63]

But why do the canons teach that God causes belief rather than merely enables it? The answer is found in the biblical testimony to the seriousness of the fall and the power of sin over us. Cornelius Plantinga comments that "we are hooked on sin and in a spiritual coma. By fallen nature we all resist God's invasion. In order to save, God must break down barriers, move past defenses, disarm rebels, and change hearts. He has to cause belief. Else we would continue to resist—and in that case there would be no hope."[64] The sole reason anyone believes is because God elects that person to belief. Election is the sole cause of the benefits of salvation. While not coercing the will, God irresistibly and efficaciously draws the elect to faith.

Election is not God's response to our faith, "but rather for the purpose of faith."[65] We are chosen not because God foresees that we shall believe, but in order that we will believe. Why do some people believe the gospel and become saved while others reject the gospel and continue in their

---

[61]Klooster, "Doctrinal Deliverances of Dort," in *Crisis in the Reformed Churches*, p. 83.
[62]Canons of Dort 3/4.16.
[63]Ibid., 3/4.14.
[64]Cornelius Plantinga Jr., *A Place to Stand: A Reformed Study of Creeds and Confessions* (Grand Rapids: Bible Way, 1979), p. 139. Cf. Canons of Dort 3/4.3.
[65]Canons of Dort 1.9.

rebellion against God? We believe that the answer given by the Canons of Dort is superior to that of the Arminian articles. The latter provide no cogent explanation, for the Arminians held that all people have been given sufficient prevenient grace to respond to the gospel call. Thus there is no reason for a person not to believe, except for the sovereignty of their own free will, a will that under the power of prevenient grace is liberated from the darkening power of sin. The Calvinist answer is divine election. Some believe

> not because they are any wiser or more intelligent than those who reject. Not because they are able to see farther or think straighter. Not in any way because they are humbler, abler, or cleaner. Not at all. Rather, they are people who have been dragged, perhaps in spite of themselves, out of the darkness and into the light. . . . For their everlasting salvation they are indebted "solely to the grace of God" ([Canons of Dort] II.7).[66]

If God does not leave so vital a matter as salvation in the hands of sin-enthralled human beings, but rather makes sure that the elect will believe, we immediately see a problem. Not all believe. One person hears the gospel as the word of life; another sees it as foolishness. The canons follow Augustine in their explanation. God has sovereignly chosen to save some but not all. The historical and experienced reality that people respond differently to the gospel is a result of the fact that grace discriminates between the elect and the nonelect. God does not save all sinners, for ultimately he does not intend to save all of them. The gift of faith is necessary for salvation, yet for reasons beyond our ken, the gift of faith has not been given to all.

While God commands all to repent and takes no delight in the death of the sinner, all are not saved because it is not God's intention to give his redeeming grace to all. Articles one through four of the Second Head of Doctrine in the Canons of Dort affirm that the atoning work of Christ

---

[66]Plantinga, *Place to Stand*, p. 145.

is of infinite value, sufficient to save all believers. Indeed, it is "more than sufficient to atone for the sins of the whole world."[67] Yet the death of Christ is effective only for "all those and only those who were chosen from eternity to salvation and given to [Christ] by the Father."[68] Thus the work of Christ is limited, in its intention and its effectiveness, to the elect. Christ did not die to save an abstraction, a class of people, but rather to save the people of God. His atoning sacrifice was particular in its intention, not general. Jesus went to the cross "for us," even for me.

If God redeems a particular people "out of all the nations," if there are those who are not Christ's sheep (Jn 10:26), what then are we to make of Scripture's offer of the gospel to all men? Clearly, God wants everybody told that he wants them saved (Ezek 18:23, 32), and the Canons of Dort declare that the gospel promise is to be spread "promiscuously" to all nations and all persons (Lk 24:47).[69] The church is commanded to preach the gospel. The Synod of Dort did not see the doctrine of particular atonement as compromising preaching in the slightest. Jesus charged his disciples to broadcast the good news of salvation to "all nations" (Mt 28:19). Yet people cannot be saved without God's powerful work in them. God wants all to hear the gospel, but he intends to save only some. Why that is the case, we do not know.

The main point regarding the debate about the atonement in both the Arminian articles and the Canons of Dort is not whether the sacrificial work of Christ is limited to the elect or universal in scope, for both parties agreed that it is limited in its ultimate effectiveness. Not all are saved. The real issue here is the efficacy of the work of Christ. Calvinists believe that from "start to finish, salvation is planned, worked, supported, and preserved by the grace of God."[70] The Calvinist knows that he has been taken hold of by God. For the Arminian believer, however, the saving work of Christ and the sinner are joined only by the individual's free ac-

---

[67]Canons of Dort, 2.3.
[68]Ibid., 2.8.
[69]Ibid., 2.5-7.
[70]Plantinga, *Place to Stand*, p. 146.

ceptance of a generally offered grace. God offers his hand, but he leaves the act of joining hands up to the sinner.

While we agree with the Arminians that the external call of the gospel is offered to all people, we Calvinists contend that the internal and graciously effective work of the Holy Spirit is given to the elect alone. And again, we do not know why God has chosen to save one but not another. As mysterious as this discrimination is, we believe that it fits the data of Scripture and is a better answer to the question, "Why are not all saved?" than that offered by Arminianism. The latter must answer that by their uncoerced free will some have not chosen to avail themselves of the gospel. But this is no answer. Lack of coercion must hold for sin as well as grace. That is to say, the Arminian notion of the free will, the will repaired by prevenient grace, is not forced by any necessity, grace or sin. If the free will cannot be forced by grace, it also cannot be coerced by stupidity, rebellion, its own desire to protect its autonomy or just plain contrariness. Universal prevenient grace is no answer. In simplest terms, given its doctrine of prevenient grace, Arminianism cannot explain why a person does not believe, why everyone does not believe.

Even though the Calvinist must admit a discrimination in the redemptive intention of God in which God intends some to be saved and others to remain unregenerate, the Arminian conception of the divine will, conditioned as it is by the decision of the human free will and thus perfectly fitted to the datum of the sovereign human free will, appears fatally flawed from any perspective in which the sovereignty of God bears any meaning. For example, if God wills and intends the salvation of all people, he wills the salvation of Judas Iscariot, while at the same time foreknowing that Judas would reject Christ. Thus God genuinely wills that which he knows will never happen, what his predestination cannot bring about, namely, the salvation of Judas. God's antecedent will, the will that all believe, is rendered hypothetical at best, and at worst null and void by his consequent will, that which his actual foreknowledge of contingents allows him to predestine.

If the Synod of Dort held that the cause of the salvation of any human being is that in eternity God elected that person in Christ, what did the canons have to say about the nonelect? Consistent with the position taken at the conference at the Hague in 1611, the canons held an Augustinian, passive view of reprobation. The Dortian position is explicitly set down in the First Head of Doctrine:

> Moreover, Holy Scripture most especially highlights this eternal and undeserved grace of our election and brings it out more clearly for us, in that it further bears witness that not all people have been chosen but that some have not been chosen or have been passed by in God's eternal election, those, that is, concerning whom God, on the basis of his entirely free, most just, irreproachable, and unchangeable good pleasure, made the following decision:
>
> > to leave them in the common misery into which, by their own fault, they have plunged themselves; not to grant them saving faith and the grace of conversion; but finally to condemn and eternally punish them (having been left in their own ways and under his just judgment), not only for their unbelief but also for all their other sins, in order to display his justice.
>
> And this is the decision of reprobation, which does not at all make God the author of sin (a blasphemous thought!) But rather its fearful, irreproachable, just judge and avenger.[71]

The canons refrain from finding the cause for man's sin and unbelief in God's decree. Rather, sin and corruption are entirely the result of Adam's fall. Human responsibility is wholly adequate to explain both the origin of sin and our historical experience of it.

The key to the Dortian conception of reprobation is its infralapsarian understanding of the divine decree. Election presupposes the fall. That is to say, the plan of salvation views humanity as fallen in Adam. God causes belief, but not unbelief. Man himself causes unbelief. The Arminian depiction of Calvinists as believing that God creates people

---

[71]Canons of Dort 1.15.

to be sinners and then damns them for being what he has made them is a gross misrepresentation. God's sovereignty in reprobation does not mean that "God predestined and created, by the bare and unqualified choice of his will, without the least regard or consideration of any sin, the greatest part of the world to eternal condemnation."[72] While the Arminian caricature of reprobation under the doctrine of absolute divine sovereignty may be a possible inference from the bare idea of divine sovereignty,[73] the Calvinists at Dort rejected a supralapsarian doctrine of reprobation (the condemnation of the unregenerate prior to their creation) on the grounds that it did not fit the biblical order of creation, fall and redemption. The reprobate are not those whom God has created to be sinners or created so that he may damn them, but rather those whom God leaves in their unbelief and permits to follow their own ways. As it was for Augustine, reprobation is God's passing by of the unregenerate. And, as was also the case for Augustine, the canons see God as relating to the elect and the nonelect in an asymmetric fashion. Yes, God is the cause of belief. It is his supernatural work of grace. But he does not need to cause unbelief. Our fall in Adam has already done that.

The concluding statement of the canons explicitly notes the Arminian contention that Calvinists teach that God is the author of sin, that he relates to sin and belief "in the same manner" such that "election is the source and cause of faith and good works, reprobation is the cause of unbelief and ungodliness." This "slanderous accusation" is one "which the Reformed churches not only disavow but even denounce with their whole heart."[74] God is not the author of sin or unbelief.

As for the doctrine of perseverance, the Remonstrance refused to affirm it even though it did not quite deny it either. The Arminians left the

---

[72]Ibid., conclusion.

[73]We hasten to add that it would truly be a legitimate inference only upon the assumption that Calvinism is synonymous with supralapsarianism and then that the entire problem is seen through the Arminian presumption of incompatibilist agency.

[74]Canons of Dort 1.15.

matter open, but given their penchant for emphasizing salvation as conditioned upon the will of man, it is not at all surprising that the Arminian tradition after the Remonstrants moved more explicitly toward a doctrine of conditional perseverance. Believers can persevere in the faith, but it is up to them to do it. Grace provides an important assistance, but the believer must see to it that he perseveres. God will only be as faithful to the work of redemption as we are. The problem here, of course, is that according to Scripture, successful perseverance is a condition for one's ultimate salvation. The Canons of Dort judged the Arminian agnosticism regarding perseverance a depressing and hopeless position. If our salvation depends on us, whether it be our merits, our will or even our strivings to keep in step with God's grace, we are most surely lost.

In contrast to the Arminians, the Calvinists at Dort rejected the notion that God allows fallen human beings to keep him from preserving and protecting his people. "Since his plan cannot be changed, his promise cannot fail, the calling according to his purpose cannot be revoked, the merit of Christ as well as his interceding and preserving cannot be nullified, and the sealing of the Holy Spirit can neither be invalidated nor wiped out."[75] To be sure, the believer might fall into grievous sin. He or she might even deny Christ. Scripture itself gives ample testimony to both. Yet God's faithfulness to his promise is infinitely greater than our responses to him. As he saves us in spite of our fallenness but for the sake of Christ, so he keeps us in spite of our best efforts—and our worst—in Jesus. "No matter how deeply God's people sin, their sin is never deeper than His grace. No matter how lasting their suspension of 'the exercise of faith,' their persistence cannot outlast God's mercy."[76] The monergistic principle that salvation is dependent upon God's grace alone, his faithfulness, his power and the triumph of Christ's redeeming work holds not merely for the beginnings of salvation but for its end as well.

---

[75]Ibid., 5.8.
[76]Plantinga, *Place to Stand*, p. 155.

CONCLUSION

We do not pretend that Calvinism provides comfortable or easy answers to every problem or question. As fallen human beings, Calvinists struggle with a sovereignty that stretches and often transcends our abilities to discern the redemptive ways of God. Why God does not save all men, we do not know. We might hazard the guess that it preserves the graciousness and wonder of grace, that no one should take grace for granted, to expect it as their due, to think that God is obligated to save. Yet ultimately we do not know why God saves one person and not another. The elect are neither intellectually nor morally superior to their unregenerate friends and neighbors. What differentiates the elect from the reprobate is no inherent power or talent or achievement but solely the gracious choice of a sovereign God.

We do know that God is not unjust by not saving all people or not saving any particular person. Egalitarian fairness—treating all persons the same—may be a cultural ideal of the modern West, but there is no biblical reason to suppose that God shares it. For his own reasons, God assumes the right to save one and not another—a Jacob, for example, and not his older, more talented brother; for Esau, left to himself and his sinfulness, is deserving of divine wrath. If there is any hint of injustice in the divine elective discrimination (and we do not believe that there is), it falls not upon God's treatment of the reprobate but upon the elect. The redeemed man does not receive the divine wrath that is due him as a sinner. Instead, he receives the gift of grace as the merits of Christ are reckoned to his account.

The central point of contention between the Calvinists and the early Arminians was whether election is unconditional or conditional upon human acceptance of the gospel, whether salvation is to be understood monergistically—God exercising his sovereign right to choose and save whom he will—or synergistically—God offering salvation to all, but leaving it up to each person to accept the gospel and thus complete the act of salvation. All other issues of dispute emanated from this core disagreement. We believe that the Canons of Dort were right in their repudiation of Arminian conditionalism. The Arminian insistence upon the inviolability of the human free will and their willingness to define God's ability to redeem human beings such that it cannot violate free will creates an anthropological idol and demeans the power and rights of God.

One might expect that the Synod of Dort would simply reverse the Arminian program: make the sovereignty of God absolute and deny the reality of human freedom. But the synod did not take this deterministic route. Yes, God is sovereign. What he wills to do, he effects, and nothing stands in his way. The canons did not limit God or his sovereignty for the sake of human free will. But they did not see any need to deny the meaningfulness of human choice and responsibility. As we shall see, free will needs to be defined more carefully—and biblically—than Arminians usually do, but neither the Canons of Dort nor we deny the responsibility of human beings in their choices or that those choices are real.

Scripture leads us to the contention that divine sovereignty—God always prevails—is not incompatible with true human freedom. God is not rendered idle by a world ruled by human freedom, but neither is the human being a puppet, a creature whose every thought, intention and move have been programmed by forces external to itself. Richard Muller states the Calvinist position thus: "The divine ordination of all things is not only consistent with human freedom; it makes human freedom possible." It is God who has established the very space in which human freedom can exist. And even as we make meaningful and responsible choices within God's world, it is "in him we live and move and have our being" (Acts 17:28).[77] We are creatures of God, and as such we are always bounded by his person, his law and, yes, his decree. Far from denouncing creaturely free will, this perspective demands that we affirm both a sovereign God and human free choice. For only an absolutely sovereign God could or would create a free human being.

---

[77]Muller, "Arminius's Gambit," p. 270. In Paul's speech at the Areopagus he declared the sovereignty of God over human affairs: "From one man he made every nation of men, that they should inhabit the whole earth; and he determined the times set for them and the exact places where they should live" (Acts 17:26).

6

FREEDOM

Incompatibilist or Compatibilist?

୶

The doctrine of divine sovereignty has always posed a problem for Arminianism. It is not too much to say that historically Arminian theology has tended to pit human freedom against divine sovereignty as if the two are mutually limiting or even mutually exclusive. If God sovereignly controls or ordains history or human destinies, then historical events and human responses to the gospel conform to an external necessity that annuls true human freedom. In short, human free will is incompatible with divine foreordination of any historical particular. One is forced, then, to choose either a determinism in which perceptions of human freedom are illusory and all things come about because God determines that they do, or an indeterminism in which human choice is bounded by no forces of necessity or coercion but is truly free and spontaneous and God is incapable of foreordaining particular future events or states of affairs.

A common term for the notion that human freedom and divine sovereignty are logically incompatible is *incompatibilism*. Whether one rejects human freedom as a determined perception within a thoroughly determined universe or one denies that God controls the flow of history in such a way that he has sovereignly ordained who will come to faith and who will not, one is an incompatibilist. Both hold that a divine sovereignty that embraces all things is impossible if human beings make truly free and uncoerced choices. Both cannot be true. There cannot be two sufficient causes for any event, one divine and one human; either God causes Jackie to believe in the gospel, or Jackie chooses to believe.

We believe that incompatibilism, whether determinist or indeterminist, is wrong. It is built upon a false, either-or assumption, an assumption that the Bible everywhere disavows. The contention that human freedom renders God incapable of exercising his kingly sovereignty or that divine ordination of history turns human beings into chess pieces who do not make meaningful choices is patently false from a biblical perspective. We believe that Scripture assumes *compatibilism,* the view that divine sovereignty and responsible human freedom are not contradictory at all.

That God sovereignly superintends and controls all things and that human beings are responsible for their choices and actions is repeatedly taught and demonstrated throughout the biblical record. God is sovereignly active in every moment. Yet that sovereign agency does not annul or limit human responsibility. Conversely, human agency is affirmed. We are not automatons. Human actions are not coerced or programmed at every moment by mysterious forces such that we act contrary to our natures and desires. Yet this human freedom does not negate or limit God's agency. This compatibilistic approach to the issue of divine sovereignty and human freedom arises, as D. A. Carson has pointed out, not from an ideological commitment but from the vast testimony of Scripture concerning the relationship between God and humanity in history.[1] God's sovereignty extends to all things, every event, yet each person is a responsible moral agent. It is a matter not of either-or but of both/and.

THE INCOMPATIBILIST CASE

As we have already seen, for Arminius and the Arminian tradition, human freedom is axiomatic. Because of this the freedom of the human will serves as a kind of grid through which all other notions and doctrines

---

[1]D. A. Carson, *How Long, O Lord? Reflections on Suffering & Evil* (Grand Rapids: Baker, 1990), p. 201.

must pass in order to be accepted. That which might qualify or question human free will must be rejected. The assumption of the unblemished integrity of human free will leads Arminian theology toward indeterminist incompatibilism: divine sovereignty and true human freedom are incompatible, and human beings are free; therefore, God cannot sovereignly govern human history, events or personal destinies.

The Arminian notion of the human free will stands upon two a priori principles, one ideological and the other psychological: (1) the conviction that necessity equals tyranny and (2) our innate sense of freedom. The first principle holds that if God foreordains an event—Jackie coming to faith in Christ—that event must happen. Whatever is ordained is ultimately governed by forces that render the human will other than truly free. The incompatibilist holds that if our decisions are qualified by any necessity—God's prior ordination that we will choose a certain course—then those decisions are not truly free and we are not truly responsible for them. If our decisions are in any sense predetermined by another, we cannot be held responsible for them because uncoerced free choice is a necessary prerequisite for moral responsibility. "To be responsible, we must be able to do otherwise."[2]

But what does it mean to be free? Arminian theologians hold to what they themselves call libertarian freedom. Burson and Walls define libertarianism as

the view that some human actions are chosen and performed by the agent without there being any sufficient condition or cause of the action prior to the action itself. . . . Actions are free precisely because it is the individual who deliberates and decides what weight to give these factors. So a free act in this paradigm cannot be reduced to anything beyond the choice of the agent.[3]

---

[2]John M. Frame, *No Other God: A Response to Open Theism* (Phillipsburg, N.J.: P & R, 2001), p. 121.

[3]Scott R. Burson and Jerry L. Walls, *C. S. Lewis & Francis Schaeffer: Lessons for a New Century from the Most Influential Apologists of Our Time* (Downers Grove, Ill.: InterVarsity Press, 1998), pp. 67-68.

Only libertarian freedom, the ability to choose the contrary, is "real freedom" according to Clark Pinnock:

> It views a free action as one in which a person is free to perform an action or refrain from performing it and is not completely determined in the matter by prior forces—nature, nurture or even God. Libertarian freedom recognizes the power of contrary choice. One acts freely in a situation if, and only if, one could have done otherwise.[4]

Although reasons and influences attend our choices, none of them "are strong enough to incline the will decisively in one direction or another. Instead, the will, despite its inclination, is neutral enough so that it can and sometimes does choose contrary to the direction the causes incline it."[5] Ultimately, the human will is free such that it can override external influences and even choose in spite of them.[6]

While the libertarian insists that free choice is not arbitrary or random, under the libertarian notion of freedom of contrary choice, human decisions must ever be independent of the determinations of human nature or character. We always have the ability to choose the contrary. Our particular characters may influence us, but they do not determine our choices. Thus the will is fundamentally independent of other aspects of human nature.

As counterintuitive as the ability to choose against our character might seem, the libertarian claims that such a notion of freedom is grounded in our intuitive sense that we are free to choose something other than what we actually chose in a particular situation, should we so will. Whenever we are faced with a choice, we feel that we could choose either way, even against our natural inclinations or strongest desires. "We

---

[4]Clark H. Pinnock, *Most Moved Mover: A Theology of God's Openness* (Grand Rapids: Baker, 2001), p. 127.

[5]John S. Feinberg, "God, Freedom, and Evil in Calvinist Thinking," in *The Grace of God, the Bondage of the Will*, ed. Thomas R. Schreiner and Bruce A. Ware (Grand Rapids: Baker, 1995), p. 469.

[6]R. K. McGregor Wright, *No Place for Sovereignty* (Downers Grove, Ill.: InterVarsity Press, 1996), p. 44.

have a strong intuitive belief that true choice is within our power," write Burson and Walls. "Most people intuitively operate under the assumption that a real live option exists: either the black jacket or the blue blazer; either Apple Jacks or bran flakes; either *Monday Night Football* or *The Movie of the Week*. There is no necessity in the matter; one is free to choose any number of ways faced with such situations."[7]

Under such an understanding of human freedom and a commitment to incompatibilism, Arminian theology has always placed serious circumscriptions upon divine agency in human history. God can never determine a human decision. He may act persuasively, but never coercively. Further, God can only will what he foresees will happen through the agency of human beings. Thus, human decision is logically prior to and determinative of the divine will.[8] The human will is free, but the divine is not.

Libertarian freedom undergirds the Arminian affirmation of a synergistic doctrine of salvation.

> While God is the primary agent in salvation, he is not the only agent. To ensure freedom, humans are agents too. . . . There is a dual agency at work in the mysterious process of salvation. God is the initiator, filling the world with prevenient and saving grace. He tenaciously seeks the lost, wooing them, convicting them and drawing them to himself. Yet sinners can be saved only if they freely cooperate with the grace that is offered.[9]

The power of contrary choice means that it is always within the ability of the human will to reject the gospel. Redemption hinges upon the will of the unregenerate human being. Grace is necessary for salvation, but it is never sufficient; that is, it is not all that is necessary. Within the Arminian view of incompatibilist freedom, divine grace and the free choice of

---

[7]Burson and Walls, *C. S. Lewis & Francis Schaeffer*, p. 66.
[8]Henry Thiessen, *Introductory Lectures in Systematic Theology* (Grand Rapids: Eerdmans, 1949), p. 157.
[9]Burson and Walls, *C. S. Lewis & Francis Schaeffer*, p. 91.

the human will are together sufficient for the redemption of the sinner. There is no salvation without grace; yet this grace is merely an offer of salvation, not a power that saves. Grace persuades, influences and provides reasons for faith, but it is the human will freely responding to the divine offer that effects redemption.

THE COMPATIBILIST RESPONSE TO INCOMPATIBILISM

It is our contention that the biblical depiction of God's sovereign power and lordship over his creatures refutes the Arminian understanding of human free will and its commitment to a doctrine of incompatibilist agency. The Arminian assumption of libertarian free will, and its insistence that anything that would qualify that doctrine—such as God's power and right to effect his will relative to human beings—is fatalistic or deterministic,[10] betrays a spirit that is decidedly foreign to the biblical portrayal of both God and human beings. Scripture is unrelenting and unapologetic in its affirmation of the sovereign government of God over all things. All of creation, from the trajectory of the smallest raindrop[11] to the fate of nations,[12] is in his hands and has a place in his plan.

A divine lordship that oversees and directs even what appears to us as random events, such as the casting of lots (Prov 16:33), certainly extends to and includes the uncoerced actions of human beings. "The king's heart is in the hand of the LORD; he directs it like a watercourse wherever he pleases" (Prov 21:1). But this applies to more than just kings and princes. "In his heart a man plans his course, but the LORD determines his steps" (Prov 16:9).[13] If the human heart—the center of human personality and the root of our freedom and our choices—is ultimately in the hand of the

---

[10]E.g., H. Ray Dunning, *Grace, Faith and Holiness: A Wesleyan Systematic Theology* (Kansas City, Mo.: Beacon Hill, 1988), pp. 257-58; H. Orton Wiley, *Christian Theology* (Kansas City, Mo.: Beacon Hill, 1941), 2:349.

[11]Cf. Ps 65:9-11; 104:10-30; 107:23-32; 135:5-7; 145:15-16; 147:15-18; Mt 5:45; 6:26-30.

[12]Acts 17:26, for example, says: "From one man [God] made every nation of men, that they should inhabit the whole earth; and he determined the times set for them and the exact places where they should live." Cf. Ps 33:10-11; 45:6-12; 47:1-9; 95:3.

[13]Cf. Ex 12:36; Ps 33:15; Prov 19:21.

Lord, his sovereign power and will are active at all times and in all events.

> The LORD brings death and makes alive;
> > he brings down to the grave and raises up.
> The LORD sends poverty and wealth;
> > he humbles and he exalts. (1 Sam 2:6-7; cf. Ps 37:23)

The kingship of God is all-inclusive, so reigning over our world that nothing escapes his sovereign sway. From the most mundane events of nature to the movements of empires to the depths of the human heart, all things are his servants. Every occurrence takes place by God's choice and in accordance with his will (1 Cor 12:18; 15:38; Eph 1:11; Col 1:19).

The great problem of the incompatibilist conception is that it reverses the biblical order of priority in the relationship between God and human beings. It says, in effect, "I am free; therefore, God is limited by my freedom." But rather than the will of God being dependent upon the choices of his creatures, Scripture teaches the absolute dependence of all creatures upon God. This is the biblical ground of compatibilism. We cannot define God's right or agency by our perception of freedom; rather we must understand what freedom means within the biblical witness to a divine sovereignty in which "not one drop of rain falls without God's sure command."[14]

The Calvinist notion of divine sovereignty is often portrayed as little more than a theological gloss upon a doctrine of philosophical determinism. But this misses the Calvinist point, and certainly misses the biblical witness to the sovereignty of God. The providential and sovereign power of God is neither an abstract nor a distant force; rather, through personal power God effects his will in the world. Calvin denied that the divine providence is "an unconcerned sitting of God in heaven, from which He merely observes the things that are done in the world."[15] God's government of the

---

[14]John Calvin *Institutes of the Christian Religion* 1.16.4 (trans. Ford Lewis Battles).

[15]John Calvin, "A Defence of the Secret Providence of God," in *Calvin's Calvinism*. trans. Henry Cole (Grand Rapids: Eerdmans, 1950), p. 224.

world is nothing less than his active, personal and kingly involvement with his creatures, for God is, to use Calvin's expression, "never idle." This means that the question of divine sovereignty and human freedom is not an abstract one, a question that can be addressed through the treatment of each as a mere idea or philosophical datum. Rather, it is one of God's personal presence, power and determination, and of our integrity and responsibility as his creatures. The error of identifying divine sovereignty with determinism or fatalism comes from the abstraction of the issue into impersonal terms. Divine sovereignty is not a blind and deterministic force any more than God himself is some impersonal *it*. The same is true when we speak of human freedom and accountability. It is *our* freedom and responsibility.

Within the incompatibilist assumption of Arminian theology, responsible human freedom and divine sovereignty conflict, and since Arminianism is committed to libertarian free will, the sovereignty of God must be limited in order to preserve human free will. Ray Dunning, for example, affirms "God's activity within the context of human freedom" through the mechanism of a self-imposed limitation on divine power and prerogatives.[16] It is difficult to imagine what such a sovereignty would look like, or if it could rightly be called a sovereignty at all, given the insistence upon the integrity of libertarian free will. However, there is no need to seek to imagine what a limited divine sovereignty might be, for Scripture gives no warrant for the supposition that such a limitation exists. John Feinberg is correct in his sweeping assertion that "no verse in Scripture says that God decided to relinquish use of his power or control to make room for our free will."[17] The God "who works out everything in conformity with the purpose of his will" (Eph 1:11) is Lord over all things. Similarly, John Frame boldly writes that "Scripture contains no hint that God has limited his sovereignty in any degree. God is Lord, from Genesis 1 to Revelation 22. He is always completely sovereign."[18]

---

[16]Dunning, *Grace, Faith and Holiness*, p. 258.
[17]John S. Feinberg, "God, Freedom, and Evil," 2:466.
[18]Frame, *No Other God*, p. 130.

In other words, the Arminian tactic of seeking to find some crawl space for divine sovereignty "within the context of human freedom" (Dunning's phrase) will not hold up to biblical analysis. No human being qualifies or defines God, but God defines and circumscribes the human.

THE COMPATIBILIST CASE

Where incompatibilism holds that divine sovereignty and responsible human freedom are logically inconsistent, and that the affirmation of one necessarily entails either the rejection or attenuation of the other, compatibilism holds that the Bible affirms both the absolute, unlimited sovereignty of God and the responsibility of human beings for their choices and actions. Further, while Scripture teaches both the sovereignty of God and the moral responsibility of human beings, the two are not equally ultimate. Human freedom must be understood in terms of the lordship of God. God's sovereign lordship over his creation includes the moral responsibility and freedom of human beings. But as we will see, creaturely freedom—within its proper biblical parameters—is not *freedom from* God, an autonomy in which human choice takes place irrespective of the divine rule, but a *freedom for* proper creaturely existence. In the words of G. C. Berkouwer, "the Divine activity is all inclusive, but not all exclusive," and "He who understands well the Biblical teaching of God's government knows that it is no despotism, compulsion, or sort of overpowering which renders creaturely activity null or impossible. He knows that it is a Divine ruling *in* and *over* all creaturely enterprise."[19]

Does an active divine sovereignty mean a limitation upon the free choices and actions of human beings? Sometimes yes. At the very least, the divine determination that a certain event will transpire means that human beings are not able to stop it from happening. John Frame explains:

> Negatively, God's purposes exclude free decisions that would otherwise be possible. Since God had planned to bring Joseph to

---

[19]G. C. Berkouwer, *The Providence of God* (Grand Rapids: Eerdmans, 1952), pp. 127, 129 (italics in original).

Egypt, his brothers were, in an important sense, not free to kill him, although at one point they planned to do so. Nor could Goliath have killed David, nor could Jeremiah have died in the womb. Nor could the Roman soldiers have broken Jesus' legs when he hung on the cross, for God's prophets had declared otherwise.[20]

God's determination that his plan will come to pass includes the free choices and actions of human beings. But any conception of God as an active agent of history who is able to ensure that his will is fulfilled (Mk 14:49) makes a libertarian doctrine of human freedom—the power of contrary choice—problematic as an a priori assumption and theological datum.

The difficulty that believers often have in relating God's sovereign lordship to human responsibility, as in the case of the Arminian doctrine of incompatibilism, comes not from Scripture but from an anthropocentric and abstract view of human freedom. The Arminian simply assumes that a divine sovereignty that is active in all events empties human effort of moral significance. Where the biblical authors derived comfort and encouragement from the realization that God is personally active in all events and leads all things to his appointed ends, Arminian incompatibilism sees only an abstract necessity that threatens the integrity of human freedom.[21] The real problem is not the sovereign activity of God, however, but a view of human freedom that dictates terms to the divine and all but seeks to push God out of his creation. The classical doctrine

---

[20]Frame, *No Other God*, pp. 64-65.

[21]Samuel Storms states the problem of Arminian incompatibilism quite bluntly: "The obvious problem with this view is that it lacks biblical warrant. No text of which I am aware says any such thing. This philosophical assumption is based on what the Arminian considers 'intellectually reasonable.' It is brought to the text as a pre-exegetical criterion to be used in deciding what a passage will be allowed to say. When confronted with texts that simultaneously assert the antecedence of divine sovereignty and the significance of human behavior, Arminians recoil, insisting that such is at best theologically contradictory and at worst morally devastating. Interestingly, neither God nor the authors of Scripture seem bothered by what agitates Arminians" (C. Samuel Storms, "Prayer and Evangelism Under God's Sovereignty," in *The Grace of God, the Bondage of the Will*, ed. Thomas R. Schreiner and Bruce A. Ware [Grand Rapids: Baker, 1995], 1:216).

of divine providence has been eclipsed by a doctrine of autonomous human agency. Interestingly, Scripture nowhere so much as hints that a God who leads history to his ordained ends by actively governing in every event presents a problem for human responsibility.

Neither does God's sovereignty make human beings mindless pawns or exonerate them of responsibility for their choices and actions, nor does human responsibility and freedom frustrate God's ability to realize his will. Scripture teaches both that God is always the sovereign king over his creation and that human beings are always accountable for their actions. Both are assumed as true throughout the biblical record, and neither is seen as limiting the other. Paul Helm goes so far as to speak of divine sovereignty and human responsibility as "fixed points" within the biblical drama.

> When we are faced with problems about the consistency of these concepts, it is tempting to modify one or both of them. But we must make every effort to avoid such a course of action. Scripture holds them together, it even speaks of them in the same breath, and so must we, for if Scripture teaches them in this way, they must each be true and so together be consistent, even though it may be difficult for us to grasp this now.[22]

BIBLICAL EXAMPLES OF COMPATIBILISM

That God sometimes acts simultaneously with human activity is evident in Philippians 2:12-13: "Continue to work out your salvation with fear and trembling, for it is God who works in you to will and to act according to his good pleasure." There is no synergistic division of labor here, as if God does part of the work of salvation and then moves aside and awaits a response from an autonomous human will. Nor does the text suggest that, because "it is God who works in you," human agency is redundant or irrelevant. In short, Philippians 2:12-13 teaches neither Arminian incompatibilism nor the Arminian caricature of Calvinism, in

---

[22]Paul Helm, "The Augustinian-Calvinist View," in *Divine Foreknowledge: Four Views*, ed. James K. Beilby and Paul R. Eddy (Downers Grove, Ill.: InterVarsity Press, 2001), p. 167.

which God acts unilaterally and the human is entirely passive.

Both God and the believer are fully active in the work of salvation, and active at the same time. God is sovereignly at work, and man is responsively active. But Paul does claim priority for divine activity over the human here. God's sovereignty extends over and is the ground for our choices and actions. Paul's call to the Philippians to work out their salvation flows out of and is energized by the fact that all of life is lived under God's absolute and active leading. For Paul, God's intimate and sovereign lordship over our lives is not an incentive for passivistic fatalism but an incentive for our action.

God often accomplishes his plan through the free choices of people. Joseph's brothers jealously sold him into slavery (Gen 37:12-36). And Potiphar's wife acted maliciously in falsely accusing Joseph of rape and imprisoning him (Gen 39:7-20). While these spiteful and vicious acts came about through the uncoerced choices of human beings, God was sovereignly in control, fulfilling his will through Joseph. He used the freely chosen misbehaviors of Joseph's brothers and Potiphar's wife to bring Joseph to high rank in the land of Egypt. Seeing the hand of God in all these events, Joseph would later say to his brothers, "God sent me ahead of you," and even, "it was not you who sent me here, but God" (Gen 45:5-8). Although God was in sovereign control, Joseph also knew that his brothers were driven by their own sinful jealousy. "You intended to harm me, but God intended it for good to accomplish what is now being done, the saving of many lives" (Gen 50:20).

What we see in the Joseph story is an explicit example of the biblical assumption of compatibilist agency. Human beings act from their own hearts and motives, uncoerced by forces external to their own moral characters. But through it all, God sovereignly acts to bring about his will. There is no hint here of the incompatibilist contention that divine sovereignty annuls human moral responsibility. Joseph's brothers were fully culpable for their mistreatment of him. D. A. Carson rightly comments: "The text will not allow the brothers to be classed as puppets and thus to escape their guilt," even though it was by their actions that God was fulfilling his will. "On the other hand," Carson continues, "neither does [the text] picture God as *post eventu* deflecting the evil action of the brothers and transforming it into something good."[23] In other words, the story does not portray the distributed action of the incompatibilist model. The motives of the human agents provide the sufficient condition for the entire event. And the sovereign will and action of God provide sufficient condition for the event as well.

A similar text, in that it too informs us of the motives of the human actors, is Isaiah 10. The prophet saw the Assyrian invasions of Israel as the chastening hand of God against a rebellious covenant people (Is 10:5-6). But the Assyrian king did not think of himself as a puppet dancing at the end of a predetermined string. Nor did he see himself as an agent of God.

> This is not what he intends,
> > this is not what he has in mind;
> his purpose is to destroy,
> > to put an end to many nations. (Is 10:7)

Indeed, the Assyrian arrogantly boasts of his own sovereignty:

> By the strength of my hand I have done this,
> > and by my wisdom, because I have understanding.
> I removed the boundaries of nations,
> > I plundered their treasures;
> > like a mighty one I subdued their kings.
> As one reaches into a nest,
> > so my hand reached for the wealth of nations;
> as men gather abandoned eggs,
> > so I gathered all the countries;
> not one flapped a wing,
> > or opened its mouth to chirp. (Is 10:13-14)

---

[23]D. A. Carson, *Divine Sovereignty & Human Responsibility: Biblical Perspectives in Tension* (Atlanta: John Knox Press, 1981), p. 10.

But immediately Isaiah retorts that the Assyrian is not autonomous, an absolute power unto himself, by reminding him that God alone is sovereign, and that he is a tool in God's hand.

Does the ax raise itself above him who swings it,
> or the saw boast against him who uses it?
As if a rod were to wield him who lifts it,
> or a club brandish him who is not wood! (Is 10:15)

Although the Assyrian is the "rod" and "club" by which God brings covenant discipline upon Israel, Isaiah clearly states that God holds the king of Assyria accountable for his actions, and will punish him for his arrogance and pride (Is 10:12). The Assyrian king carried out the will of God, yet he acted out of his own motives. He acted freely from his own character. Thus Calvin could write of the Assyrians that "We must not suppose that there is a violent compulsion, as if God dragged them against their will; but in a wonderful and inconceivable manner he regulates all the movements of men, so that they still have the exercise of their will."[24] Carson appropriately concludes: "This one passage—and there are dozens like it in the prophets—demonstrates beyond doubt that Isaiah, at least, was a compatibilist."[25]

The Bible teaches that God is always fully sovereign; that is, he is active in all events and he always accomplishes his will. His plan for his creatures is never stymied or frustrated by human choices or behaviors. Yet Scripture also teaches that human beings are morally responsible creatures. We make truly free choices and undertake enterprises that emanate from our own natures or characters. As such, we are fully accountable for them. God's sovereign action and human moral accountability are *compatible* because Scripture teaches both of them, even though they seem to overlap, qualify one another or even call each other into question. God is sovereign in creation, human history and our lives;

---

[24]John Calvin, *Commentary on the Book of the Prophet Isaiah* (Grand Rapids: Eerdmans, 1947), 1:352.
[25]Carson, *How Long, O Lord?* p. 208.

yet that sovereignty does not minimize or mitigate our responsibility. We truly make free choices, choices that come from our own desires rather than from impersonal determining forces; yet our freedom does not frustrate the sovereign will of God.

Perhaps no event in the biblical story brings the sovereign plan of God and human accountability together as clearly as the crucifixion of our Lord. It is in the cross that the sovereign plan of God and the machinations of human beings come together most starkly.

> This man was handed over to you by God's set purpose and foreknowledge; and you, with the help of wicked men, put him to death by nailing him to the cross. (Acts 2:23)

> You handed him over to be killed, and you disowned him before Pilate, though he had decided to let him go. You disowned the Holy and Righteous One and asked that a murderer be released to you. You killed the author of life, but God raised him from the dead. . . . This is how God fulfilled what he had foretold through all the prophets, saying that his Christ would suffer. (Acts 3:13-15, 18)

> Indeed Herod and Pontius Pilate met together with the Gentiles and the people of Israel in this city to conspire against your holy servant Jesus, whom you anointed. They did what your power and will had decided beforehand should happen. (Acts 4:27-28)

> The people of Jerusalem and their rulers did not recognize Jesus, yet in condemning him they fulfilled the words of the prophets that are read every Sabbath. (Acts 13:27)

The interplay between God's sovereign decree and human activity here is striking. Luke makes it eminently clear that the crucifixion of Christ was not an accident of history. God had "decided beforehand" that Jesus would die on a cross. The betrayal, hatred and injustice that led up to and issued in the crucifixion all occurred according to God's "set purpose and foreknowledge." Jesus was betrayed, handed over to the authorities and crucified because God sovereignly decreed that it would happen (Lk 22:22).

Now if God ordained that the crucifixion of Jesus would take place, we must say that Judas, Pilate and the others were not free in the libertarian sense of absolute power to choose the contrary. Judas could not have not betrayed Jesus. Herod and the Jews could not have chosen not to be murderous. Does this mean then that they were not free? If they acted according to the purpose of God, were they manipulated as if they were no more than pawns? That is the incompatibilist contention, but Scripture nowhere suggests such an inference. God did not ordain the actions of Herod or Pilate as if they were puppets. None of those involved in the death of Jesus acted contrary to their wills or in violation of their character. They did as they chose to do. Jesus was crucified because Judas, Herod, Pilate and the others conspired to kill him. Their choices were part of God's eternal plan, but that fact did not remove one bit of human accountability. Divine sovereignty and human responsibility cannot be pitted against one another.

We could look at many other texts in which the sovereign plan and action of God and the responsible choices and actions of human beings are in evidence. Besides the texts we have examined, Leviticus 20:7-8; 1 Kings 8:46-61; 11:11-39; 12:1-15; John 6:37-40; and Acts 18:9-10; 27:22-44 easily come to mind.[26] We invite the reader to examine each of these texts.

John Feinberg cogently suggests that Scripture itself argues for the compatibility of divine sovereignty and responsible human action. The evangelical doctrine of verbal inspiration holds that the Bible is fully the product of human authors while at the very same time it is also the authoritative Word of God. The human authors were not stenographers re-

---

[26]We might add Ex 8:15, 32; 9:34, in which we are told that Pharaoh hardened his heart against God, and Ex 9:12; 10:1, 20; Rom 9:17-18, which say that it was God who hardened Pharaoh's heart. Both God's will and Pharaoh's character provide sufficient condition for Pharaoh's behavior. Thus a compatibilist understanding of free will is a natural inference from these texts when taken together.

cording dictation. The writings of Paul are differentiated from those of John or Moses not merely by content but also by the writing styles, personal concerns and personalities that are revealed in their respective writings. While each of the individual books of the Bible bears the imprint of a human author, the Holy Spirit so guided the writing that the product was the Word of God (2 Tim 3:16; 2 Pet 1:20-21). "The Holy Spirit so superintended their work that even the words they chose were directed by the Holy Spirit."[27] Thus the Bible was written both by human beings and by the Holy Spirit. This is compatibilist double agency. Scripture is fully the product of human beings. Yet it is also fully the product of God. Does the fact that the Spirit of God guided the human authors take anything away from their agency? Not at all. Feinberg writes,

> No evidence suggests that the writers were forced to write contrary to their wishes. They apparently wrote freely. But it seems hard to reconcile this notion of the dual authorship of Scripture with anything other than some form of compatibilism. Again we have evidence that one and the same action can be under God's control so that his will is done, and at the same time can be the act of the person who does it freely.[28]

BIBLICAL FREEDOM

The incompatibilist seeks to find some room for the sovereignty of God within the assumption of libertarian freedom. But incompatibilism fails badly as a way of understanding the relationship between divine sovereignty and human freedom. First, it assumes a libertarian view of freedom. Human beings always possess the power of contrary choice. Second, incompatibilism insists that such a notion of freedom is the necessary condition for moral accountability: I cannot be held responsible if I could not choose to do otherwise. Third, in this view the sovereignty of God is necessarily limited by human freedom. If

---

[27]Feinberg, "God, Freedom, and Evil," p. 469.
[28]Ibid.

God has ordained that I perform some act, I could not choose otherwise and thus am not truly free.[29] While this collection of assumptions constitutes a coherent whole, each is no more than an assumption. And while they all are taken as having a self-evident power within Arminian theological circles, we can find no evidence that Scripture teaches or assumes any of them.

As we have already noted, the Bible does not limit the sovereignty of God. Rather, the Scriptures everywhere proclaim the sovereign kingship of God over all things. Indeed, the Bible begins with this very theme. God is the mighty Creator, the great King of the universe. The sovereignty of God is nonnegotiable. It is the precondition for all else. Human freedom and responsibility must be understood in the context of the absolute and active kingship of God over all his creatures.

The Bible nowhere refers to freedom in the libertarian sense, and never suggests that God's foreordination of an event frees the human participants in that event from responsibility. John Frame states the matter with bluntness:

> Scripture never suggests that libertarian freedom, or lack of it, has any relevance at all to moral responsibility. . . . Scripture never judges anyone's conduct by reference to libertarian freedom. Scripture never declares someone innocent because his conduct was not free in the libertarian sense. . . . Scripture never refers to freedom in a demonstrably libertarian sense. . . .
>
> Nor does Scripture indicate that God places any positive value on libertarian freedom (even granting that it exists). This is a significant point, because the freewill defense against the problem of evil argues that God places such a high value on human free choice

---

[29]Burson and Walls, *C. S. Lewis & Francis Schaeffer*, p. 90. Much like Arminius long before them, Burson and Walls contend that if libertarian freedom is true (and they accept the ability to choose the contrary as a self-evident truth), then divine sovereignty must be rethought in terms of that freedom. If God ordains an act, it is determined such that I could not do otherwise, and thus freedom is a "mere illusion," for "there really is no alternative to what God has willed."

that he gave it to creatures even at the risk that they might bring evil into the world. One would imagine, then, that Scripture would abound with statements to the effect that causeless free actions by creatures are terribly important to God, that they bring him glory and are essential to human personhood and dignity. But Scripture never suggests that God honors causeless choice in any way or even recognizes its existence.[30]

Frame finds no biblical warrant for a libertarian notion of human freedom. Quite the contrary. Scripture seems to deny the very sort of independence that libertarian freedom demands. Human beings are never independent of God. Whereas incompatibilism holds that libertarian freedom—independence from all causes and forces external to the will—is the prerequisite for responsibility, the Bible seems to assume the opposite: responsibility is the necessary condition for freedom. The gift of responsible choice has meaning and significance not because of any connection to libertarian freedom but because it is an essential aspect of our imaging God. Freedom in Scripture is not independence from God and his will but dependence upon God and our faithful participation in his kingdom.

True freedom, freedom in the biblical sense, is the liberty to obey God without restraint, without sin standing in the way. Christians have always, and quite rightly, understood Jesus as the exemplar of true humanity. There is no evidence that Jesus held the ability of contrary choice—the ability to disobey—as a value. Rather, from first to last, he is the One who aligns himself with the Father's plan, fulfills what is written of him, and always does that which pleases the Father (Jn 8:28; cf. 4:34). Jesus was free in the highest sense. He was free to do what he wanted to do—fulfill the Father's will—and no sin impeded his ability.

As we will argue in the next chapter, human beings since the fall are born as sinners, selfishly disposed toward the satisfaction of the self

---

[30]Frame, *No Other God*, p. 125.

rather than toward the worship of God, the service of their fellow human beings and the stewardly care of God's world. Scripture teaches that the sinner is a slave to sin. A slave is not free but bound. Any discussion of freedom within a Christian or biblical context must do justice to this fundamental biblical principle: sin reigns over the unregenerate heart. The sinner is not free to please or love God. Biblical freedom, the ability to do that which is pleasing to God (Jn 8:34-36; cf. Rom 6:15-23; 2 Cor 3:17), freedom from sin, is given to us by the redemptive work of Christ. Where the Arminian asserts that freedom is the precondition for grace, the Calvinist holds that grace is the prerequisite for freedom. Yet this freedom is not a condition of moral responsibility. Those who are enslaved to sin are as morally responsible as those who are free in Christ. The sinner is responsible for the sin that enslaves him because even as he follows its dictates he does so willingly, freely. He does what he wants to do. The sinner follows the deepest desires of his heart in his sin. Even though bound to sin, he chooses to sin.

In their assumption of libertarian free will, Burson and Walls state that one is free to choose one cereal over another for breakfast, free to wear one garment rather than another, free to watch one television program and not another. From such freedom of choice, the case for libertarianism is assured. But is it? What if they had used less trivial examples? What if they had illustrated their point with choices that count for something? Should we assume that the choice to commit adultery or remain faithful to our marriage vows is as facile as our choice of cereal? Am I responsibly free only if I have the liberty to choose either to embrace my children when I get home from work or bludgeon them with a baseball bat?

Jesus said: "The good man brings forth good things out of the good stored up in his heart, and the evil man brings evil things out of the evil stored in his heart. For out of the outflow of his heart his mouth speaks" (Lk 6:45; cf. Mt 7:15-20; 12:33-35). A person chooses and acts according to his character. The will is not independent of the person and nature who chooses. We do what we want to do (Deut 30:19; Mt 17:12; Jas 1:14), even though our characters, which are themselves determined by a myriad of forces external to us and outside of our control, determine what we want to do. Personal character is not nearly as spontaneous as those who see the will as the power of contrary choice like to suggest.

If we are bounded by God's plan, by our sinful blindness and slavery, and by an almost countless number of sociological and environmental factors, how then do we account for our sense of freedom, that from moment to moment we can choose one option over another? We sense that we are free because none of the things that go into making us the persons that we are constrains us such that we choose or every act contrary to our natures or against our wills. We do as we please. But we are not so absolutely free as to be able to please as we please. The compatibilist holds that every human choice and action has a sufficient cause outside of the human will. Freedom in the compatibilist sense is the contention that even if every choice we make and every act we perform is determined by forces outside ourselves, and ultimately by God's ordaining guidance, we are still free, for we still act according to our desires.

If the ability of contrary choice, the undetermined free will, is as central to human integrity and flourishing as Arminianism insists, then we should expect it to be an appropriate eschatological value, something that we should prize and seek because it will characterize the blessedness of heaven. But this is not what we find in the biblical depiction of the consummation. Sin will be no more, for the redeemed will enjoy an everlasting and unbroken fellowship with God (Rev 21:1-4). This means that the ultimate life of the redeemed will not include libertarian freedom, the ability to choose sin rather than obedience, apostasy rather than faithfulness. Will we then be free? In the compatibilist sense of free, yes. We will follow our deepest desires. We will do as we want to do. And we will—with our whole hearts—want to love and obey God and serve our neighbor.

SIN AND THE SOVEREIGNTY OF GOD

The incompatibilist commitment to the freedom of the will as the highest value and first principle of doctrinal construction moves Arminianism to argue that human choices and actions have no meaning if God directs them by his ordaining power. But Scripture is unapologetic in its affirmation of God's sovereign and continual covenant presence. John Frame does not overstate the biblical position when he says that God's providential care oversees and directs all of creation. God "does not set it in motion and leave it to run on its own. He remains with and in the world, to control it, to evaluate it, to bless and to judge it. He is the potter and the world is his clay."[31] Our lives and responsible choices are made meaningful not because they are run by a random and autonomous power of choice but because God cares for us (Ps 8:4) and calls us to faithful service in his kingdom (Gen 1:26-28), even as our lives are "fully planned by him, dependent on him, and under his control."[32]

One of the perceived strengths of libertarianism is that it provides a simple and lucid solution to the problem of evil. Sin came into the world as a consequence of our first parents' misused freedom, and all subsequent sin is traceable to human choice. God is not the cause or author of sin; human beings are. And since there are human choices and behaviors that God does not cause—our sin—then the Adamic fall and the reality of our own sin constitute an argument for incompatibilist agency.

While we applaud the affirmation of the holiness and goodness of God and the insistence that God does not cause sin, the libertarian view fails to represent the complexity of the biblical depiction.[33] Scripture

---

[31]Frame, *The Doctrine of God*, pp. 147-48.

[32]Ibid., p. 148.

[33]Frame finds the libertarian attempt to protect the goodness of God through the notion of incompatibilist agency (God does good, we sin) faulty on systematic grounds. "Traditional Arminians, although they don't believe that God causes evil, do believe that he is able to prevent it and that he made the world knowing in advance that evil would enter it. But if God created the world, knowing that sin and evil would certainly enter it, how is his action different from causing or foreordaining evil? It was he who set the process in motion, knowing where it would go. All the things and persons in the world are

does not so conveniently absent sin from the sovereignty of God as libertarianism suggests. The ordination of God somehow stands over and guides all events. "Who can speak and have it happen if the Lord has not decreed it? Is it not from the mouth of the Most High that both calamities and good things come?" (Lam 3:37-38).[34] Pharaoh hardened his heart against the Lord (Ex 8:15), but we are also told that God hardened Pharaoh's heart so that Pharaoh would not hear and obey God's commands (e.g., Ex 4:21; 7:3; 9:12; 10:1). There are many examples of human sin conforming to the plan of God in the Old Testament (e.g., 1 Sam 2:12-15; 2 Sam 16:5-10; 24:1; 1 Kings 22:21-28). The clearest New Testament example is, of course, the crucifixion of Christ. The death of Jesus on the cross took place "by God's set purpose and foreknowledge" (Acts 2:23). But it could not have happened apart from the sin of human beings. It was God's plan that human beings would murder his Son.

But how can God bring about sin? After all, Scripture insists that God is good, that he hates sin, and that he tempts no one to evil. "God is light; in him there is no darkness at all" (1 Jn 1:5). "He is the Rock, his works are perfect, and all his ways are just. A faithful God who does no wrong, upright and just is he" (Deut 32:4). Human beings are responsible for their sins because they do them freely, that is, without constraint. As John Feinberg puts it, "No one forces us kicking and screaming against our will to do evil. We do it in accord with our wishes."[35] But our sin never takes place outside the sovereign rule of God. The Bible insists that God is good

---

his creations. The order of events begins with him. If he sets everything in motion, knowing what will happen, how is that different from intending the result?" Seeing the problem here, openness theologians have sought to make libertarian freedom absolute by denying the doctrine of divine foreknowledge. In making the world, God gave human beings the gift of libertarian freedom, and thus assured that he himself would not know what they would do with that gift. Frame comments: "But doesn't this make God into a kind of mad scientist, who 'throws together a potentially dangerous combination of chemicals, not knowing if it will result in a hazardous and uncontrollable reaction'? Doesn't this view make God guilty of reckless endangerment? So we see that open theism exacerbates the problem of evil, rather than solving it" (*No Other God*, pp. 135-36).

[34]Cf. Is 45:6-7; Prov 16:4.

[35]Feinberg, "God, Freedom, and Evil," p. 471.

and that he hates evil, but it also teaches that his sovereign plan governs all things. That God is supremely good and has a good purpose for ordaining sin is a problem that Scripture itself recognizes (Job 38—42; Rom 9:17-24). Yet in these very texts God reminds us that he is the transcendent One, the Creator and Lord of all things. He is the potter, and we are but clay in his hands.

There simply is no neat way to systematize the countless biblical passages that insist that God is holy and good with those that openly declare that God is sovereign even over human sin and that he has included that sin in his plan (e.g., Hab 1:12-13; Rom 9:22-24). But this should not greatly surprise us. Sin is by its very nature irrational.[36] It never makes sense. We do not understand our own sin. And adding God and his sovereign plan to the equation only deepens the mystery of sin and evil. D. A. Carson has wisely written,

> One of the common ingredients in most of the attempts to overthrow compatibilism is the sacrifice of mystery. The problem looks neater when, say, God is not behind evil in any sense. But quite apart from the fact that the biblical texts will not allow so easy an escape, the result is a totally nonmysterious God. And somehow the god of this picture is domesticated, completely unpuzzling.[37]

Just as the Bible gives us no neat explanation for the ultimate origin of sin, it does not provide an answer to how a supremely good and holy God can sovereignly ordain the sinful acts of human beings. It simply affirms both. Sin ought not to be. It does not fit with any conception of a good and just God. Yet it is, and he is. Carson continues: "The mystery of providence defies our attempt to tame it by reason. I do not mean it is illogical; I mean that we do not know enough to be able to unpack it and domesticate it."[38]

Yet we can say that, as the Canons of Dort asserted, God relates differ-

---

[36]For a concise discussion of the irrationality of sin, see Anthony A. Hoekema, *Created in God's Image* (Grand Rapids: Eerdmans, 1986), pp. 130-32.

[37]Carson, *How Long, O Lord?* p. 225.

[38]Ibid., p. 226.

ently to sin than he does to obedience. God relates to sin and faithfulness asymmetrically. Scripture constrains us to say that God is not the cause of sin, yet somehow, in ways we cannot fathom, his sovereign plan includes the sinful acts of human beings. "To put it bluntly," writes Carson, "God stands behind the evil in such a way that not even evil takes place outside the bounds of his sovereignty, yet evil is not morally chargeable to him."[39]

Exactly how God relates to the sinful behaviors of human beings we do not know. While the "causal joint"[40] between divine sovereignty and human responsible freedom belongs to the mystery of God's providence, in accordance with the biblical testimony we must affirm that both are true, that God's sovereign plan takes nothing away from our moral accountability and that creaturely responsibility poses no limitation to the almighty guidance and direction of God. Just as a small portion of an iceberg that breaks the surface of the North Atlantic indicates the existence of a much larger mass below the waterline, which indeed buoys up that which is visible, so too God's actions in our lives hint that there are depths to the providence of a transcendent God that we cannot begin to fathom. The appeal to mystery scandalizes some Arminian thinkers.[41] But to envision the sovereign governance of God as existing on the same level with and as equally discernible as immanent causes and agents is surely to denigrate divine transcendence and betray a simplistic conception of the divine.[42] The rationalist bent of Arminianism, seen so evidently in its

---

[39]Ibid., p. 213.

[40]Austin Farrer, *Faith and Speculation* (New York: New York University Press, 1967), p. 65.

[41]See for example the discussion of mystery in Burson and Walls, *C. S. Lewis & Francis Schaeffer*, pp. 83-88. Jacob Arminius's rationalism also tended to denigrate mystery. As Peter O. G. White notes, "Arminius's confidence in the capacity of human reason exceeded that of Beza. . . . He refused to take refuge in the inscrutability of God; if a doctrine was incomprehensible, it ought to be repudiated" (*Predestination, Policy, and Polemic* [Cambridge, Mass.: Cambridge University Press, 1991], p. 25).

[42]William Placher writes that seventeenth-century rationalism—of which Arminianism is a species—"grew more confident about human capacities—about their ability to understand God and God's role in the world and to contribute to human salvation—and narrowed their understanding of what counted as reasonable articulation for faith" (*The Domestication of Transcendence: How Modern Thinking About God Went Wrong* [Louisville, Ky.: Westminster John Knox, 1996], p. 3).

doctrine of incompatibilist agency, helped to create a theological vision that would give itself to an emphasis upon the human will and reason in which rational neatness would overshadow divine transcendence and the wonder of grace.

Scripture tells us that God loves his people with an infinite love, that his wisdom is unfathomable and that he is unremittingly holy and good. It also tells us that God is sovereign over both the evil and the good. We do not know how it is that God sovereignly directs and ordains our freely chosen paths and, yes, our sinful acts as well as the good that we do. Yet since we have faith in his goodness, we will trust that "God always has the best reason for his plan"[43] (Rom 8:28). This is the comfort of the biblical proclamation of the sovereign kingship of God. He assures us that the world in which we live is not a mad chaos but is ever under his fatherly control.

---

[43]Calvin *Institutes* 1.17.1.

7

INABILITY

Hypothetical or Actual?

❧

Arminians and Calvinists believe much in common with regard to sin—original sin, depravity and the inability of lost persons to choose God on their own—but their theologies diverge when we consider who actually is unable to believe the gospel. For each point discussed in relation to these themes, we will cite John Wesley for Arminianism and John Calvin for Calvinism, mentioning other important exponents in footnotes.

Arminians and Calvinists alike believe in original sin. Although Wesley wrote thousands of pages of sermons, explanatory notes on Scripture, essays, journals and letters, he wrote only one full-length theological treatise. It is significant that this treatise was on the topic of original sin. Wesley affirmed original sin while commenting on Romans 5. First, he explained Romans 5:12: "*As by one man*—Adam; who is mentioned, and not Eve, as being the representative of mankind; *sin entered into the world*—actual sin, and its consequence, a sinful nature; *and death.*" Second, he interpreted Romans 5:19: "*As by the disobedience of one man, many,* that is, all men, *were constituted sinners*—Being then in the loins of their first parent, the common head and representative of them all."[1]

---

[1]John Wesley, *New Testament Notes,* Romans 5:12, cited in Kenneth J. Collins, *The Scripture Way of Salvation: The Heart of John Wesley's Theology* (Nashville: Abingdon, 1997), p. 33 (italics in original).

Calvin also believed in original sin and offered this definition: "Original sin, therefore, seems to be a hereditary depravity and corruption of our nature, diffused into all parts of the soul, which first makes us liable to God's wrath, then also brings forth in us those works which Scripture calls 'works of the flesh' [Gal. 5:19]."[2]

Arminians and Calvinists alike believe in total depravity: because of the fall, every aspect of human nature is tainted by sin. Wesley preached on Genesis 6:5, "Is man by nature filled with all manner of evil? Is he void of all good? Is he wholly fallen? Is his soul totally corrupted? Or, to come back to the text, is 'every imagination of the thoughts of his heart evil continually'? Allow this, and you are so far a Christian. Deny it, and you are but an heathen still."[3]

Calvin likewise affirmed total depravity. "All parts of the soul were possessed by sin. . . . The whole man is overwhelmed—as by a deluge—from head to foot, so that no part is immune from sin and all that proceeds from him is imputed to sin."[4]

Arminians and Calvinists alike believe that sinners are unable to choose God on their own. Wesley, after citing Genesis 6:11, Ephesians 2:3 and Romans 8:6, 8 as proof, explained, "Without supernatural grace we can neither will nor do what is pleasing to God."[5]

Calvin also held to inability. "Because of the bondage of sin by which the will is held bound, it cannot move toward good, much less apply itself thereto; for a movement of this sort is the beginning of conversion to God, which in Scripture is ascribed entirely to God's grace."[6]

Evangelical Arminians and Calvinists, therefore, agree on many basic ideas regarding original sin, total depravity and inability. Do they then

---

[2]John Calvin, *Institutes of the Christian Religion*, trans. Ford Lewis Battles (Philadelphia: Westminster Press, 1960), 2.1.8.

[3]John Wesley, "Original Sin," in *The Works of John Wesley*, ed. Albert C. Outler (Oxford: Clarendon, 1975-1983), 2:183-84, cited in Collins, *Scripture Way of Salvation*, p. 37.

[4]Calvin *Institutes* 2.1.9.

[5]John Wesley, "The Doctrine of Original Sin," in *John Wesley's Scriptural Christianity*, ed. Thomas Oden (Grand Rapids: Zondervan, 1994), p. 171.

[6]Calvin *Institutes* 2.3.5.

agree on every point of the doctrine of sin? The answer is no, because they part company in their understanding of the way inability applies to actual human beings.

Wesley scholar Kenneth J. Collins accurately contrasts Wesley's teaching with that of Calvin.

> At least initially, there does appear to be great similarity between Wesley's doctrine of original sin and that of . . . Calvin, especially in the emphasis on total depravity. Upon closer examination, however, there are important differences to be noted largely due to different conceptions of grace. For instance, when Wesley uses the vocabulary of total depravity, he is referring to what he calls, "the natural man," that is, to a person who is utterly without the grace of God. But does such a person actually exist? Not according to Wesley, for in the sermon "On Working Out Our Own Salvation" (1785) he states: "For allowing that all souls of men are dead in sin by nature, this excuses none, seeing that there is no man that is in a state of mere nature; there is no man, unless he has quenched the Spirit, that is wholly void of the grace of God. No man living is entirely destitute of what is vulgarly called 'natural conscience.' But this is not natural; it is more properly termed 'preventing grace.'"[7]

Collins is right; Wesley and Calvin have different conceptions of grace and inability. According to Calvin, inability is the condition of actual human beings, and grace, therefore, must be irresistible if anyone is to be saved. Calvin declared, God "does not move the will in such a manner as has been taught and believed for many ages—that it is afterward in our choice either to obey or resist the motion—but by disposing it efficaciously."[8]

---

[7]Collins, *Scripture Way of Salvation*, pp. 38-39, quoting Wesley, "On Working Out Our Own Salvation," in *The Works of John Wesley*, ed. Albert C. Outler (Oxford: Clarendon, 1975-1983), 3:207.

[8]Calvin *Institutes* 2.3.10.

Consequently, for Calvin, inability describes sinful human beings as they are—unable to do anything, even believe, apart from God's sovereign grace. In terms of our "knowing God's fatherly favor in our behalf, in which our salvation consists, . . . the greatest geniuses are blinder than moles!"[9]

It is important to note that Wesley's view of inability influenced subsequent Arminian theology.[10] We must ask: Does Scripture present inability as "a logical abstraction that does not correspond to actual men and women," words used by a Wesley scholar to summarize Wesley's view?[11] Or does Scripture present inability as the actual state of affairs of unsaved persons, as Calvinism holds? In sum, is inability hypothetical (Arminianism) or actual (Calvinism)?

We will argue that Scripture teaches a Calvinist and not an Arminian view of inability, basing our argument on three passages of Scripture: John 6:44, 65; 1 Corinthians 2:14-15; and 2 Corinthians 4:3-4.

JOHN 6:44, 65

Jesus shocks his hearers by teaching that they must eat his flesh and drink his blood to gain eternal life (Jn 6:48-58), that he will return to the Father (Jn 6:62), and that "no one can come to me unless the Father has enabled him" (Jn 6:65).

Jesus' shocking words in John 6:65 reflect his earlier assertion in John 6:44, "No one can come to me unless the Father who sent me draws him." In order to understand these two verses we will outline the Father's and Son's works on behalf of God's people according to John 6:35-45, 54, 65.

- The Father gives people to the Son (Jn 6:37). This is one of John's pictures of election.

---

[9]Calvin *Institutes* 2.2.18. See also 2.3.1.

[10]H. Orton Wiley, *Christian Theology* (Kansas City, Mo.: Beacon Hill, 1941), 2:353-54; H. Ray Dunning, *Grace, Faith and Holiness: A Wesleyan Systematic Theology* (Kansas City, Mo.: Beacon Hill, 1988), p. 278.

[11]Umphrey Lee, *John Wesley and Modern Religion* (Nashville: Cokesbury, 1936), pp. 124-25, approvingly quoted by Collins, *Scripture Way of Salvation*, p. 39.

- The Father draws them to the Son (Jn 6:44, 65). This is akin to Paul's idea of effectual calling.
- These people come to the Son (Jn 6:35, 37, 44, 45, 65). The parallelism of John 6:35 shows that coming to Jesus means believing in him.
- The Son keeps the people given to him by the Father (Jn 6:37, 39). This means that once saved by Christ, they are not lost.
- Jesus will raise them from the dead on the last day (Jn 6:39, 40, 44, 54). Here Jesus predicts the resurrection of the righteous.

These works of salvation form the theological framework for John 6:44, 65 and lead us to affirm two important truths. First, there is harmony between the Father and Son in salvation. The Father gives people to his Son and draws them to him. The Son saves, keeps and will raise the same people. Second, there is continuity in the identity of God's people. These are the same people whom the Father gives to and draws to the Son. And the same people believe in the Son, are preserved by him and will be raised by him.

Studying John 6:44, 65 within the framework of the saving deeds of the Father and Son yields much fruit. Jesus replies to the Jewish leaders' unbelieving complaints: "Stop grumbling among yourselves. . . . No one can come to me unless the Father who sent me draws him, and I will raise him up at the last day" (Jn 6:43-44). Jesus' words are arresting. He tells his hearers that their unbelief indicates that they are not God's people. When he says, "No one can come to me" (remember Jn 6:35, where coming to Jesus parallels believing in him), he means, "No one can believe in me unless the Father who sent me draws him." Sinners cannot believe in the Son unless they are drawn to him by the Father. Jesus is not speaking of inability hypothetically but is confronting actual grumbling, unbelieving hearers with the fact that they are not the people of God. He tells them not merely that they *do not* believe but that they *cannot* believe.

Arminian interpreters have appealed to the parallel use of the same word, *draw* (*helkō*), in John 12:32 and have concluded that God draws everyone to Jesus.[12] There Jesus says, "But I, when I am lifted up from the earth, will draw all men to myself." He means that when he is crucified (see Jn 12:33), he will bring "all men" to himself in salvation. "All men" here does not mean every individual, however, but Gentiles as well as Jews. We say this because of the context, in which after "some Greeks" ask to see Jesus (Jn 12:20-22) he apparently ignores them and talks about his approaching cross (Jn 12:23-28). But he doesn't really ignore the Greeks; he includes them in "all men" whom he will draw by his death. Jesus thus speaks of all without distinction (e.g., all kinds of people, Greeks as well as Jews) and not all without exception (i.e., every individual).

In addition, a careful reading of John 6:44 precludes the idea that the Father draws all persons to his Son. Jesus said, "No one can come to me unless the Father who sent me draws him, and I will raise him up at the last day." Because of the continuity in the identity of the people of God that we noted earlier, if we understand John 6:44 to say that every person is drawn, then we must conclude that every person will be raised up by Jesus for salvation on the last day. But this is universalism, the view that everyone will finally be saved, a view rejected by evangelical Calvinists and Arminians alike.

Consequently, the Father does not draw all persons to Christ in John 6:44. That verse teaches that unsaved persons are unable to trust Jesus as Savior unless the Father draws them to Jesus. The Father does this for those whom he has given to the Son, that is, those whom he has chosen. And the Son will raise them for final salvation.

The conclusions we reached for John 6:44 are reinforced by John 6:65. There Jesus says to a grumbling crowd, "For this reason I have told you that no one can come to me unless it has been given to him by the Father" (our own translation). Once more Jesus affirms that unsaved persons are unable to believe in him unless the Father has enabled them to do so.

In the verses immediately preceding John 6:44 and 65, unsaved peo-

---

[12]Grant Osborne, "Exegetical Notes on Calvinist Texts," in *Grace Unlimited*, ed. Clark H. Pinnock (Minneapolis: Bethany House, 1975), p. 171.

ple grumble about Jesus. Jesus addresses them and thereby ascribes inability to actual unbelieving people. This contradicts the Arminian idea of a hypothetical inability.

1 CORINTHIANS 2:14-15

After speaking of the source of the apostles' gospel (1 Cor 2:11-13), Paul shifts gears to talk about the recipients of the gospel: "The man without the Spirit does not accept the things that come from the Spirit of God, for they are foolishness to him, and he cannot understand them, because they are spiritually discerned. The spiritual man makes judgments about all things, but he himself is not subject to any man's judgment" (1 Cor 2:14-15).

Paul contrasts two types of people: "the man without the Spirit" (literally "the natural man," 1 Cor 2:14), with "the spiritual man" (1 Cor 2:15). It is crucial to understand that the difference between the two is the absence and presence of the Spirit, respectively. The natural man is natural, that is, unspiritual, because he does not have the Holy Spirit. And the spiritual man is spiritual because he has the Spirit.

The way Paul describes the two types of people is also significant. The spiritual man "makes judgments about all things." Paul means that the person who has the Spirit has access to spiritual wisdom, to "the mind of Christ" (1 Cor 2:16). By contrast, "The man without the Spirit does not accept the things that come from the Spirit of God."

In the context of 1 Corinthians 2, it is easy to identify "the things that come from the Spirit of God." They are "the testimony about God" (1 Cor 2:1), "Jesus Christ and him crucified" (1 Cor 2:2), "my preaching" (1 Cor 2:4), "a message of wisdom" (1 Cor 2:6), "God's secret wisdom" (1 Cor 2:7), "what God has prepared for those who love him" (1 Cor 2:9), "what God has freely given us" (1 Cor 2:12) and "words taught by the Spirit" (1 Cor 2:13). The expression "the things that come from the Spirit of God," therefore, refers to the apostles' gospel. That is why 1 Corinthians 2:14 is so amazing. Paul teaches that unsaved persons lack the Spirit and therefore do not believe the gospel. The present tense "*does* not *accept*" doesn't point to a particular rejection of the gospel but indicates the general state of affairs.[13] Unsaved people lack the Spirit and reject the gospel.

The situation is even worse. "The things that come from the Spirit of God . . . are foolishness to him" (1 Cor 2:14). The lost person considers the gospel "foolishness." Why? Because he or she is devoid of the Spirit and therefore lacks God's wisdom. Yet the situation is still worse. Paul explains that those without the Spirit "cannot understand them because they are spiritually discerned." In other words, the unsaved cannot understand the gospel because it is spiritually understood.

Paul's contrast between the unsaved and the saved is acute. People devoid of the Spirit do not accept the gospel. Indeed, it is foolishness to them and they cannot understand it. But people who possess the Spirit have the spiritual wisdom that comes from God.

It remains for us to test the Calvinist and Arminian models of inability against Paul's teaching. When Paul speaks of "the man without the Spirit" in 1 Corinthians 2:14, is he speaking of a hypothetical situation? Is he speaking of unsaved persons before they are enabled to believe by prevenient grace? No, on both counts. Instead, he is speaking of the state of affairs of unsaved people who do not understand God's wisdom in the gospel (1 Cor 2:8). He is contrasting actual persons in 1 Corinthians 2:14 and 15, those who don't have the Spirit with those who do. He is explaining why unsaved persons don't believe the apostles' message— because they don't have the Spirit of God and therefore can't understand that message. We conclude that this passage presents a concrete inability and not a theoretical one.

2 CORINTHIANS 4:3-4

Paul had proclaimed in 2 Corinthians 3:7-18 the glory of new covenant ministry. Paul, however, is the object of attacks; his enemies maintain that he is a heretic and that his message is not glorious but full of darkness.

Paul answers his accusers to defend the gospel. He insists that his preaching did not involve deception but presented an honest expression

---

[13]It is a gnomic present.

of God's truth (2 Cor 4:1-2). He candidly admits that some reject and others believe his gospel. But he refuses to fault the gospel. "And even if our gospel is veiled, it is veiled to those who are perishing" (2 Cor 4:3). Contrary to his detractors' claims, the gospel is not a message of darkness (falsehood and sin); it is full of God's light. Because unbelievers are lost and perishing, they don't "see the light."

Paul explains, "The god of this age has blinded the minds of unbelievers, so that they cannot see the light of the gospel of the glory of Christ, who is the image of God" (2 Cor 4:4). Paul teaches that Satan exerts a negative influence on the minds of unsaved people to keep them from believing the gospel. The gospel is luminous, Paul insists. The darkness in lost persons is the result of the devil's blinding their thinking.

The situation of unsaved persons according to 2 Corinthians 4:4 is even worse than that described in 1 Corinthians 2:14. There Paul pointed to the absence of the Spirit to account for sinners' inability to believe the gospel. Here he points to the presence and activity of Satan.

Does Calvinism or Arminianism better describe the inability depicted in this text? Does the inability describe a theoretical situation that has been overcome by preparing grace given to all, so that all are able to believe? Clearly not. The inability is not hypothetical but actual. Paul describes people who hear the gospel but do not believe it. They "are perishing" (2 Cor 4:3). The reason for their unbelief (given here) is that Satan has blinded their minds so that they cannot embrace Christ.

2 Corinthians 4:6 confirms this conclusion. "For God, who said, 'Let light shine out of darkness,' made his light shine in our hearts to give us the light of the knowledge of the glory of God in the face of Christ." The saving grace of God does not nullify inability in order to grant all sinners free will. Instead, God's grace enlightens sinners, with the result that they believe and know Christ. Just as the sovereign God spoke light into being at creation, so he causes the light of the gospel to penetrate dark hearts, overcoming the devil's blinding influence. God's sovereign grace effectively overcomes the actual inability of many sinners.

CONCLUSION

This, then, is our case for a Calvinist view of inability based on John 6:44, 65; 1 Corinthians 2:14-15; and 2 Corinthians 4:3-4. Arminianism and Calvinism are evangelical theologies that hold many important truths in common, including original sin, depravity and inability. Here, however, the two theologies diverge. Briefly stated, Arminianism holds to a hypothetical inability and Calvinism an actual inability.

Was inability, in the passages we examined, a former condition superseded by prevenient grace? Was the situation described in those passages such that, in fact, all people are enabled by God to believe the gospel? If so, then the Arminian view of inability is more biblical and should be embraced as such.

Or did the passages teach an actual inability, in which persons being addressed by Christ and described by Paul were in the terrible condition of being unable to rescue themselves? The second option is correct. Jesus was not speaking theoretically but was describing the concrete condition of the unbelieving crowd when he said, "No one can come to me unless the Father who sent me draws him" and "No one can come to me unless the Father has enabled him" (John 6:44, 65).

Paul, likewise, was not speaking hypothetically when he wrote, "The man without the Spirit does not accept the things that come from the Spirit of God, for they are foolishness to him, and he cannot understand them" (1 Cor. 2:14) and "The god of this age has blinded the minds of unbelievers, so that they cannot see the light of the gospel" (2 Cor. 4:4). We conclude, then, that the Calvinist doctrine of inability and not the Arminian doctrine is true.

The truth of inability has important practical ramifications. Because unsaved persons can do nothing to save themselves, we who know the Lord must depend totally upon him when we present the gospel to the lost.

James Packer expresses the connection between sinners' actual inability and the preaching of the gospel of God's grace better than we could:

Without the Holy Spirit there would be *no faith and no new birth*—in short, *no Christians.* The light of the gospel shines; but "the god of this world hath blinded the minds of them which believe not" (2 Cor. 4:4), and the blind do not respond to the stimulus of light. . . .

What follows, then? Should we conclude that preaching the gospel is a waste of time, and write off evangelism as a hopeless enterprise, foredoomed to fail? No; because the Spirit abides with the Church to testify of Christ. To the apostles, He testified by *revealing* and *inspiring.* . . . To the rest of men, down the ages, He testifies by *illuminating:* opening blinded eyes, restoring spiritual vision, enabling sinners to see that the gospel is indeed God's truth, and Scripture is indeed God's Word, and Christ is indeed God's Son. . . . It is the sovereign prerogative of Christ's Spirit to convince men's consciences of the truth of Christ's gospel; and Christ's human witnesses must learn to ground their hopes of success, not on clever presentation of the truth by man, but on powerful demonstration of the truth by the Spirit. . . . (1 Cor. 2:1-5, RSV). And because the Spirit does bear witness in this way, men come to faith when the gospel is preached. But without the Spirit there would not be a Christian in the world.[14]

---

[14]J. I. Packer, *Knowing God* (Downers Grove, Ill: InterVarsity Press, 1973), pp. 62-63.

8

GRACE

Resistible or Irresistible?

❧

Prevenient grace is God's grace that precedes the salvation of sinners and prepares them to believe. The concept of prevenient grace appears in the writings of Augustine, Calvin, Arminius and Wesley, among many others. Both Arminians and Calvinists believe in prevenient grace, although each defines it differently. Arminians teach that God gives prevenient grace to all, enabling them to believe or reject the gospel. Calvinists hold that God gives prevenient grace only to the elect, and this grace unfailingly brings them to saving faith. Prevenient grace in the Wesleyan mode is thus universal and resistible, while in the Calvinist mode it is particular and irresistible.

A DESCRIPTION OF AN ARMINIAN VIEW
OF PREVENIENT GRACE

The concept of prevenient grace developed in Arminian theology, and we will present the best view from that theological camp—that of Wesley and his theological descendants. First, their view is Trinitarian, as Dunning implies.[1] It is based on the Father's love, flows from the Son's cross and is conveyed to sinners by the Holy Spirit.

---

[1] H. Ray Dunning, *Grace, Faith and Holiness*, pp. 197, 338-339. See also Theodore Runyon, *The New Creation: John Wesley's Theology Today* (Nashville: Abingdon, 1998), p. 34.

Second, according to Arminianism, prevenient grace is necessary for salvation. Tom Oden summarizes John Wesley's view: "Fallen men and women cannot turn to repent without grace preceding them."[2]

Third, Arminians hold that prevenient grace is universal. John Wesley comments on his key text for prevenient grace, John 1:9: "Everyone has some measure of that light, some faint glimmering ray, which sooner or later, more or less, enlightens every man coming into the world."[3] The Arminian idea of prevenient grace is broad, encompassing general revelation and, especially, conscience.

Calvinists also teach that there is a universal focus to God's grace. We call it common grace and define it as "every favour of whatever kind or degree, falling short of salvation, which this undeserving and sin-cursed world enjoys at the hand of God."[4] God's common grace restrains evil (Gen 20:6) and bestows good (Ps 145:15, 16) so that no one is a stranger to God's kindness. But no biblical passage teaches that people are enabled by common grace to know salvation, as Arminians claim for universal prevenient grace.

Fourth, prevenient grace precedes salvation, as Oden emphasizes: "The initiative comes from grace prevening prior to our first awakening to the mercy and holiness of God. . . . Grace works ahead of us to draw us toward faith, to begin its work in us."[5] Both Arminianism and Calvinism insist that grace precedes and enables salvation.

Fifth, Arminianism holds that prevenient grace restores free will to sinners. Wesley, after teaching that our ability to choose God was lost in the Fall, explains, "I only assert, that there is a measure of free will supernaturally restored to every man."[6] Here is a key difference between Calvinism and Arminianism. Calvinism holds to the actual inability of

---

[2]Thomas Oden, *John Wesley's Scriptural Christianity* (Grand Rapids: Zondervan, 1994), p. 135.

[3]John Wesley, quoted in Kenneth J. Collins, *The Scripture Way of Salvation: The Heart of John Wesley's Theology* (Nashville: Abingdon, 1997), p. 39.

[4]John Murray, *Collected Writings* (Edinburgh: The Banner of Truth Trust, 1977), 2:96.

[5]Oden, *John Wesley's Scriptural Christianity*, p. 246.

[6]John Wesley, quoted in Collins, *Scripture Way of Salvation*, p. 42.

sinners to move toward God in salvation. Arminianism holds to a hypothetical inability overcome by prevenient grace granting sinners an ability to believe and be saved.[7]

Sixth, in Arminianism, the result of prevenient grace restoring free will is a gracious synergism ("a vision of divine/human cooperation")[8] in which God and people work together in salvation. Robert Rakestraw sums up the result of this synergism: "For Wesley, even though one cannot in any sense save oneself by good works or by any inherent goodness, that one is ultimately the determining factor in the decision of his or her justification."[9] Prevenient grace is the first aspect of grace, a grace that also includes convicting, justifying, regenerating, sanctifying and glorifying grace. And, although God's grace initiates each stage of salvation, "at each stage we are called to receive and respond to the grace being incrementally given."[10] Arminianism, then, holds that via the process set in motion by God's preparing grace, our choices finally determine our salvation.

Seventh, therefore, according to Arminianism, saving grace is resistible. Theologian Ken Grider explains: "We can either accept Christ or reject Him—and our eternal destiny depends upon our free response to God's offer of salvation."[11]

We arrive at a summary description: Prevenient grace, according to Arminianism, is the necessary grace of the Trinity, given to all persons, that precedes salvation, restores free will and enables sinners to cooperate with God in salvation if they choose to believe. Calvinists also maintain that God's prevenient grace is Trinitarian, is necessary and precedes salvation. Calvinists differ with Arminians, however, in maintaining that preceding grace is irresistibly given to those whom God has chosen and always results in their believing and being saved.

---

[7]Oden, *John Wesley's Scriptural Christianity,* p. 169.

[8]Collins, *Scripture Way of Salvation,* p. 44.

[9]Robert V. Rakestraw, "John Wesley as a Theologian of Grace," *Journal of the Evangelical Theological Society* 27.2 (1984): 199.

[10]Oden, *John Wesley's Scriptural Christianity,* p. 247.

[11]J. Kenneth Grider, *A Wesleyan-Holiness Theology* (Kansas City, Mo.: Beacon Hill, 1994), p. 245.

THE IMPORTANCE OF PREVENIENT GRACE
FOR ARMINIAN THEOLOGY

The idea of prevenient grace is of critical importance for Arminianism. Universal preceding grace "is one of the most central concepts in all of Wesley's theology."[12] "Prevenient grace plays a crucial role in Wesleyan evangelical teaching."[13]

The Arminian view of prevenient grace is the glue that holds together their entire systematic theology. Collins agrees, "Wesley's doctrine of prevenient grace allows him to hold together, without any contradiction, the four motifs of total depravity, salvation by grace, human responsibility, and the offer of salvation to all."[14]

Universal and resistible prevenient grace, then, is the genius of Arminian systematic theology, enabling it to be evangelical and synergistic at the same time. If a strong biblical case can be made for it, its proponents will have gone a long way toward demonstrating the truthfulness of their system. But if their appeal to the Bible is unconvincing, the whole system will come into question.

AN EVALUATION OF AN ARMINIAN VIEW
OF PREVENIENT GRACE

Given the importance of prevenient grace for Arminianism, we expected to find carefully argued biblical defenses of the doctrine. But we had to comb the Arminian literature to find arguments for prevenient grace. The arguments can be divided into biblical and theological categories (though we will treat Scriptural passages under both).

Biblical Arguments

John 1:9. This was John Wesley's favorite proof text for universal prevenient grace. He wrote, "The will of man is by nature only free to evil. Yet

---

[12]Rakestraw, "John Wesley as a Theologian of Grace," p. 202. Cf. Grider, *Wesleyan-Holiness Theology,* p. 49.

[13]Oden, *John Wesley's Scriptural Christianity,* p. 244.

[14]Collins, *Scripture Way of Salvation,* p. 45.

. . . every man has a measure of free-will restored to him by grace. . . . Natural free-will, in the present state of mankind, I do not understand: I only assert, that there is a measure of free-will supernaturally restored to every man, together with that supernatural light which 'enlightens every man that comes into the world.'"[15]

John 1:9, however, viewed in its literary and historical contexts, does not support the Arminian view of prevenient grace. Although John's prologue speaks of revelation in creation in John 1:3-5, John 1:9 speaks of revelation in the incarnate Son. It speaks of the Son's incarnation using the metaphor of the light shining in a dark world, and John 1:14 does the same, using the metaphor of the Word becoming flesh.

The King James Version, used by Wesley, mistranslated John 1:9 as, "That was the true Light, which lighteth every man that cometh into the world." Almost all modern translations (including the NRSV, NJB, NEB, NASB and ESV) render it similarly to the NIV: "The true light that gives light to every man was coming into the world" (Jn 1:9). The words "coming into the world" go not with "every man" but with "the true light was." Rendered in this way, verse 9 sets the stage for John 1:10, which begins, "He was in the world." John speaks of the incarnation (v. 9) and its results (v. 10).

The four following verses confirm our understanding of John 1:9. They provide historical context, telling of two responses to the incarnate Son's illumination. John 1:10-11 speaks of an unbelieving response to Jesus on the part of his human creatures (v. 10), even the Jews (v. 11). By contrast, John 1:12-13 speaks of a believing response. If we interpret verse 9 in light of its subsequent context, "every man" does not mean every person, but all who came in contact with Jesus' earthly ministry. Verse 9 does not make a statement about the cosmos or of God illuminating all persons, but it describes Jesus' giving "light to every man" who saw his signs and heard his words.

Romans 2:4. Grider cites this text to argue that prevenient grace

---

[15]Oden, *John Wesley's Scriptural Christianity*, p. 250.

gives helpless sinners the assistance they need to be saved.[16] An examination of the context shows that Arminians overreach when they cite Romans 2:4 to support their view of prevenient grace. Paul exposes the Jewish hypocrisy of condemning Gentiles' sins while the Jews do the same things (Rom 2:1-3). Continuing, Paul writes, "Or do you show contempt for the riches of his kindness, tolerance and patience, not realizing that God's kindness leads you towards repentance?" (Rom 2:4). Paul does not teach that God gives prevenient grace to all persons. Rather, the blessings he mentions were given to Israel as God's covenant people. His point is that Israel's rejection of those blessings increases its judgment.

Arminian theologians can correctly point to Romans 2:4 to show, in the words of Calvinist Leon Morris, "That which is good and kind in God is directed towards bringing people to *repentance*."[17] But Paul does not say that God's kindness enables *all* sinners to believe the gospel. In fact, what is fast becoming a consensus among Pauline scholars is the conclusion that Paul uses the present-tense verb *leads* here to indicate desired or intended action on God's part.[18] Anders Nygren, for example, interprets Paul's words, "Do you not know that God's kindness is meant to lead *you* to repentance?"[19]

In sum: Arminians correctly cite Romans 2:4 as evidence of God's goodness in directing sinners toward repentance. But a closer examination of the verse reveals that Paul is making not a universal statement but a particular one showing that the Jews are condemned along with the Gentiles.

---

[16]Grider, *Wesleyan-Holiness Theology*, p. 353.

[17]Leon Morris, *The Epistle to the Romans* (Grand Rapids: Eerdmans, 1988), p. 113 (italics in original).

[18]That is, as a conative.

[19]Anders Nygren, *Commentary on Romans* (Philadelphia: Fortress, 1972), p. 117 (italics in original); cf. Thomas R. Schreiner, *Romans*, Baker Exegetical Commentary on the New Testament (Grand Rapids: Baker, 1998), p. 108; H. C. G. Moule, *The Epistle to the Romans*, The Expositor's Bible (New York: Armstrong & Son, 1894), p. 8; James D. G. Dunn, *Romans 1-8*, Word Biblical Commentary 38A (Dallas: Word, 1988), p. 91; Murray, *The Epistle to the Romans*, New International Commentary on the New Testament (Grand Rapids: Eerdmans, 1959), p. 60; Morris, *Epistle to the Romans*, p. 113 n. 30.

Theological Arguments

God's love. Arminians also offer theological arguments for their view of prevenient grace. Perhaps the most important one is based upon God's nature as love. Dunning explains: "The Wesleyan holds that God's love is a manifestation of His nature, and consequently it is universal rather than selective. . . . None is excluded, for this would involve a violation of God's own nature. . . . It is this aspect of the doctrine of God that provides the theological grounding for the Wesleyan doctrine of prevenient grace."[20]

Vernon Grounds cites biblical passages to support this argument.[21] To avoid duplication, we'll consider those verses that refer to God's love generally here—John 3:16, Romans 11:32 and 2 Peter 3:9—and those that refer to Christ's atonement—John 1:29, Romans 5:17-21, 1 Timothy 2:6 and Hebrews 2:9—under the next category.

John 3:16. "For God so loved the world that he gave his one and only Son, that whoever believes in him shall not perish but have eternal life." What motivated the Father to send his Son to die for sinners was his great love. Calvinists have not always properly understood John 3:16. We reject attempts to limit the meaning of "world" here to "the world of the elect," for example. It is better to follow the lead of D. A. Carson, who sees this verse as indicating "God's salvific stance towards his fallen world."[22] But although John 3:16 speaks of the universality of God's love for sinners, it does not teach what Arminians claim about what that love does for sinners. It says nothing about universal prevenient grace bestowing ability to unbelievers.

Romans 11:32. "For God has bound all men over to disobedience so that he may have mercy on them all." While discussing the last verse we admitted that Calvinists sometimes mishandle texts speaking of God's love for the "world" (or "all"). We now add that Arminians sometimes do

---

[20]Dunning, *Grace, Faith and Holiness,* pp. 196-97.

[21]Vernon Grounds, "God's Universal Salvific Grace," in *Grace Unlimited,* ed. Clark Pinnock (Minneapolis: Bethany House, 1975), pp. 26-27.

[22]D. A. Carson, *The Difficult Doctrine of the Love of God* (Wheaton, Ill.: Crossway, 2000), p. 17.

the same. The verses that precede Romans 11:32 shed light on the meaning of *all,* used two times in that verse.

> *Israel* has experienced a hardening in part until the full number of the *Gentiles* has come in. . . . Just as *you* who were at one time disobedient to God have now received mercy as a result of *their* disobedience, so *they* too have now become disobedient in order that *they* too may now receive mercy as a result of God's mercy to *you.* For God has bound *all men* over to disobedience so that he may have mercy on them *all.*" (Rom 11:25, 30-32; italics added)

All plainly means both Jews and Gentiles. It will not do to claim that Paul is speaking of every human being. He speaks, rather, of the *class* of Jews and the *class* of Gentiles, though not necessarily of every person within those classes. More important, once again Paul does not say that God's mercy enables sinners to believe, the very thing that Arminians claim.

2 Peter 3:9. "The Lord is not slow in keeping his promise, as some understand slowness. He is patient with you, not wanting anyone to perish, but everyone to come to repentance." For two reasons this verse is not a good proof text for universal grace, let alone universal prevenient grace in the Arminian sense. First, before Peter says that God doesn't want "anyone to perish, but everyone to come to repentance," he says, "he is patient with *you*" (italics added). In light of the preceding pronoun *you,* Peter means "anyone" of you and "everyone" of you. Richard Bauckham agrees, "But *pantas* ('all') is clearly limited by *humas* ('you'). . . . In Jewish thought it was usually for the sake of the repentance of his own people that God delayed judgment. Here it is for the sake of the repentance of 2 Peter's Christian readers."[23]

Second, 2 Peter 3 must be read in light of the preceding chapter. There Peter in no uncertain terms condemns the false teachers who will harass his readers.

---

[23]Richard Bauckham, *Jude, 2 Peter,* Word Biblical Commentary 50 (Waco, Tex.: Word, 1983), p. 313.

There will be false teachers among you. They will secretly introduce destructive heresies . . . bringing swift destruction on themselves. . . . Their condemnation has long been hanging over them,
and their destruction has not been sleeping. . . . Like beasts they
too will perish. They will be paid back with harm for the harm they
have done. . . . Blackest darkness is reserved for them. (2 Pet 2:1,
3, 12, 13, 17)

It is hard to believe that 2 Peter 3:9 teaches that God wants the false
teachers, whom he condemns in 2 Peter 2, to repent. Instead, 2 Peter 3:9
means that God will certainly bring about the consummation of all things.
That he has not done so already shows not an unwillingness on his part
but his long-suffering. He patiently waits for all of Peter's professed Christian readers to repent because he wants to spare them judgment.

Christ's atonement. As Dunning notes, "Wesley insists that prevenient grace is ultimately grounded in Christ's death on the Cross."[24] In
the preceding section we dealt with verses cited in support of the universality of God's saving grace in terms of God's love. We now proceed
to examine those having to do with Christ's atonement.

John 1:29. "The next day John saw Jesus coming toward him and said,
'Look, the Lamb of God, who takes away the sin of the world!'" If we understand "takes away" as meaning "forgives" and "the world" as meaning
"all persons," the verse teaches that everyone will be saved, a view rejected by Arminians and Calvinists. So, interpreters either qualify "the
world" or explain "takes away" in a way that comes short of accomplishing forgiveness. We would prefer to understand "takes away" in a strong
sense and to take "the world," along with D. A. Carson, as speaking "of
all human beings without distinction, though not . . . of all without exception."[25] But we will not insist on that. Instead, for the sake of argument we will assume that "takes away" means "makes forgiveness avail-
able" and that "world" means "all persons." Even then Arminianism

---

[24]Dunning, *Grace, Faith and Holiness,* pp. 333, 339.
[25]D. A. Carson, *The Gospel According to John* (Grand Rapids: Eerdmans, 1991), p. 151.

would not have proved universal prevenient grace because once more there is no mention of God's preceding grace granting sinners the ability to believe.

Romans 5:18-19. "Consequently, just as the result of one trespass was condemnation for *all men,* so also the result of one act of righteousness was justification that brings life for *all men.* For just as through the disobedience of the one man *the many* were made sinners, so also through the obedience of the one man *the many* will be made righteous" (italics added).

Romans 5:18-19 is not a good proof text for God's universal love for sinners. We say that because of the parallelism of the two verses. Notice the words "all men" (in v. 18) and "the many" (in v. 19) italicized above. Interpreters miss Paul's intention if they teach that all were condemned from verse 18 or that many (and not all) will be saved from verse 19. Of course these are both biblical truths; our point is that it is not wise to appeal to Romans 5:18-19 as support. One could just as well teach that all will be justified from verse 18 or that not all were made sinners from verse 19!

Paul does not contrast "all" in Romans 5:18 with "many" in Romans 5:19. If he did, he would contradict himself twice in the space of two verses! Rather, he contrasts both Adam and Christ with "all" in verse 18 and with "many" in verse 19. Paul contrasts the one man Adam with the many he affects, even all who belong to him. And Paul does the same for Christ. He means that even as Adam brought death and condemnation to his race, so also Christ, the second Adam, brought life and justification to his. So, Romans 5:18-19 is not a good proof text for God's universal saving love.

1 Timothy 2:5-6. "For there is one God and one mediator between God and men, the man Christ Jesus, who gave himself as a ransom for all men—the testimony given in its proper time." Paul here affirms that Christ, the only mediator between God and human beings, died "as a ransom for all" (ESV). This passage does not mention the concept of grace, prevenient grace or the Arminian view of prevenient grace.

Hebrews 2:9. "But we see Jesus, who was made a little lower than the angels, now crowned with glory and honor because he suffered death, so that by the grace of God he might taste death for everyone." Citing Psalm 8, the writer to the Hebrews laments that human beings since the Fall have forfeited the glory and dominion that was theirs at creation (Heb 2:6-8). But he rejoices that Jesus has become a man and as the resurrected second Adam has reclaimed the glory lost by Adam in the Fall and will bring "many sons to glory" (Heb 2:9-10). The writer teaches that Jesus "suffered death, so that by the grace of God he might taste death for everyone" (Heb 2:9). Although the verse says it was by God's grace that Christ died for all, there is no mention of the effects of grace, effects demanded by the Arminian view of prevenient grace.

Synergism. Arminians also argue for universal prevenient grace from synergism, their view that God and sinners (enabled by grace) cooperate in salvation. After citing passages that show that God grants repentance to sinners, Grider argues:

> Repentance is what God gives to people, what he grants to their cooperating hearts. That God has a part in one's repentance, although not an overriding part, is shown in Hebrews. . . . The implication is that God works toward their repentance, but that, if they will not respond, it is not possible for God to force them to do so. . . . The drawing of the Holy Spirit . . . is necessary before people repent and turn utterly to God. . . . "His Spirit will not contend with man forever" (Gen 6:3), but He contends sufficiently—if the sinner will respond.[26]

Grider thinks that setting side by side Scriptures that speak of God's initiative in salvation with those that insist on human beings' response to God proves prevenient grace. But he assumes what he intends to prove. We agree that many passages speak of God's saving initiative and many others speak of human response. But we disagree with Grider about how to combine those facts theologically. We affirm divine monergism based on the same verses, but the mere affirmation does not prove our case for

---

[26]Grider, *Wesleyan-Holiness Theology*, pp. 353-55.

Calvinism. And it is the same for Arminianism. The fact that Arminians point to passages teaching that God saves and that people receive salvation does not prove the Arminian view of prevenient grace.

Conclusion

We agree with the assessments of New Testament scholar Tom Schreiner, who concludes an essay on the Arminian case for prevenient grace in this way:

> What was most striking to me in my research was how little scriptural exegesis has been done by Wesleyans in defense of prevenient grace. It is vital to their system of theology. . . . Nonetheless, not much exegetical work has been done in support of the doctrine. Wesleyans contend that prevenient grace counteracts the inability of humanity due to Adam's sin, but firm biblical evidence seems to be lacking. One can be pardoned, then, for wondering whether this theory is based on scriptural exegesis.[27]

The case for an Arminian view of universal prevenient grace is weak. Neither the biblical nor the theological argument works. Consequently, because of the critical importance of prevenient grace to the Arminian system of theology, that system suffers a serious blow.

IRRESISTIBLE GRACE

It is not enough to find the Arminian view of universal prevenient grace wanting. We must also present a case for the Calvinist view of irresistible (prevenient) grace. Before doing so, we will describe the Calvinist view and clear up misconceptions.

A Description of the Calvinist View of Irresistible Grace

Calvinists and Arminians agree that the grace of God is Trinitarian (Eph

---

[27]Thomas R. Schreiner, "Does Scripture Teach Prevenient Grace in the Wesleyan Sense?" in *Still Sovereign*, ed. Thomas R. Schreiner and Bruce A. Ware (Grand Rapids: Baker, 2000), p. 246. See also Millard J. Erickson, *Christian Theology*, 2nd ed. (Grand Rapids: Baker, 1998), p. 938.

2:4-5; Rom 16:20; Rev 1:4), necessary for salvation (Eph 2:8-9) and prevenient (1 John 4:10, 19). Calvinists part company with Arminians,
however, when they affirm that God's grace is efficacious (John 6:37, 39),
particular (John 17:6, 9, 11) and irresistible. This last description is our
current concern—irresistible grace.

Misconceptions of the Calvinist View of Irresistible Grace

The term "irresistible grace" itself is misleading; it was coined by the
Arminians at the Synod of Dort, not by the Calvinists. It suggests that God
grabs poor sinners by the scruff of the neck and forces them to believe.
This is a caricature of Calvinism. We have "preferred to speak of 'invincible' or 'unconquerable' grace, or to say that God's saving grace was 'finally
irresistible.'"[28] Sinners are hostile to God, and when God touches their
lives with his sovereign grace, he frees them from sin's bondage. As a result
they willingly trust Christ. God doesn't force sinners to believe against
their will; he liberates their will by his Spirit. He doesn't violate their personalities; he sets them free to be the people whom he intended.

Another misconception concerns the fact that many sinners successfully resist God's grace and die in their sins. How can Calvinists say that
God's grace is irresistible? The answer is that we don't teach that God's
grace is irresistible for all; rather, God's grace is irresistible only for God's
people. God's invincible grace eventually brings all of the elect to salvation.

A Defense of the Calvinist View of Irresistible Grace

Belief in irresistible or unconquerable grace is based upon at least five
lines of biblical evidence.

God's predestination inevitably results in faith. Jesus said, "All that
the Father gives me will come to me, and whoever comes to me I will
never drive away" (Jn 6:37). Jesus assures that all the elect (all the Father
gives him) "will come to" him. John 6:35 had equated "coming to" him
with "believing in" him. Thus, when Jesus says that all the Father gives

---

[28]Anthony Hoekema, *Saved by Grace* (Grand Rapids: Eerdmans, 1989), p. 105.

him will come to him, he means that all those whom God has chosen will believe in him. Although Jesus doesn't use the word *grace,* he teaches the concept of irresistible grace when he says that *all* of the elect *will* believe in him. God's predestination inevitably results in saving faith for the people of God.

Luke, too, combines predestination and the irresistibility of grace when he describes the Gentiles' warm reception of Paul and Barnabas in Pisidian Antioch on the first missionary journey. Luke writes, "When the Gentiles heard this, they were glad and honored the word of the Lord; and all who were appointed for eternal life believed" (Acts 13:48). Those "appointed for eternal life" are those whom God had chosen for salvation. Luke thus teaches that all those chosen for eternal life believed. That means that God's predestination inevitably results in saving faith; his grace is irresistible.

God irresistibly draws or calls people to Christ. Jesus teaches the invincibility of grace when he says to his grumbling audience, "No one can come to me unless the Father who sent me draws him, and I will raise him up at the last day" (Jn 6:44; cf. Jn 6:65). Jesus means that no one can believe in him unless the Father draws him. Drawing here means bringing people effectively to Christ. People are not able to choose God on their own; the Father has to draw them, to enable them to believe in his Son. An Arminian objector might respond, "Yes, and that is exactly what God does for all people by virtue of prevenient grace. He draws, enables everyone to believe in Jesus." Our response? That is not what Jesus is saying, as the preceding context attests. In the context preceding John 6:44, we learn that "the Jews began to grumble about him" (Jn 6:41). For that reason, Jesus prefaces verse 44 with "Stop grumbling among yourselves" (Jn 6:43). In context Jesus is not teaching the grumblers a lesson about God's universal prevenient grace; rather, he is putting them in their place by implying that they are not the people of God as they assume.

In Romans 8:29-30, God's effective calling of his people to salvation testifies to irresistible grace. Paul comforts those "who have been called according to his purpose" (Rom 8:28) by outlining that purpose: "For those God foreknew he also predestined. . . . And those he predestined, he also called; those he called, he also justified; those he justified, he also glorified" (Rom 8:29-30). Paul describes God's saving actions on behalf of his people: God foreknew, predestined, called, justified and glorified them. These actions are so certain that the apostle expresses each in the past tense. By using the literary device of climax, Paul indicates that it is the same people whom God foreknew, predestined, called, justified and glorified. The calling spoken of here, then, cannot be the universal gospel call; it must be the special effective call. That is because those God called, he justified and glorified. Because not everyone will be glorified, not everyone is called in the sense spoken of here.

Paul paints a panorama of God's sovereign grace. From the beginning (foreknowledge) to the end (glorification) salvation is the work of God. And the intermediate links in the golden chain of salvation are unbreakable. The same persons whom God foreloved, he predestined, *called,* justified and glorified. The effective calling of God's people is not in doubt. And that means that God's grace is finally irresistible.

God unfailingly opens hearts. The book of Acts depicts God's grace in action. It speaks of "the gospel of God's grace" (Acts 20:24), of "those who by grace believed" (Acts 18:27), and renders this more precisely in Acts 16:14, where he says "the Lord opened [Lydia's] heart."[29] On the second missionary journey, Paul, Timothy and Silas traveled to Philippi, where they shared the gospel with a group of women who had gathered by a river to pray. "One of those listening was a woman named Lydia, a dealer in purple cloth from the city of Thyatira, who was a worshiper of God. The Lord opened her heart to respond to Paul's message" (Acts 16:14). Luke focuses on Lydia and tells us that she became "a believer in the Lord" (Acts 16:15) because she is a beautiful example of what God's grace accomplishes. Her responding to Paul's message in faith is ascribed to God's working in her life to bring her to himself: "The Lord opened

---

[29]We learned this line of reasoning from our esteemed colleague David Clyde Jones.

her heart to respond to Paul's message." And so she did. Luke with simplicity and power portrays God's invincible grace in action.

God successfully illuminates those blinded by Satan. It is not surprising that two of the passages for irresistible grace are the same ones we used to show the inability of sinners to save themselves: John 6:44, 65 and 2 Corinthians 4:3-6. The context of the latter passage concerns two very different responses to Paul's preaching the gospel. Those who reject it give evidence that they "are perishing" (2 Cor 4:3), in whose case "the god of this age has blinded the minds of unbelievers, so that they cannot see the light of the gospel of the glory of Christ, who is the image of God" (2 Cor 4:4).

They would be hopeless except for the sovereign grace of God. Paul appeals to Genesis 1: "For God, who said, 'Let light shine out of darkness,' made his light shine in our hearts to give us the light of the knowledge of the glory of God in the face of Christ" (2 Cor 4:6). Philip Hughes explains, "As creation was irresistibly effected through the all-powerful word and will of God, so also the new creation in Christ is irresistibly effected through that same all-powerful word and will. The Creator God is one and the same with the Redeemer God."[30] God's saving grace is irresistible.

God's regeneration invariably results in faith. To believers rejected by false teachers John says, "I write these things to you who believe in the name of the Son of God so that you may know that you have eternal life" (1 Jn 5:13). John fulfills his purpose by describing the fruit of regeneration. Five times he says that those who have been born of God show it in their lives. Each time John uses the perfect tense—"has been born of God"—to show past action with ongoing results. We quote the ESV because it translates these verses consistently.[31] It is helpful to compare the verses.

---

[30]Philip Edgcumbe Hughes, "Grace," in *Evangelical Dictionary of Theology,* ed. Walter A. Elwell, 2nd ed. (Grand Rapids: Baker Academic, 2001), p. 521.

[31]The NIV disappoints because it inconsistently translates the perfect tense in one of the five passages. Its rendering of 1 John 5:1, "Everyone who believes that Jesus is the Christ is born of God," could be understood as teaching that regeneration is the result of faith.

Everyone who practices righteousness has been born of him.
(1 Jn 2:29)

He cannot keep on sinning because he has been born of God.
(1 Jn 3:9)

Whoever loves has been born of God. (1 Jn 4:7)

Everyone who believes that Jesus is the Christ has been born
of God. (1 Jn 5:1)

We know that everyone who has been born of God does not
keep on sinning. (1 Jn 5:18)

God always produces results in the lives of those who have been regenerated. John assures his readers that they *do* evidence the fruit of eternal life. Those who have been born of God are characterized by godliness
(1 Jn 2:29; 3:9; 5:18), love (4:7) and faith in Christ (5:1). The important
point for our discussion is that faith is as much a result of regeneration
as are godliness and love. "Everyone who believes that Jesus is the Christ
has been born of God" (1 Jn 5:1 ESV).

John's point is that saving faith in Christ is the result of God's regeneration. The perfect-tense verb in 1 John 5:1, "has been born," indicates
that the new birth is the cause of faith in Christ, even as the new birth is
the cause of godliness and love in the passages cited above. As a result
of God's grace in regeneration, all those who have been born of God believe savingly in the Son of God.

CONCLUSION

Arminianism holds that God gives prevenient grace to all, restoring free
will and enabling sinners to believe the gospel. Although Arminian
scholars have made biblical and theological arguments to support this,
examination reveals that the arguments are not persuasive. John 1:9 and
Romans 2:4, the two biblical passages most often cited, do not teach *universal* grace at all. Theological arguments based on God's love, the atone-

ment and synergism fare no better. The texts appealed to don't teach that God's grace enables all sinners to turn to him in faith. We conclude that the case for universal prevenient grace is unconvincing. As a result, because of the critical importance of prevenient grace to Arminian theology, that theology is guilty of assuming its conclusions. We detect a pattern of convenient exegesis of Scripture, whereby a key theological assumption (prevenient grace) determines the meaning of texts cited to support that assumption.

We affirm that there is a universal aspect to God's grace. This is common grace—God's general benevolence to all persons in the curbing of evil and granting of manifold blessings. We confess, along with Paul, that God "has not left himself without testimony: He has shown kindness by giving you rain from heaven and crops in their seasons; he provides you with plenty of food and fills your hearts with joy" (Acts 14:17). But the Bible never teaches that we are enabled by this general benevolence to exercise saving faith. Rather, in spite of God's common grace, people remain in darkness, under the powerful influence of Satan, until the Son sets them free. Common grace is not saving grace and therefore does not support the Arminian idea of universal prevenient grace.

The chief distinction between common grace and special saving grace is that the former is given indiscriminately to all but the latter is not. Special grace is given only to those whom God has chosen. For reasons known only to God, he has not chosen to save all human beings. He wants the gospel to be broadcast to all; he doesn't delight in the destruction of any, but he has ordained the salvation of billions, not all. God's predestination of his people affects their lives. By grace he irresistibly brings them to salvation. This grace is prevenient and enables salvation, but it does so not in a universal but in a particular fashion.

In at least five different ways, as we argued, the New Testament teaches that God's saving grace is invincible. If people properly understand the biblical portrayal of humanity's plight since the Fall, they will also understand the necessity of irresistible grace. There is good reason that the Canons of Dort combined human sinfulness and irresistible grace (by combining the third and fourth main points of doctrine). We are *actually* (not merely hypothetically) unable to rescue ourselves and thus need sovereign grace if we are to be saved. And that is exactly what our heavenly Father provides—unconquerable, invincible, irresistible grace.

9

ATONEMENT

Governmental or Substitutionary?

∽

We agree with the main outlines of John Wesley's theology as they summarize Christian orthodoxy, but we take issue with a number of his views, including those on predestination, inability and grace. As we turn to the doctrine of Christ's saving work, we are in a curious position, for here at our starting place we agree with Wesley against most of his theological successors. Tom Oden summarizes (with liberal quoting of Scripture) Wesley's powerful testimony to substitutionary atonement:

> Just here we stand at the "inmost mystery of the Christian faith," where "all the inventions of men ought now to be kept at the utmost distance" to allow Scripture to speak of one Mediator who has "become the guarantee of a better covenant" (Heb 7:22), who "took up our infirmities and carried our sorrows," who was "pierced for our transgressions, he was crushed for our iniquities; the punishment that brought us peace was upon him, and by his wounds we are healed." "The Lord has laid on him the iniquity of us all," who was "led like a lamb to the slaughter," who was "cut off from the land of the living; for the transgression of my people he was stricken" . . . (Isa 53:4-9). . . .

> In this way the suffering Messiah atones for the sins of the people and restores them to God's favor. "Christ redeemed us from the

curse of the law by becoming a curse for us" (Gal 3:13). "He himself bore our sins in his body on the tree, so that we might die to sins and live for righteousness" (1 Pet 2:24).[1]

Wesley clearly and strongly affirms substitutionary atonement, especially in the language of penal satisfaction. Ken Collins correctly notes: "It was neither the moral influence theory nor the ransom theory, but penal substitution in some form or other, to which Wesley continually returned."[2] Our thesis is that Wesley was correct to teach substitutionary atonement and that his heirs have erred to depart from it.

SCRIPTURE TEACHES SUBSTITUTIONARY ATONEMENT

Isaiah 53:5-6, 11b, 12b. Isaiah communicates the Servant's vicarious suffering using various images in Isaiah 53:5. "But he was pierced for our transgressions, he was crushed for our iniquities." The verbs *pierced* and *crushed* intensely portray the Servant's sufferings. His sufferings were vicarious—they were endured "for our transgressions," "for our iniquities." Next, Isaiah writes, "The punishment that brought us peace was upon him." Here is legal substitution. The Servant takes upon himself the punishment that evildoers deserve and accomplishes for them what they could not achieve—salvation ("peace"). We read finally in Isaiah 53:5, "by his wounds we are healed." Here in medicinal language, the prophet again conveys the idea of substitution. The Messiah heals others by taking their wounds upon himself.

Isaiah points to Leviticus 5 when he depicts the Servant's death as "a guilt offering" (Is 53:10). Against this background, Isaiah's words mean that God will offer the Servant as a sacrifice in his death. As the ram was the guilt offering substituted for the Old Testament worshiper, so the Messiah is the guilt offering substituted for all believers.

---

[1]Thomas C. Oden, *John Wesley's Scriptural Christianity* (Grand Rapids: Zondervan, 1994), pp. 216-17.
[2]Kenneth J. Collins, *The Scripture Way of Salvation: The Heart of John Wesley's Theology* (Nashville: Abingdon, 1997), pp. 85-86.

"The LORD has laid on him the iniquity of us all" (Is 53:6). Isaiah speaks of God laying our sins on the Servant who bears our sins; he dies instead of us who deserve to die. Also, Isaiah says the Servant "will bear their iniquities" and "bore the sin of many" (Is 53:11, 12). The Servant is the sin-bearer. Just as the Old Testament animals bore the sins of repentant worshipers who offered them in sacrifice, so the Servant bears sin and makes atonement for believers. He dies as a substitutionary sacrifice.

Again Isaiah speaks of substitution: "For the transgression of my people he was stricken" (Is 53:8). The Servant suffered unto death for the transgressions of Israel. He took the awful penalty that the Israelites should have paid when "he was stricken."

Mark 10:45. James and John selfishly asked for special favors; the other ten disciples, upon hearing of the brothers' request, "became indignant with" them (Mk 10:41). Jesus uses this occasion as an opportunity to teach his disciples: "Not so with you. Instead, whoever wants to become great among you must be your servant, and whoever wants to be first must be slave of all" (Mk 10:43-44). If the disciples aspire to places of greatness later, they must accept humble places of service now.

Jesus uses his life as an example. "For even the Son of Man did not come to be served, but to serve" (Mk 10:45). Jesus, the disciples' Lord, came not as a glorious king, but as a humble servant, who gave himself on the cross.

Next comes the ransom saying: "The Son of Man" came "to give his life as a ransom for many" (Mk 10:45). Jesus gives his life by becoming "obedient to death—even death on a cross" (Phil 2:9). He teaches that his death will be substitutionary when he speaks of giving his life "as a ransom for many." William Lane captures well the substitutionary force:

> The ransom metaphor sums up the purpose for which Jesus gave his life. . . . The prevailing notion behind the metaphor is that of deliverance by purchase. . . . Because the idea of equivalence, or substitution, was proper to the concept of a ransom, it became an integral element in the vocabulary of redemption in the OT.

The thought of substitution is reinforced by the qualifying phrase "a ransom *for the many.*" The Son of Man takes *the place* of the many, and there happens to him what would have happened to them. . . . The many forfeited their lives, and what Jesus gives in their place is his life.[3]

2 Corinthians 5:21. Luther labeled 2 Corinthians 5:21 "a happy exchange": "God made him who had no sin to be sin for us, so that in him we might become the righteousness of God." Paul affirms Christ's sinlessness when says "he . . . who knew no sin" (ESV). This qualifies him to make atonement for his people.

The verse also teaches that the Father gave his Son to save sinners: "God made him . . . to be sin for us" (2 Cor 5:21). Paul shockingly identifies the sinless Son of God with our sins. Although these words don't demand the idea of substitution, here they imply it because they complete the thought, "God made him . . . to be sin *for us.*" The Father's identifying the Son with our sin was for our benefit. The Son substituted himself for *our* sins; he died in our place.

Galatians 3:13. In Galatians Paul argues that salvation has always been by God's grace through faith, not by law keeping. "All who rely on observing the law are under a curse, for it is written: 'Cursed is everyone who does not continue to do everything written in the Book of the Law'" (Gal 3:10, quoting Deut 27:26). Here Paul continues his strategy (begun in Gal 3:6, 8) of refuting his foes by citing the Old Testament. Next he emphasizes that "clearly no one is justified before God by the law, because 'The righteous will live by *faith*'" (Gal 3:11, quoting Hab 2:4; italics added). Law corresponds not to believing but to doing, for "The man who *does* these things will live by them" (Gal 3:12, citing Lev 18:5; italics added). No one will be saved by law keeping; all who depend on the law are cursed. But how, then, can anyone be saved?

Paul answers: "Christ redeemed us from the curse of the law by be-

---

[3]William L. Lane, *The Gospel According to Mark,* New International Commentary on the New Testament (Grand Rapids: Eerdmans, 1974), pp. 383, 384.

coming a curse for us" (Gal 3:13). Paul appeals to substitution to explain *how* Christ sets free the prisoners of sin: "Christ redeemed us . . . by becoming a curse for us."[4] And he backs up his assertion with the Old Testament: "Cursed is everyone who is hung on a tree" (Gal 3:13, quoting Deut 21:23). F. F. Bruce summarizes the Old Testament context of Paul's quotation in Galatians 3:10: "The curse of Deuteronomy 27:26 was pronounced at the end of a covenant-renewal ceremony and had special reference therefore to the covenant-breaker. Christ accordingly underwent the penalty prescribed for the covenant-breaker."[5]

John Stott is emphatic: "This is probably the plainest statement in the New Testament of substitution. The curse of the broken law rested on us; Christ redeemed us from it by becoming a curse in our place. The curse that lay on us was transferred to him. He assumed it, that we might escape it."[6]

Colossians 2:13-14. God solves the problem of spiritual uncleanness by providing forgiveness: "He forgave us all our sins" (Col 2:13). Paul describes the way God forgave us, "having canceled the written code, with its regulations, that was against us and that stood opposed to us" (Col 2:14). Paul depicts the law as our enemy in the sense that it is a sin detector that "was against us and . . . stood opposed to us" (Col 2:14).

But how can a holy God cancel "the written code, with its regulations"? He cannot simply dismiss sin, waving it off by divine prerogative. Rather, "he took it away, nailing it to the cross" (Col 2:14). God removed our accuser, the law, by hammering it to Christ's cross. This is a vivid picture of legal substitution. The holy law of God, because of our disobedience, had become "a signed certificate of debt in which the signature le-

---

[4]"'For our sake' renders a Greek phrase (*hyper hēmōn*) which in itself need not mean any more than 'on our behalf'; the sense 'in our place,' however, is conceded by many scholars as at least a derived meaning warranted here by the context" (Ronald Y. K. Fung, *The Epistle to the Galatians,* New International Commentary on the New Testament [Grand Rapids: Eerdmans, 1988], p. 149).

[5]F. F. Bruce, *Commentary on Galatians,* New International Greek Testament Commentary (Grand Rapids: Eerdmans, 1982), p. 164.

[6]John Stott, *The Cross of Christ* (Downers Grove, Ill.: InterVarsity Press, 1986), p. 346.

galized the debt, a promissory note signed by the debtor.[7] God nailed the law, viewed as our bond of indebtedness, to Christ's cross. The sinless One died with our record of debt nailed to his cross.

1 Peter 3:18. Peter gives powerful incentive for his readers to live for God, regardless of the cost. "For Christ died for sins once for all, the righteous for the unrighteous, to bring you to God" (1 Pet 3:18). Jesus suffered[8] for doing good—even unto death—and he calls his people to do the same.

While presenting Christ as an example of one enduring unjust suffering patiently, Peter affirms the uniqueness of Christ's saving work when he says, "Christ died for sins *once for all*" (1 Pet 3:18; italics added). The Son of God died *once* for sins; he will not die again. His death is unique and unrepeatable. Furthermore, Jesus' death is substitutionary, for, "Christ died for sins" (1 Pet 3:18). Peter Davids explains the significance of this expression in light of its Old Testament background.

> The reason Christ suffered was "on behalf of sins." This formula was well known from the sin offerings of the OT (Lev 5:7; 6:23; Ps 39:7; Isa 53:5, 10; Ezek 43:21-25) and NT explanations of the death of Christ (Rom 8:3; 1 Cor 15:3; 1 Thess 5:10; Heb 5:3; 10:6, 8, 18, 26; 1 John 2:2; 4:10). It is the formula of substitutionary atonement, the death of the victim on behalf of the sins of another.[9]

The apostle also teaches that Christ's death made a substitutionary atonement when he writes, "the righteous for the unrighteous" (1 Pet 3:18). A literal translation of these words is, "the just one for the unjust ones." Wayne Grudem comments,

---

[7]Murray J. Harris, *Colossians and Philemon: Exegetical Guide to the Greek New Testament* (Grand Rapids: Eerdmans, 1991), p. 107. Cf. W. Bauer et al., *A Greek-English Lexicon of the New Testament and Other Early Christian Literature,* ed. Frederick Danker, 2nd ed. (Chicago: University of Chicago Press, 1979), p. 880.

[8]Many manuscripts read "suffered" instead of "died."

[9]Peter H. Davids, *The First Epistle of Peter,* New International Commentary on the New Testament (Grand Rapids: Eerdmans, 1990), p. 135.

Christ's death was *for sins,* a compressed way of saying that he paid the penalty for our sins. This is made more explicit when Peter adds *the righteous for the unrighteous.* . . . Precisely because Christ had no guilt of his own to pay for (he was "righteous"), he could be the substitute who died in our place, bearing the punishment we deserved.[10]

Conclusion. Scripture teaches that Christ's saving work involves his incarnation, sinless life, death, resurrection, ascension, session, intercession and second coming. And at the center of his saving work stands the cross. The cross accomplishes much: it propitiates God, ratifies the new covenant, reconciles and redeems sinners, is a sacrifice, defeats God's enemies and more. And at the center of the cross stands substitution, or as John Stott puts it, "substitution . . . is the heart of the atonement itself."[11]

ARMINIANS ERR IN REJECTING SUBSTITUTIONARY ATONEMENT

The Scriptures, therefore, bear abundant witness that the atonement is substitutionary. John Wesley, as we have noted, strongly affirmed substitution, yet his theological descendants, with few exceptions,[12] have not followed his lead. Ray Dunning explains, "The Atonement theory that John Wesley seemed to espouse was antithetical to his central soteriological claims."[13] Arminians reject Wesley's adoption of legal penal substitution because they believe penal substitution leads to Calvinist conclusions, including limited atonement and irresistible grace.

Matters are complicated by the fact that Arminians teach that Christ suffered as our representative, even as our substitute, but not our *penal*

---

[10]Wayne Grudem, *1 Peter,* Tyndale New Testament Commentary (Grand Rapids: Eerdmans, 1988), pp. 155-56 (italics in original).

[11]John Stott, *Cross of Christ,* pp. 202-3.

[12]Jack Cottrell is one non-Calvinist theologian who has taught substitutionary atonement. See his *What the Bible Says About God the Redeemer* (Joplin, Mo.: College Press, 1987).

[13]H. Ray Dunning, *Grace, Faith and Holiness: A Wesleyan Systematic Theology* (Kansas City, Mo.: Beacon Hill, 1988), p. 362. For a recent rejection of penal substitution, see Joel B. Green and Mark D. Baker, *Recovering the Scandal of the Cross* (Downers Grove, Ill.: InterVarsity Press, 2000).

substitute. These distinctions are best understood in light of the view that Arminians have adopted instead of Wesley's view—the governmental view of the atonement. This view, first articulated by Arminius's student Hugo Grotius, claims that Jesus did not receive the specific punishment due our sins. Rather, his death was in the best interests of God's moral government and provided a powerful example of God's hatred of sin. Arminian theologian Ken Grider explains:

> Arminians teach that what Christ did he did for every person; therefore what he did could not have been to pay the penalty, since no one would then ever go to eternal perdition. Arminianism teaches that Christ suffered for everyone so that the Father could forgive those who repent and believe; his death is such that all will see that forgiveness is costly and will strive to cease from anarchy in the world God governs. This view is called the governmental theory of the atonement. . . . Arminians assert that Scripture always states that Christ suffered (Acts 17:3; 26:23; 2 Cor 1:5; Phil 3:10; Heb 2:9-10; 13:12; 1 Pet 1:11; 2:21; 3:18; 4:1, 13)—and never that he was punished because the Christ who was crucified was guiltless and sinless. They also hold that God the Father would not be forgiving us at all if his justice was satisfied by the real thing that justice needs: punishment.[14]

The governmental view of the atonement is inadequate for a number of reasons. First, the Bible teaches both that Christ suffered and that he was punished for our sins. That is the plain sense of the Scriptures we studied earlier in this chapter. How could Scripture more clearly communicate that Christ paid the penalty for our sins than by saying that he was crushed for our iniquities, that his punishment brought us peace (Is 53:5), that God made him to be sin for us (2 Cor 5:21), that he became a curse for us (Gal 3:13), that our certificate of debt was nailed to his cross (Col 2:13-14)? It is wrong to pit suffering and punishment against

---

[14]J. Kenneth Grider, "Arminianism," in *Evangelical Dictionary of Theology*, ed. Walter A. Elwell, 2nd ed. (Grand Rapids: Baker, 2001), pp. 97-98.

each other because at times Scripture teaches that Christ saves us by enduring the suffering of punishment.

Second, the governmental view of the atonement is inadequate because of the weak sense it gives to Christ's substitution. In the final analysis, the governmental view sees Christ's death primarily as didactic, as a teaching tool. As Grider wrote, Christ's "death is such that all will see that forgiveness is costly." In this view Christ's death is a replacement (a substitute!) for a substitutionary atonement and not a substitutionary atonement itself, as Wiley explains:

> The governmental theory of the atonement, therefore, makes prominent the sacrifice of Christ as a substitute for penalty. It maintains that the death on the cross marked God's displeasure against sin, and therefore upholds the divine majesty and makes possible the forgiveness of sins. On this theory, the sacrifice of Christ is regarded as the substitute for public rather than retributive justice.[15]

Third, the governmental view of the atonement is inadequate because it insists that God the Father would not forgive us at all if he punished Christ for our sins. "It is either punishment or forgiveness, surely, not punishment and forgiveness. . . . One cannot both punish and forgive, surely."[16] To the contrary, we insist that there can be justice and forgiveness. Indeed, as we saw above, God grants us forgiveness through Christ's penal substitutionary atonement. Scripture combines God's justice (righteousness), Christ's atonement and forgiveness in one passage, when it speaks of

> Christ Jesus, whom God put forward as a propitiation by his blood, to be received by faith. This was to show God's righteousness, because in his divine forbearance he had passed over former sins. It was to show his righteousness at the present time, so that he

---

[15]H. Orton Wiley, *Christian Theology* (Kansas City, Mo.: Beacon Hill, 1941), 2:275-76.
[16]J. Kenneth Grider, *A Wesleyan-Holiness Theology* (Kansas City, Mo.: Beacon Hill, 1994), pp. 329, 331.

might be just and the justifier of the one who has faith in Jesus. (Rom 3:24-26 ESV)

Fourth, the governmental view of the atonement is inadequate because it denies the necessity of Jesus dying for sins. Since this view holds that God can forgive sin without the sinner—or Christ—paying its exact consequences, the necessity of the specific atonement provided by Christ is called into question. Grider explains:

> If we say that the Atonement provided is the only kind that was open to God, we get into an evangelical rationalism. . . .
>
> We can say only that some kind of atonement was necessary if the holy God was to forgive and cleanse us sinful human beings. We can speak of the appropriateness of the method of atonement that He chose. But God was surely free to choose the method of atonement: a different kind of death, or even a method other than death.[17]

We conclude our rejection of the governmental view of the atonement by applauding Wesley—who followed Scripture even though it meant a less than perfect theological system—and lamenting that his heirs abandoned a key biblical emphasis. We heartily endorse the words of John Stott: "Substitution is not a 'theory of the atonement.' Nor is it even an additional image to take its place as an option alongside the others. It is rather the essence of each image and the heart of the atonement itself."[18]

PARTICULAR ATONEMENT IS AN IMPLICATION OF SUBSTITUTIONARY ATONEMENT

Although we agree with Wesley against his successors that Scripture teaches substitutionary atonement, we agree with them against Wesley that substitutionary atonement fits better with limited than unlimited

---

[17]Ibid., p. 323.
[18]Stott, *Cross of Christ*, pp. 202-3; cf. Robert Letham, *The Work of Christ* (Downers Grove, Ill.: InterVarsity Press, 1993), pp. 132-39.

atonement. Unlimited atonement is the view that Christ died to make possible the salvation of every human being. Over against this is the view of limited atonement: Christ died only to save the elect. We prefer to label our position particular or definite atonement: although certain benefits of Christ's death come to everyone and although God adopts a posture of love toward a world that hates him, Christ's atonement was designed not merely to make salvation possible, but actually to secure the salvation of those whom God has chosen. It is, therefore, specifically designed to save a definite or particular people.

Weak Calvinist arguments. Calvinists have not always argued well for limited atonement. For example, Calvinists have adduced passages of Scripture that say Christ died for the church (Eph 5:25), the sheep (Jn 10:15) and others as evidence for limited atonement. But this line of reasoning is not persuasive.[19] It only stands to reason that Scripture, when talking about Christ's sheep or his church, would say Christ died for them. That does not mean that he did not die for others. But this argument could be strengthened if some Scripture passages indicated that some are excluded.

Another less than convincing argument for limited atonement involves deduction from other doctrines. For example, some argue from particular election to particular atonement. God chose some people, and not all, for salvation. Therefore, he sent his Son to atone for those he chose. However, "four-point Calvinists" agree with the premise but don't reach the same conclusion. They hold to unconditional election but reject limited atonement because they maintain that the Bible teaches unlimited atonement. It is necessary that a doctrine fit a theological system to be true; it is not sufficient, however. To be true, a doctrine must pass not only a test of logical coherence but also a test of empirical fit with the Bible's data. To be true, limited atonement must not only be systematically consistent with Calvinism; it must also be taught in Scripture.

---

[19]For more discussion of weak Calvinist proofs for limited atonement (and weak Arminian proofs for unlimited atonement), see Millard J. Erickson, *Christian Theology*, 2nd ed. (Grand Rapids: Baker, 1998), pp. 843-51.

Our experience shows that such arguments for limited atonement only convince those convinced already. What is needed is for a case to be made from Scripture, and not just from systematic theology.

Our case for particular atonement. Although substitutionary atonement is taught in numerous places in both Testaments, particular atonement is not as prominent. It is, however, implied in a number of passages that speak of Christ's substitutionary death. We will present from Scripture three pieces of evidence for definite atonement: trinitarian harmony, exclusion passages and efficacy passages.

First, we argue on the basis of trinitarian harmony from Ephesians 1:3-14. The passage divides thematically as follows: Ephesians 1:3-6: the Father's election; Ephesians 1:7-12: the Son's redemption; and Ephesians 1:13-14: the Spirit as seal.

If we follow the pronouns through the passage, a strong case can be made for trinitarian harmony in salvation. The Father "chose us . . . before the creation" for sanctification and "predestined us to be adopted as his sons" (Eph 1:4-5). Paul says about the Son, "In him we have redemption through his blood, the forgiveness of sins" (Eph 1:7). The continuity of pronouns indicates that the people whom God chooses for salvation are the same ones Christ redeems through his substitutionary atonement. The Son works in harmony with his Father. And even as the Father does not choose every human being for salvation, so the Son does not atone for everyone's sins. He atones for the sins of the elect.

The Spirit too, as God's seal on believers, works in concert with the Father and Son. The same people whom the Father predestined (Eph 1:5) the Son redeemed (Eph 1:7) and were sealed with the Spirit (Eph 1:13). The three divine persons work in harmony in salvation. But an unlimited atonement sets the Son against the Father and Spirit. For, in such a scenario, the Father chooses a particular people, he only sets the seal of the Spirit on believers, but the Son dies to redeem everyone. Robert Letham, who labels limited atonement "effective atonement" and unlimited atonement "provisional atonement," sounds the alarm:

The doctrine of the Trinity requires . . . effective atonement. . . .
This is by far the most serious problem with provisional atonement. It introduces disorder into the doctrine of God. The Father
and the Holy Spirit have different goals from the Son.[20]

Ephesians 1:3-14, therefore, presents the Father, Son and Spirit
working in unison to save their people, and this implies a definite or limited atonement.

John shows the same harmony in the work of salvation between the
Father and the Son when he reports the Son's prayer to the Father for
those whom the Father gave him, that is, those whom the Father chose.
Although the Son was Lord over all, he gave eternal life only to those the
Father gave him (Jn 17:2). The Son revealed the Father only to those the
Father gave him (Jn 17:6). The Son is in accord with the Father: "I pray
for them. I am not praying for the world, but for those you have given
me, for they are yours" (Jn 17:9-10).

The Son predicts his substitutionary atonement, "For them I sanctify
myself, that they too may be truly sanctified" (Jn 17:19). Jesus consecrates himself to his priestly work of dying on the cross for the people
the Father gave him, the elect. Why? That they might become saints,
sanctified by the Son's priestly consecration at Calvary.

Finally, the Son asks the Father to bring to heavenly glory the ones
whom the Father had given him (Jn 17:24). John portrays a harmony between the Father and Son. The Son works as mediator and redeemer for
the ones the Father gave him, the people he chose for salvation. To them
alone the Son reveals the Father and gives eternal life; for them alone he
prays; he asks the Father to take them alone to heaven. And for them
alone the Son consecrates himself in death in order to sanctify them in salvation (Jn 17:19). This implies a particular atonement, designed to save
those whom the Father gave to the Son. An unlimited atonement, by contrast, would disrupt the harmony between Father and Son and put them

---

[20]Letham, *Work of Christ*, p. 237.

at odds: the Father choosing some and the Son dying to save all.

Our second piece of evidence for particular atonement is the occurrence of exclusions in substitutionary atonement passages. It is true that for biblical passages to say that Jesus died for the church or his sheep does not prove that he did not die for others. But for those same passages to contain exclusionary elements is another matter. In John 10, Jesus twice says that he lays down his life for the sheep (Jn 10:11, 15). And yet he declares to the Jewish leaders, "You do not believe because you are not my sheep" (Jn 10:26). That is, Jesus follows his statements about dying for his sheep by a stark denial that some are his sheep. It would be difficult to maintain that he lays down his life to save them, for he just excluded them from the number of his sheep.

Exclusions also appear in John 17. Though the Father gave Jesus "authority over all people," Jesus gives eternal life only to those the Father gave him (Jn 17:2). And, although God loves the world (Jn 3:16), in John 17 Jesus does not pray for "the world"; he prays for those the Father gave him (Jn 17:9). And, as we saw above, the Son makes atonement for the same people (Jn 17:19). In light of the exclusions in John 17:2 and 9, it is implied that Jesus' consecration of himself for "them" (Jn 17:19), includes those the Father gave him and excludes "the world" (Jn 17:9). That is, within the context of Jesus' prayer, he excludes some from eternal life. When he speaks of dying for the elect, we are correct in excluding from those whom the Father gave him those whom Jesus himself excludes.

Our third piece of evidence for particular atonement concerns the efficacy of the cross. Does Scripture present Christ's substitutionary atonement as *potential,* making possible the salvation of all, or as *effective,* securing the salvation of God's people? We will argue for the latter based on Revelation 5:9. Christ, the Lion and the Lamb, takes the scroll and is worshiped as the elders and living creatures prostrate themselves before him and sing this song:

> You are worthy to take the scroll
>   and to open its seals,

because you were slain,
>   and with your blood you purchased men for God
>   from every tribe and language and people and nation.
> You made them to be a kingdom and priests to serve our God,
>   and they will reign on the earth. (Rev 5:9)

The Lamb was "slain," that is, slaughtered in his sacrifice on the cross. John explains what the Lamb's unique sacrifice accomplishes: with his blood he purchased human beings.

Notice the results of the Lamb's redeeming work. The song says, "with your blood you purchased *men* for God from every tribe and language and people and nation" (Rev 5:9; italics added). The italicized word is supplied. This is a partitive construction: the preposition "from" introduces the whole out of which what precedes is a part. So translations must supply a word (marked by italics) to indicate the part:

You purchased *men* for God from every tribe. (NIV)
You ransomed for God *saints* from every tribe. (NRSV)
You ransomed *people* for God from every tribe. (ESV)
You bought *men* for God of every race. (JB)
You purchased for God *men* from every tribe. (NASB)
You bought for God *people* from every tribe. (CEV)

The point is that Jesus via his substitutionary atonement redeemed a part of the human race out of the bigger whole, "every tribe and language and people and nation." Christ's atonement here is not potential, but actual; his blood purchases people for God from among the nations. The words "tribe, language, people and nation" refer to the same entity—humankind from the perspectives of people group, tongue, location and political entity, respectively. Here John helps us understand the meaning of Christ's dying for "the world" and "all" in Scripture. Christ ransoms people out of "every tribe and language and people and nation," that is, from out of the world. This verse does not teach a universal but a particular atonement. It doesn't say that Christ died for every human being; it says that he died for people from every nation. The concept of "world" here, therefore, is collective rather than distributive. Christ died for the world—understood as all without distinction, not all without exception. Such an interpretation is impossible because Christ's blood actually delivers people *out of* every tribe and so on.

This suggests that we are justified in understanding *world* in other atonement passages in a collective rather than a distributive sense. The Lamb redeemed persons from "every tribe and language and people and nation." He died to redeem persons in "every tribe," including Masai, Zulu, Yoruba, Xhosa, Tutsi and Hutu. He died to redeem persons in "every language," including Japanese, Korean, Indonesian and Tagalog. He died to redeem persons among "every people," including those born in mainland China, Taiwanese and American-born Chinese, among others. He died to redeem persons in "every nation," including Mexico, Brazil, Peru and Chile.

To recapitulate: we believe in particular substitutionary atonement because Scripture implies it when it speaks of Father, Son and Spirit working harmoniously to save the people of God (Eph 1:3-14; Jn 17:2, 6, 9-10, 19, 24; cf. 1 Pet 1:1-2). We hold to definite atonement because sometimes when the Bible speaks of Christ's saving death, it excludes some persons (John 10:11, 15, 26; 17:2, 9, 19). We teach limited atonement because Scripture describes the cross as effective, not making salvation possible for all, but actually securing salvation for multitudes (Rev 5:9; cf. 1 Pet 1:18-19).

Arminian objections to particular atonement. Arminian arguments for unlimited atonement and criticisms of limited atonement overlap. We will examine four important ones and thereby clarify our case for definite atonement.[21]

First, Arminians point to passages that say Christ died for "the world" or "all" in an attempt to prove unlimited atonement. Representative among these are:

---

[21]These examples are from Wiley, *Christian Theology*, 2:296, and Erickson, *Christian Theology*, pp. 846-49.

We all, like sheep, have gone astray,
  each of us has turned to his own way;
and the LORD has laid on him
  the iniquity of us all. (Is 53:6)

We have put our hope in the living God, who is the Savior of all men, and especially of those who believe. (1 Tim 4:10)

He is the atoning sacrifice for our sins, and not only for ours but also for the sins of the whole world. (1 Jn 2:2)

The pronouns "we" and "us" in Isaiah 53:6 refer not to all people but to Israelites. This is confirmed by Isaiah's reference to "my people," the nation of Israel, in Isaiah 53:8. Isaiah 53:6 means all we Israelites have strayed like sheep and the Lord has laid on the suffering servant the iniquity of all us Israelites. Thus, contextually considered, Isaiah 53:6 is not a good proof text for unlimited atonement.

The same is true for 1 Timothy 4:10. Ironically, this verse does not refer to Christ or his cross. We say this because of the way the word *Savior* is used in the pastoral epistles, where it occurs ten times. When it refers to God the Father, it appears without Christ's name: "God our Savior" (1 Tim 1:1; 2:3; Tit 1:3; 2:10; 3:4) and "the living God, who is the Savior of all men" (1 Tim 4:10). But when it refers to Christ, his name is used: "our Savior, Christ Jesus" (2 Tim 1:10), "Christ Jesus our Savior" (Tit 1:4), "our great God and Savior, Jesus Christ" (Tit 2:13), and "Jesus Christ our Savior" (Tit 3:6). Because *Savior* appears without qualification in 1 Timothy 4:10, it speaks of God the Father and not of Christ and thus is not a good proof text for unlimited atonement.

First John 2:2 is a better proof text, for it speaks of Christ being "the atoning sacrifice for our sins, and not only for ours but also for the sins of the whole world." A universal dimension of Christ's work is plainly in view. The apostle John, a Jewish Christian, says that Christ's atonement was not only for his fellow Jews but also for Gentiles. We say this because of the only other reference to "the whole world" in 1 John: "We know that we are children of God, and that the whole world is under the control of the evil one" (1 Jn 5:19). Here "the whole world" is in contrast to "children of God" and refers not to every person but to sinners viewed collectively as God's enemies. First John 2:2 means that Christ atoned for "the whole world," that is, for the world viewed as a whole, for Gentiles as well as Jews, but not necessarily for each and every Jew or Gentile.

Second, Arminians cite as evidence for unlimited atonement texts that teach that some for whom Christ died will perish. These include: Romans 14:15, 1 Corinthians 8:11 and 2 Peter 2:1. The first two references are not good proofs for unlimited atonement. Paul deals with the same theme in Romans 14 and 1 Corinthians 8—Christian freedom in the matter of eating or not eating certain foods. Paul appeals to stronger Christians who have no scruples about eating "unclean" (nonkosher) foods (Rom 14:15) or foods sacrificed to idols (1 Cor 8:11). In both cases he warns them against flaunting their Christian liberty to the hurt of weaker believers: "Do not by your eating destroy your brother for whom Christ died" (Rom 14:15); "So this weak brother, for whom Christ died, is destroyed by your knowledge" (1 Cor 8:11). There is not clear evidence that the destruction spoken of in Romans 14:15 and 1 Corinthians 8:11 refers to hell. In fact, it is likely that those two verses warn of the "judgment" mentioned elsewhere in 1 Corinthians—not damnation but fatherly discipline involving weakness, sickness or death (1 Cor 11:30, 32). Erickson, who holds to unlimited atonement, agrees.[22]

Second Peter 2:1 is a difficult text for those who support limited atonement because it seems to teach that Christ died for false prophets: "But there were also false prophets among the people, just as there will be false teachers among you. They will secretly introduce destructive heresies, even denying the sovereign Lord who bought them." Wayne Grudem summarizes the best Calvinist treatment, that of John Gill in 1735:

---

[22]Erickson, *Christian Theology*, p. 850.

When Peter speaks of false teachers who bring in destructive heresies, "even denying the Master who bought them" (2 Peter 2:1), it is unclear whether the word "Master" (Gk. δεσπότης) refers to Christ (as in Jude 4) or to God the Father (as in Luke 2:29; Acts 4:24; Rev. 6:10). In either case, the Old Testament allusion is probably to Deuteronomy 32:6, where Moses says to the rebellious people who have turned away from God, "Is not he your Father *who has bought you?*" (author's translation). Peter is drawing an analogy between the past false prophets who arose among the Jews and those who will be false teachers within the churches. . . . From the time of the exodus onward, any Jewish person would have considered himself or herself one who was "bought" by God in the exodus and therefore a person of God's own possession. In this sense, the false teachers arising among the people were denying God their Father, to whom they rightfully belonged. So the text means not that Christ redeemed these false prophets, but simply that they were rebellious Jewish people (or church attenders in the same position as the rebellious Jews) who were rightly owned by God because they had been brought out of the land of Egypt (or their forefathers had), but they were ungrateful to him. Christ's specific redemptive work on the cross is not in view in this verse.[23]

Third, Arminians contend that divine commands to preach the gospel to every person—including Matthew 28:19-20 and Acts 1:8—are incompatible with the idea of a limited atonement and imply an unlimited atonement.

We agree that God commands us to take the gospel to the ends of the earth and to every person in it. We are embarrassed that at times Reformed Christians have not been as zealous as others to propagate the gospel. But we deny that there is a necessary connection between Calvinism and a lack of evangelistic zeal. Indeed, we cite as evidence of the

---

[23]Wayne Grudem, *Systematic Theology* (Grand Rapids: Zondervan, 1994), p. 600.

compatibility of belief in limited atonement and a fire for spreading the gospel Jonathan Edwards, George Whitefield, Asahel Nettleton, Charles H. Spurgeon and Francis Schaeffer.

Fourth, Arminians argue that limited atonement contradicts scriptural declarations of God's universal love in John 3:16-17, Romans 5:8 and elsewhere. This too, by implication they claim, is an argument for unlimited atonement.

Romans 5:8 is not a good text to show God's universal love because in context it speaks of God's love for Christians before they believed. It is easily harmonized with the Calvinistic idea of God's unique love for the elect. But John 3:16-17 teaches that God loves all sinners, a truth unfortunately not endorsed by all Calvinists. Scripture compels us to teach that God loves people in three different senses. First, he loves each person by virtue of common grace. This love preserves the human race but does not save anyone. Second, he loves his elect by planning their salvation, accomplishing it in Christ and applying it to them by the Holy Spirit. Also, we hold that God loves people in a third sense, the one we would attribute to John 3:16-17. Although the world hates God, the Bible depicts God's posture toward all sinners as one of love, as D. A. Carson explains:

> *God's salvific stance toward his fallen world.* God so loved *the world* that he gave his Son (John 3:16). I know that some try to take κόσμος ("world") here to refer to the elect. But that really will not do. All the evidence of the usage of the word in John's Gospel is against the suggestion. True, *world* in John does not so much refer to bigness as to badness. In John's vocabulary, *world* is primarily the moral order in willful and culpable rebellion against God. In John 3:16 God's love in sending the Lord Jesus is to be admired not because it is extended to so big a thing as the world, but to so bad a thing; not to so many people, as to such wicked people. . . . On this axis, God's love for the world cannot be collapsed into his love for the elect.[24]

---

[24]D. A. Carson, *The Difficult Doctrine of the Love of God* (Wheaton, Ill.: Crossway, 2000), p. 17 (italics in original).

Carson distinguishes this sense from "God's particular, effective, selecting love toward his elect,"[25] the second sense of God's love for people listed above. We agree that Scripture speaks of the saving love of God for human beings in these two distinguishable senses: God's gracious posture toward a world that hates him and God's special effective love for his chosen ones. We admit that Calvinists have not always admitted the first sense and sometimes have resorted to forced exegesis of passages such as John 3:16.

We agree, therefore, with Arminians that John 3:16 and similar texts speak of God's love for every person. We understand these passages to teach that God assumes a saving posture toward his fallen world. When asked how we reconcile these passages with those that teach God's special love for the elect, we admit that our theology contains rough edges. But we would rather have an imperfect theology and be faithful to the whole witness of Scripture than to mute the voice of some texts as Calvinists have sometimes done (John 3:16 and similar passages) and as Arminians do (the texts that teach God's special love for the elect). Carson sounds a needed word of caution:

> If the love of God is exclusively portrayed as an inviting, yearning, sinner-seeking, rather lovesick passion, we may strengthen the hands of Arminians, semi-Pelagians, Pelagians, and those more interested in God's inner emotional life than in his justice and glory, but the cost will be massive. There is some truth in this picture of God, as we shall see, some glorious truth. Made absolute, however, it not only treats complementary texts as if they were not there, but it steals God's sovereignty from him and our security from us. . . .
>
> If the love of God refers exclusively to this love for the elect, it is easy to drift toward a simple and absolute bifurcation: God loves the elect and hates the reprobate. Rightly positioned, there is truth to this assertion; stripped of complementary biblical truths, that same assertion has engendered hyper-Calvinism. I use the term ad-

---

[25]Ibid., p. 18.

visedly, referring to groups within the Reformed tradition that have forbidden the free offer of the Gospel.[26]

We affirm that biblical passages dealing with the cross are of two types. Some speak of God's loving stance toward an evil world and others speak of his effective love only for the elect. We choose to hold the two types of atonement passages in creative tension—as Scripture does. The alternatives to doing so are to blunt the force of one of the two types of atonement texts. But these two solutions are rationalistic because they affirm some biblical data and suppress other equally biblical data.

Furthermore, we do not regard this problem as insoluble for the mind of God. If we are correct that God has revealed both types of atonement passages in his Word, then they do not pose a problem for God. But we admit that our present state of knowledge prohibits us from explaining how God can love all persons savingly in the one sense and only love some savingly in another sense.

CONCLUSION

We affirmed in this chapter that one foundational biblical teaching is substitutionary atonement, as taught in Isaiah 53:5-6, 11, 12; Mark 10:45; 2 Corinthians 5:21; Galatians 3:13; Colossians 2:13-14; and 1 Peter 3:18. Christ died in the place of his people, bearing the penalty that their sins deserved.

Next we argued that the Arminian tradition strayed when it moved away from Wesley's doctrine of substitutionary atonement and instead adopted the governmental view. We found that view inadequate because it substitutes a weak sense of substitution for the biblical sense of penal substitution, teaches that the Father forgives us without punishing the Son for our sins and denies the necessity of the atonement.

Then, we argued that substitutionary atonement implies a particular (limited) rather than an indefinite (unlimited) atonement. Particular

---

[26]Ibid., p. 22.

atonement reflects the Bible's emphasis on trinitarian harmony in salvation (Eph 1:3-14; Jn 17:19), accounts for passages that exclude some from Christ's saving work (Jn 10:11, 15, 26; 17:2, 9, 19) and expresses the efficacy of the cross (Rev 5:9). By contrast, unlimited atonement disrupts the harmony of the Trinity, cannot accommodate places where the Bible excludes some from the atonement, and affirms a potential, rather than an effective, atonement.

Finally, we responded to Arminian objections to definite atonement and in the process affirmed that Christ died for all in a collective sense (all without distinction) rather than in a distributive sense (all without exception). We lamented the fact that Calvinists have not always been zealous for evangelism, but we cited examples of famous Calvinist evangelists as proof that there is not a necessary connection between limited atonement and a lack of gospel zeal. We also affirmed that the Bible teaches two seemingly contradictory, but ultimately complementary, truths: (1) God loves a sinful world, and (2) he has a special effective love only for the elect. Only by affirming these two truths simultaneously do we do justice to scriptural teaching. If we refuse to hold the two truths in tension and downplay the first, we err in the direction of hyper-Calvinism; if we downplay the second, we err in the direction of Arminianism.

It is fitting for us to conclude with Zinzendorf's stirring hymn that John Wesley translated in 1740, "Jesus, Thy Blood and Righteousness."

Jesus, thy blood and righteousness
My beauty are, my glorious dress;
'Midst flaming worlds, in these arrayed,
With joy shall I lift up my head.

Bold shall I stand in thy great day,
For who aught to my charge shall lay?
Fully absolved through these I am,
From sin and fear, from guilt and shame.

When from the dust of death I rise
To claim my mansion in the skies,
Ev'n then this shall by all my plea,
Jesus hath lived, hath died, for me.

Jesus, be endless praise to thee,
Whose boundless mercy hath for me—
For me a full atonement made,
An everlasting ransom paid.

O let the dead now hear thy voice;
Now bid thy banished ones rejoice;
Their beauty this, their glorious dress,
Jesus, thy blood and righteousness.[27]

---

[27]Nikolaus Ludwig von Zinzendorf, 1739; translated by John Wesley, 1740.

Names Index

Arminius, Jacobus, 9, 15, 39, 93, 94, 98, 99, 100, 101, 102, 103, 104, 105, 106, 107, 108, 109, 110, 111, 112, 113, 114, 115, 116, 119, 135, 137, 153, 160, 173, 199

Augustine, bishop of Hippo, 19, 20, 21, 22, 23, 24, 25, 26, 27, 28, 29, 30, 31, 32, 33, 34, 35, 36, 37, 38, 39, 40, 41, 92, 95, 120, 128, 132, 173

Bangs, Carl, 100, 101, 105, 106, 109, 110

Berkouwer, G. C., 144

Beza, Theodore, 9, 93, 94, 95, 96, 97, 99, 101, 103, 160

Brown, Harold O. J., 31, 97, 98

Burson, Scott, 138, 140, 153, 155, 160

Calvin, John, 82, 92, 93, 94, 95, 98, 120, 142, 143, 149, 162, 163, 164, 165, 173

Carson, D. A., 137, 147, 148, 149, 159, 160, 179, 181, 211, 212

Cassian, John, 35, 37, 39

Collins, Kenneth J., 162, 163, 164, 165, 174, 176, 193

Dunning, Ray, 15, 42, 62, 141, 143, 144, 165, 173, 179, 181, 198

Episcopus, Simon, 111, 112

Feinberg, John, 139, 143, 151, 152, 158

Frame, John, 97, 98, 113, 114, 138, 143, 144, 153, 154, 157, 158

Gomarus, Franciscus, 99, 100, 101, 111

Grider, J. Kenneth, 15, 43, 56, 62, 65, 117, 175, 176, 177, 183, 199, 200, 201

Grotius, Hugo, 199

Hasker, William, 105, 117

Helm, Paul, 146

Hughes, Philip E., 9, 72, 73, 83, 88, 188

Klein, William W., 42, 52

Marshall, I. Howard, 52, 74, 75, 76, 77

McKnight, Scot, 82, 83, 88

Molina, Luis de, 106, 107

Muller, Richard, 94, 99, 101, 106, 107, 108, 135

Nicole, Roger, 82, 83, 86

Oden, Thomas C., 163, 174, 192, 193

Olson, Roger, 28

Osborne, Grant R., 49, 74, 75, 76, 77, 167

Packer, James I., 9, 26, 171, 172

Pelagius, 19, 20, 21, 22, 23, 28, 32, 33, 34, 35, 36, 39, 41, 92

Pinnock, Clark, 42, 49, 58, 67, 74, 75, 105, 139, 167, 179

Schreiner, Thomas R., 55, 99, 139, 145, 178, 184

Stott, John, 196, 198, 201

Suárez, Francisco, 106

Thomas Aquinas, 94, 107, 120

Uytenbogaert, Hans, 112

Vincent of Lérins, 35, 36, 39

Walls, Jerry, 138, 140, 153, 155, 160

Wesley, John, 15, 162, 163, 164, 165, 173, 174, 175, 176, 177, 181, 192, 193, 198, 199, 201, 213, 214, 215

Wiley, H. Orton, 15, 42, 62, 65, 109, 110, 117, 141, 165, 200, 207

Subject Index

ability, 17, 18, 21, 23, 24, 26, 27, 29, 31, 32, 34, 35, 36, 41, 60, 105, 109, 110, 117, 135, 139, 140, 146, 153, 154, 155, 156, 160, 174, 175, 179, 182

apostasy, 67, 74, 76, 80, 81, 82, 83, 84, 85, 87, 88, 89, 90, 91, 114, 118, 156

Arminian-Calvinist controversy (seventeenth century), 19

atonement, 19, 72, 78, 85, 120, 121, 129, 179, 181, 193, 194, 195, 197, 198, 199, 200, 201, 202, 203, 204, 205, 206, 207, 208, 209, 211, 213, 214, 215

  governmental view of, 199, 200, 201, 213

  particular (limited), 10, 11, 12, 15, 29, 35, 42, 95, 100, 103, 104, 107, 108, 109, 111, 114, 119, 120, 129, 134, 136, 139, 168, 173, 178, 185, 190, 198, 202, 203, 204, 205, 206, 207, 209, 210, 211, 212, 213, 214

  substitutionary, 192, 193, 197, 198, 200, 201, 203, 204, 205, 206, 207, 213

  universal (unlimited), 119, 202, 203, 204, 207, 208, 209, 210, 211, 214

Augustinianism, 40

Augustinian-Pelagian controversy, 20, 40

Canons of Dort, 93, 119, 123, 124, 125, 126, 127, 128, 129, 133, 134, 135, 159, 190

compatibilism, 19, 137, 142, 144, 152, 159

Contra-Remonstrants, 10

decretal theology, 96, 100, 103

divine sovereignty, 30, 101, 111, 127, 132, 135, 136, 137, 138, 142, 143, 144, 145, 146, 147, 151, 152, 153, 160

  and human freedom, 14, 27, 42, 60, 64, 99, 103, 106, 107, 108, 111, 135, 136, 137, 138, 140, 143, 144, 145, 152, 154

Dort, Synod of (1618-1619), 10, 13, 19, 92, 93, 112, 119, 123, 124, 129, 130, 135, 185

effectual calling, 166

election

  conditional, 42, 44, 54, 101, 119, 121, 202

evangelism, 53, 172, 214

Five Arminian Articles, 112

five points of Arminianism, 119, 120, 123

five points of Calvinism, 119

foreknowledge (of God), 54, 55, 56, 75, 104, 105, 106, 130, 150, 158, 187

free will, 21, 24, 25, 26, 32, 35, 36, 61, 62, 99, 105, 106, 108, 109, 110, 111, 114, 115, 117, 118, 119, 120, 126, 128, 130, 135,

136, 138, 141, 143, 151, 156, 170, 174, 175, 189

  and contingent agents, 105

  libertarian, 27, 41, 105, 117, 138, 139, 141, 143, 145, 151, 152, 153, 154, 155, 156, 157, 158

grace, 13, 14, 17, 18, 19, 20, 21, 22, 23, 27, 28, 29, 30, 31, 32, 33, 34, 35, 36, 37, 38, 39, 40, 41, 47, 48, 57, 65, 66, 79, 81, 82, 86, 87, 89, 90, 92, 96, 104, 108, 109, 110, 112, 113, 115, 116, 117, 118, 119, 120, 122, 125, 126, 127, 128, 129, 130, 131, 132, 133, 134, 140, 141, 155, 161, 163, 164, 165, 170, 171, 173, 174, 175, 176, 177, 178, 179, 181, 182, 183, 184, 185, 186, 187, 188, 189, 190, 191, 192, 195

  common, 125, 174, 190, 211

  irresistible, 29, 185, 186, 188, 190, 191, 198

  prevenient, 27, 29, 38, 81, 108, 109, 110, 115, 116, 117, 119, 120, 128, 130, 140, 169, 171, 173, 174, 175, 176, 177, 178, 179, 180, 181, 182, 183, 184, 185, 186, 189, 190

  resistible, 120

  universal, 180, 189

Heidelberg Catechism, 100
hyper-Calvinism, 212, 214
inability, 9, 19, 23, 29, 108,
  117, 118, 120, 124, 162,
  163, 164, 165, 166, 168,
  169, 170, 171, 174, 175,
  184, 188, 192
incompatibilism, 19, 136,
  137, 138, 140, 144, 145,
  146, 152, 154
infralapsarianism, 98, 102
libertarianism, 138, 155,
  157, 158
middle knowledge (scientia
  media), 106, 107, 108
monergism, 28, 36, 38, 39,
  41, 122, 183
open theism, 158
Orange, Synod of (529
  A.D.), 37, 38, 40
particular atonement, 114,

129, 202, 203, 204, 205,
  206, 207
Pelagianism, 21, 37, 39, 40
perseverance of the saints,
  41, 67
preceding grace, 38, 109,
  175, 176, 182
predestination, 19, 21, 30,
  35, 38, 41, 43, 50, 52,
  53, 54, 56, 57, 62, 63,
  65, 75, 95, 96, 98, 99,
  100, 102, 104, 105, 111,
  112, 120, 130, 185, 186,
  190, 192
  doctrine of, 37, 38, 42,
    94, 97, 100, 101, 120
  double predestination,
    30, 95
  temporal, 56, 65
provisional atonement,
  203, 204

Remonstrants, 9, 10, 112,
  115, 133
reprobation, 96, 97, 98,
  102, 104, 120, 122, 131,
  132
Semi-Augustinianism, 39,
  40
supralapsarianism, 96, 97,
  98, 100, 101, 102, 113,
  122, 124, 132
synergism, 36, 37, 38, 40,
  109, 110, 122, 175, 183,
  190
will of God, 24, 25, 33, 37,
  38, 87, 93, 94, 95, 96,
  103, 108, 111, 142, 149,
  150, 188
  antecedent, 103, 104,
    110, 130
  consequent, 130

Scripture Index

Genesis
1, *143, 188*
1:26-28, *157*
6:3, *183*
6:5, *163*
6:11, *163*
12:1, *46*
12:1-3, *43*
12:3, *47, 64*
15:1, *43, 46*
15:6, *43*
17:7, *43, 46*
20:6, *174*
22:2, *46*
25:21-22, *44*
25:23, *44, 46*
25:31-33, *47*
26:7, *47*
27:19, *47*
27:24, *47*
27:35, *47*
28:15, *44*
31:20, *47*
31:31, *47*
33:3, *47*
33:8, *47*
35:9-15, *47*
37:12-36, *147*
39:7-20, *147*
45:5-8, *147*
50:20, *147*

Exodus
4:21, *158*
7:3, *158*
8:15, *151, 158*
8:32, *151*
9:12, *151, 158*
9:34, *151*
10:1, *151, 158*
10:20, *151*
12:36, *141*

Leviticus
5, *193*
5:7, *197*
6:23, *197*
18:5, *195*
20:7-8, *151*

Deuteronomy
4:37, *45, 48, 64*
7:6, *46, 48*
7:6-8, *45, 64*
7:7, *45, 48, 65*
7:7-8, *46*
7:8, *48, 65*
10:14-15, *45, 46, 64*
10:15, *46, 48*
14:2, *46, 48*
17:2-3, *85*
21:23, *196*
27:26, *195, 196*
29:29, *48*
30:19, *156*
32:4, *158*
32:6, *210*
32:35, *86*
32:36, *86*

Joshua
24:2-3, *43, 47, 64*

1 Samuel
2:6-7, *142*
2:12-15, *158*

2 Samuel
16:5-10, *158*
24:1, *158*

1 Kings
8:46-61, *151*

11:11-39, *151*
12:1-15, *151*
22:21-28, *158*

Job
38—42, *159*

Psalms
8:4, *157*
33:10-11, *141*
33:15, *141*
37:23, *142*
39:7, *197*
45:6-12, *141*
47:1-9, *141*
65:9-11, *141*
95:3, *141*
104:10-30, *141*
107:23-32, *141*
135:5-7, *141*
145:15, *174*
145:15-16, *141*
145:16, *174*
147:15-18, *141*

Proverbs
16:4, *158*
16:9, *141*
16:33, *141*
19:21, *141*
21:1, *141*

Isaiah
5:20, *22*
10, *148*
10:5-6, *148*
10:7, *148*
10:12, *149*
10:13-14, *148*
10:15, *149*
45:6-7, *158*
53:5, *193, 199*

53:5-6, *193, 213*
53:6, *194, 208*
53:8, *194, 208*
53:10, *193*
53:11, *193, 194, 213*
53:12, *194, 213*
64:6, *31*

Lamentations
3:37-38, *158*

Ezekiel
18:23, *129*
18:32, *129*
43:21-25, *197*

Habakkuk
1:12-13, *159*
2:3-4, *87*
2:4, *195*

Malachi
1:2, *47*
1:2-3, *44*

Matthew
5:45, *141*
6:26-30, *141*
7:15-20, *155*
7:21-23, *88*
7:23, *55, 70, 90*
12:33-35, *155*
17:12, *156*
22:14, *49*
24:22, *48*
24:24, *48*
24:31, *48*
25:41, *70*
28:19, *129*
28:19-20, *210*

Mark
10:41, *194*
10:43-44, *194*
10:45, *194, 213*
13, *48*
13:20, *48*
13:22, *48*
13:26-27, *49*
14:49, *145*

Luke
2:29, *210*
6:45, *155*
18:7-8, *49*
22:22, *151*
22:31-32, *67, 74*
22:32, *67*
22:33-34, *67*
24:47, *129*

John
1:3-5, *177*
1:9, *174, 176, 177,
  189*
1:10, *177*
1:10-11, *177*
1:12-13, *177*
1:14, *177*
1:29, *179, 181*
2:2, *114, 208, 209*
3, *29*
3:2, *29*
3:16, *114, 179, 205,
  211, 212*
3:16-17, *211*
3:36, *112*
5:24, *73*
6:1-15, *49*
6:25-59, *49*
6:35, *49, 68, 166,
  185*
6:35-45, *49, 165*
6:36, *49*
6:37, *49, 50, 52, 65,
  68, 73, 74, 165,
  166, 185*
6:37-40, *64, 151*

6:39, *65, 68, 74,
  166, 185*
6:39-40, *68, 74*
6:40, *68, 166*
6:41, *186*
6:43, *186*
6:43-44, *166*
6:44, *68, 74, 165,
  166, 167, 171,
  186, 188*
6:45, *166*
6:48-58, *165*
6:54, *165, 166*
6:62, *165*
6:65, *165, 166, 167,
  171, 186, 188*
6:66, *80*
6:70, *50, 51, 79*
6:71, *80*
8:28, *154*
8:34-36, *155*
10, *118, 205*
10:11, *205, 207,
  214*
10:14, *55*
10:15, *202, 205,
  207, 214*
10:25-27, *50*
10:26, *129, 205,
  207, 214*
10:26-27, *50*
10:26-30, *50*
10:27-30, *68*
10:28, *65, 68, 74*
10:28-29, *76, 77*
10:29, *68, 73*
12:20-22, *167*
12:23-28, *167*
12:32, *166*
12:33, *167*
13:5, *115*
15, *79, 80*
15:2, *78*
15:4-5, *78*
15:4-9, *78*
15:5, *115*
15:6, *78*

15:7, *78*
15:8, *79*
15:9, *78, 79, 81, 90*
15:10, *79*
15:12, *78, 79, 81,
  90*
15:14, *79*
15:14-19, *50*
15:16, *50, 51, 64,
  79, 80, 90*
15:17, *78, 79, 81,
  90*
15:18-19, *51*
15:19, *51, 80*
17, *68, 205*
17:1-2, *52*
17:2, *51, 65, 204,
  205, 207, 214*
17:6, *51, 65, 185,
  204, 207*
17:7-8, *51*
17:9, *51, 65, 185,
  205, 207, 214*
17:9-10, *51, 204,
  207*
17:11, *185*
17:15, *68*
17:19, *204, 205,
  207, 214*
17:24, *51, 65, 204,
  207*

Acts
1:8, *210*
2:10-11, *59*
2:23, *150, 158*
3:13-15, *150*
3:18, *150*
4:24, *210*
4:27-28, *150*
7, *116*
13:27, *150*
13:42-44, *52*
13:45-46, *52*
13:47-49, *52*
13:48, *52, 53, 64,
  65, 186*

13:50-51, *52*
14:17, *190*
16:14, *187*
16:15, *187*
17:3, *199*
17:26, *135, 141*
17:28, *135*
18:5-8, *53*
18:9, *53*
18:9-10, *52, 151*
18:9-11, *65*
18:10, *53*
18:11, *53*
18:27, *187*
20:24, *187*
26:23, *199*
27:22-44, *151*

Romans
1—8, *178*
1:16, *59*
2:1-3, *178*
2:4, *177, 178, 189*
2:9, *59*
2:10, *59*
3, *59*
3:24-26, *201*
3:29, *59*
4:19, *60*
5, *25, 162*
5:6, *69*
5:8, *69, 211*
5:9, *69*
5:9-10, *69, 73*
5:10, *69*
5:12, *124, 162*
5:17-21, *179*
5:18, *182*
5:18-19, *182*
5:19, *162, 182*
6:15-23, *155*
7, *99*
8:3, *197*
8:6, *163*
8:8, *163*
8:28, *54, 75, 161,
  187*

8:28-30, *54, 74, 77*
8:28-39, *69*
8:29, *54, 55, 56, 64,*
65, 75, 90
8:29-30, *54, 65, 70,*
75, 186, 187
8:30, *65, 73*
8:31, *70*
8:31-32, *73*
8:32, *70*
8:33, *70, 73*
8:34, *68, 70, 74*
8:35, *70*
8:35-39, *73*
8:38-39, *71*
8:39, *71*
9, *63, 64, 99*
9—11, *59*
9:6, *60, 61*
9:6-9, *60*
9:6-13, *61*
9:6-23, *62*
9:6-24, *54, 59, 63*
9:6-29, *60*
9:8, *60*
9:9, *60*
9:10-13, *44, 60, 63,*
64
9:11, *56, 61*
9:11-12, *45, 47*
9:11-13, *47, 61*
9:13, *44, 63, 65*
9:14, *61*
9:14-15, *61*
9:15, *63, 65*
9:15-16, *63*
9:16, *61, 63, 64,*
65
9:17, *61*
9:17-18, *151*
9:17-24, *159*
9:18, *61, 63, 65*
9:19, *61*
9:19-24, *63, 65*
9:20, *62*
9:21, *62*
9:22-23, *62, 63*

9:22-24, *64, 159*
9:23, *63, 65*
9:23-24, *63*
9:24, *59, 63, 65*
9:30—10:21, *60*
10, *64*
10:12, *59*
11:1-32, *60*
11:13, *59*
11:25, *180*
11:30-32, *180*
11:32, *179, 180*
11:33, *30*
14, *209*
14:2, *59*
14:5, *59*
14:14, *59*
14:15, *209*
14:19, *59*
15:7, *59*
16:20, *185*

1 Corinthians
2, *168*
2:1, *168*
2:2, *168*
2:4, *168*
2:6, *168*
2:7, *168*
2:8, *169*
2:9, *168*
2:11-13, *168*
2:12, *168*
2:13, *168*
2:14, *125, 168, 169,*
170
2:14-15, *165, 168,*
171
2:15, *168*
2:16, *168*
7:14, *86*
8, *209*
8:11, *209*
11:29-34, *73*
11:30, *209*
11:32, *209*
12:18, *142*

15:3, *197*
15:38, *142*

2 Corinthians
1:5, *199*
1:21-22, *71*
1:22, *71*
3:7-18, *169*
3:17, *155*
4:1-2, *170*
4:3, *170, 188*
4:3-4, *165, 171*
4:3-6, *188*
4:4, *125, 170, 188*
4:6, *170, 188*
5:21, *195, 199, 213*
13:5, *88*

Galatians
3:6, *195*
3:6-9, *72*
3:8, *47, 195*
3:10, *195, 196*
3:11, *195*
3:12, *195*
3:13, *193, 195, 196,*
199, 213
4:8-9, *55*

Ephesians
1, *56, 57, 58, 59*
1:1, *58*
1:3, *58*
1:3-4, *57, 59*
1:3-6, *203*
1:3-14, *203, 204,*
207, 214
1:4, *55, 56, 57, 58,*
65, 98
1:4-5, *54, 56, 57,*
64, 65, 203
1:5, *65, 203*
1:6, *56, 58*
1:7, *58, 203*
1:7-12, *203*
1:9, *58*

1:11, *54, 56, 57, 58,*
65, 142, 143
1:11-13, *64*
1:12, *56, 59*
1:13, *59, 71, 203*
1:13-14, *71, 76, 77,*
203
1:14, *56, 71, 74, 89*
2:1, *124*
2:3, *163*
2:5, *124*
2:8-9, *30, 185*
4:30, *71, 74, 76*
5:25, *202*

Philippians
1:6, *73*
2:9, *194*
2:12-13, *90, 146*
3:10, *199*

Colossians
1:19, *142*
1:19-20, *78*
1:21-22, *81*
1:21-23, *77, 79, 90*
1:22, *78*
1:22-23, *78*
1:23, *78*
2:13, *196*
2:13-14, *196, 199,*
213
2:14, *196*

1 Thessalonians
1:4-5, *65*
5:10, *197*

2 Thessalonians
2:13, *65*

1 Timothy
1:1, *208*
2:3, *208*
2:5-6, *182*
2:6, *179*
4:10, *208*

2 Timothy
1:8-9, *65*
1:9, *55, 57, 98*
1:10, *208*
1:12, *73*
2:10, *65*
3:16, *152*

Titus
1:3, *208*
1:4, *208*
2:10, *208*
2:13, *208*
3:4, *208*
3:6, *208*

Hebrews
1:5—2:5, *82*
2:1-4, *81*
2:6-8, *183*
2:9, *179, 182, 183*
2:9-10, *183, 199*
2:16, *72*
3:1—4:13, *82*
3:6, *80*
3:7—4:11, *81*
3:12, *80*
3:13, *79*
3:14, *78, 80, 90*
5:3, *197*
5:11-14, *91*
5:11—6:3, *82*
5:11—6:12, *81, 82, 87*
5:12, *82*
6:1-12, *71*
6:3, *82*
6:4, *83*

6:4-5, *83*
6:4-6, *82, 83, 84, 85, 88, 91*
6:4-8, *88*
6:4-12, *82*
6:5, *83*
6:7-8, *84*
6:8, *84*
6:9, *91*
6:9-12, *85, 87, 88*
6:10, *84*
6:11, *82*
6:11-12, *78*
6:13-18, *73*
6:13-20, *91*
6:14, *71*
6:17, *72*
6:17-18, *72*
6:17-20, *71, 74*
6:18, *89*
6:19-20, *72, 73*
7:22, *192*
7:23-25, *72*
7:24-25, *74*
7:25, *68, 72, 73, 74*
9:13, *86*
9:15, *72*
10:6, *197*
10:8, *197*
10:18, *197*
10:26, *85, 197*
10:26-39, *81, 82, 85*
10:27, *82*
10:28, *85*
10:29, *82, 86*
10:30-31, *86*
10:31, *82*
10:32-34, *86*

10:35-36, *87*
10:35-39, *78*
10:37-38, *87*
10:39, *82, 87*
12:14, *79, 81, 90*
12:25-29, *82*
13:12, *199*

James
1:14, *156*
2:5, *64*
2:14-26, *88*

1 Peter
1:1-2, *207*
1:3-5, *73, 89*
1:4, *73, 74*
1:5, *73, 74*
1:11, *199*
1:15, *89*
1:17, *89*
1:18-19, *207*
1:22, *89*
2:21, *199*
2:24, *193*
3:18, *197, 199, 213*
4:1, *199*
4:13, *199*

2 Peter
1:5-9, *88*
1:10, *64*
1:20-21, *152*
2, *181*
2:1, *181, 209, 210*
2:3, *181*
2:12, *181*
2:13, *181*

2:17, *181*
3, *180*
3:9, *179, 180, 181*

1 John
1:5, *158*
2:2, *197, 208*
2:3-6, *79*
2:9-11, *79*
2:19, *80, 81, 90*
2:29, *79, 189*
3:3-10, *79*
3:9, *189*
3:11-18, *79*
4:7, *189*
4:7-21, *79*
4:10, *185, 197*
4:19, *185*
5:1, *188, 189*
5:13, *88, 188*
5:18, *189*
5:19, *209*

Jude
4, *210*

Revelation
1:4, *185*
3:5, *53*
5:9, *205, 206, 207, 214*
13:8, *53, 65*
17:8, *53, 65*
20:12, *53*
20:15, *53, 65*
21:1-4, *156*
21:27, *53, 65*
22, *143*